How to Draw Art for Comic Books

CORBEN
ELDER
FOSTER
KANE
KUBERT
KURTZMAN
RAYMOND
SPIEGELMAN
SPRANG
WILLIAMSON

Lessons from the Masters

Edited and Designed by Hal Schuster,
with production assistance from James R. Martin

Library of Congress Cataloging-in-Publication Data
Van Hise, James, 1949—
How to Draw Art for Comic Books

1. Art I. Title
ISBN 1-55698-254-2

 Published by Pioneer Books, Inc., 5715 N. Balsam Rd., Las Vegas, NV, 89130.
International Standard Book Number: 1-55698-254-2

First Printing 1989

contents...

An introduction...

Comic art is something you grow up with, which becomes more and more fascinating as you grow older. A lot who love comics toy with drawing, but you have to possess native artistic talent to become proficient. You can't teach someone to draw if their hand is incapable of rendering what's in their mind's eye. A person who has never drawn so much as a doodle can't be taught art from the ground up. That's why art schools only admit students after reviewing a portfolio to judge your basic skills; to find out what abilities they'll have to work with.

Gil Kane explains the internal aspects of becoming an artist. At one point he reveals, "You need to equip yourself with an emotional identification with the form, and then ultimately an objective view that allows you to step back and begin to put perspective structure in terms of the material. And then ultimately you need a direction to go in. Something that the work has to be about, otherwise you get a kind of uneventful virtuosity." In other words, you have to *feel* art to draw; it has to exist as an extension of yourself. It must be more than just lines on paper.

Sometimes it's difficult to judge just how much an artist can improve from their early work. I've seen pieces published in fan publications during the '60s by Jim Starlin which seems to suggest little innate ability or chance of improving, and yet a decade later his work had improved dramatically. The same is true of the early work of Frank Miller. These artists worked hard and applied themselves, and over a period of years, their work blossomed. The more they learned, the more their talent was enriched. The operative word here is *years*. An artist cannot improve overnight. Some artists are put off by this, particularly when they see that the work of contemporaries is far in advance of their own. Some artists possess a gift that manifests itself early, and their work at age 16 is superior to that of artists a decade older, but this is unusual and hardly a standard to measure against. Each individual is different, which is why there are so many different , but excellent and appropriate, styles of art. Each artist develops their own vision. It's why popular artists often try to hide their work of ten and fifteen years before; they see how far they've come and hindsight provides a more objective view of their work. A beginning pianist doesn't hope to play a complicated concerto after just thirty days. Sharpening artistic abilities is much the same. It takes time for talent to be nourished and to grow, but with time comes increased skill as well as increased confidence.

Knowing what has come before is vital to a comics artist. The form has grown during this century just as an artist's personal skills stretch and grow over decades of practice and performance. The more you learn of the artists of the past and the work they did, the more you become aware of the influences that shaped the work of the current crop of artists, including your favorite. It is an endless cycle. An artist working in illustration before the turn of the century may have shaped an early newspaper strip artist who in turn affected an artist of the Golden Age who shaped the work of an artist now working in the comic book field. It's a progression of form and talent which grounds you in both the best of the form, as well as the worst. The more you learn, the more you can avoid the pitfalls and cliches which entrap artists. And the better you understand what makes a good comic book page, where the emphasis of the action should be placed and how the story should flow, the easier you can recognize the strengths and weaknesses in your own work. You'll understand why one story is dramatically effective while a similar one falls flat under other hands.

Drawing for comics is not an easy path to follow. Some artists, even after achieving professional acceptance, still pursue their art career only in their spare time until they can secure regular work. This is in the nature of a freelance business. The freelancer, unless he lands a job as a staff artist with a guaranteed monthly income, works from job to job, like a movie actor who goes from film to film, never certain what they'll be doing in six months. It's a business filled with demands and the pressure of deadlines, one where the ability to meet a deadline can make or break a career. When starting out, an artist must accept that he'll have little choice but to follow the artistic demands of an employer, no matter how unreasonable they may seem. This is why after years of struggling, after artists achieve popular acceptance, they step back and slow down, using their new-found clout to demand greater flexibility in deadlines. Only then can they work at a more leisurely pace and enjoy their work, rather than feeling someone is breathing down their necks, waiting for the job to get finished.

Drawing comics is a job much like most any other. A career in comic book art means bosses, deadlines and demands just as in any other job. You may be able to work at home and set your own hours, but that doesn't mean you're not expected to deliver on time. Some artists can't handle this freedom and, even if they have a month to finish a job, put it off until the last week and then claim insufficient time. This only makes things more difficult for everyone, including yourself if you expect to work for that publisher again. It's very easy for an artist to schedule his workload; he knows how long it takes to draw. And if he sets daily quotas for himself, even if they seem meagre ones, he will complete the work on time. Good work habits lead to enjoy an enjoyable, productive career that is personally satisfying to the artist. Art is a career like any other. If treated like one from the beginning it can be enjoyed far more than working any nine to five job, and will provide the personal enrichment an artist requires.

The artists appearing in this volume form an interesting cross-section of the field. Most of them have enjoyed careers spanning decades. They bring their years of collective expertise to this discussing of the basic points a cartoonist needs to understand in developing his craft. Although most of them have spent their careers drawing and inking comic books, some have made different applications of comic art. Dick Sprang is perhaps the most popular artist to draw **Batman** during the Forties and Fifties; Joe Kubert has drawn superheroes since the Forties, but is also well known for his work in war comics, which requires another approach altogether. Harvey Kurtzman has drawn war, horror and science fiction comics (at E.C. in the Fifties) but achieved greater recognition for his work in humor, from the creation of **Mad** to his work in **Playboy** on "Little Annie Fanny." Richard Corben started out in the field of advertising art and gradually moved into comics, showing that one can adapt and move from one application of commercial art into another. Al Williamson has drawn numerous comic book stories as well as spending over a decade on a syndicated daily newspaper strip. He also taught drawing for a year at the Joe Kubert School. Will Elder's career parallels that of his friend Kurtzman in many respects and he tells what it is like collaborating with another artist. Art Spiegelman comes from a very different sort of comic art, having achieved distinction in the realm of underground comics as both artist and editor, and popular recognition for his graphic novel **Maus**. Gil Kane has drawn comics since the Forties and chooses in this book to deal less with the external side of drawing and more with the internal aspect of what should motivate an artist to draw. Kane has worked in comic books, drawn newspaper strips and spent a good number of years in the field of animation.

Since several of these artists refer to the influence of Hal Foster and Alex Raymond, masters of the comic strip page, chapters on both discussing their respective techniques and importance in the field are included. The work of Foster and Raymond provides examples through which one can see how their work of fifty years ago continues to influence comics artists today.

Cartooning is a labyrinth of complicated rules which shape artistic expression and determine financial success; rules which an artist must learn to survive. Just think of How to Draw Art for Comic Books as a guide provided by a number of pioneers who have led the way.

---JAMES VAN HISE
October 9, 1989

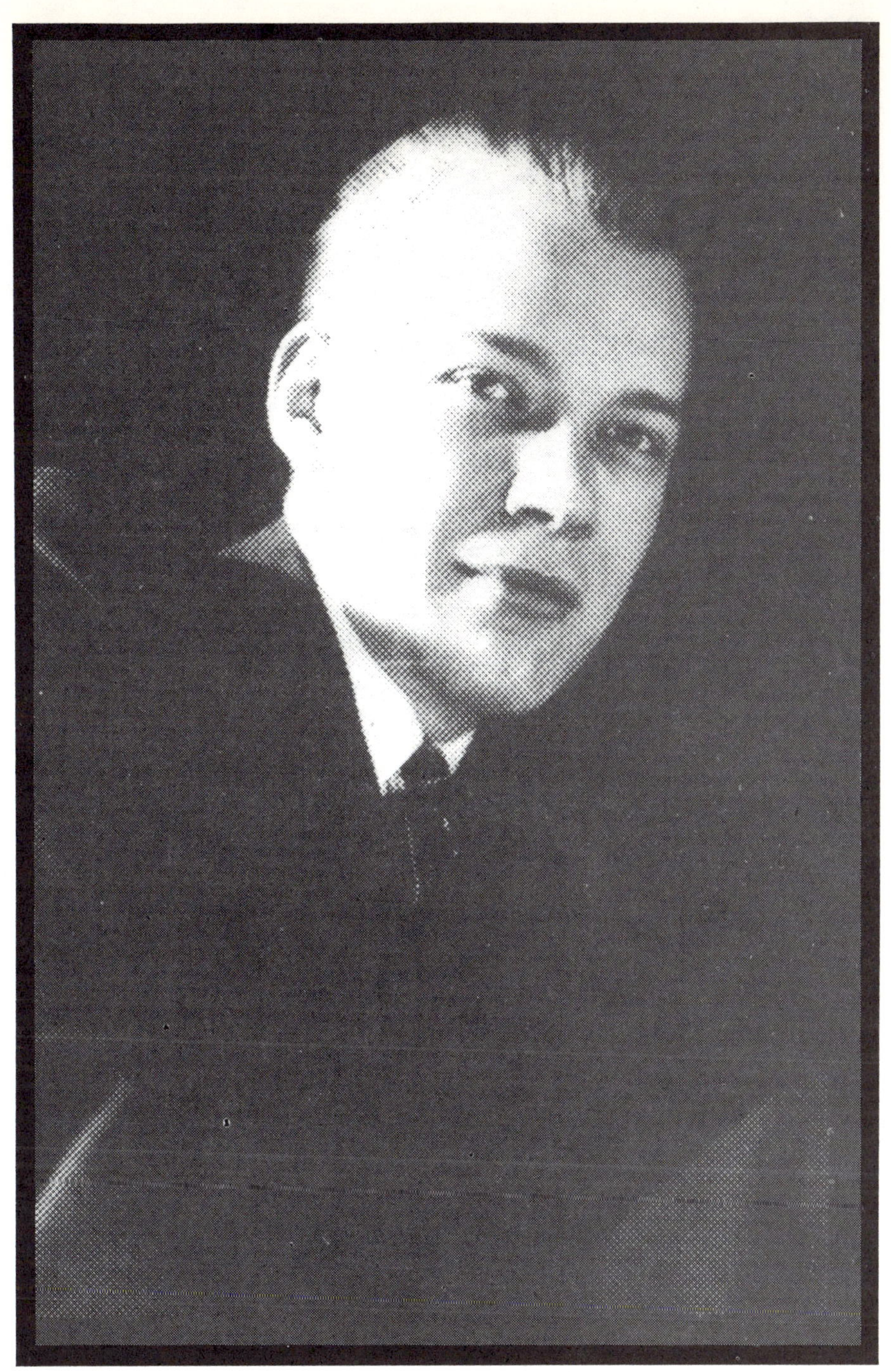

Chapter One
DICK SPRANG

Born July 28, 1915 in Fremont, Ohio, Sprang's first work as an artist began when he was fifteen. This consisted of such odd jobs as painting signs, billboards, street banners and lobby posters for Fremont's two movie theaters. Following his high school graduation, he worked in the art department of the ***Toledo News-Bee*** *where he learned layout, advertising art, editorial cartooning and composition, as well as about printing and meeting deadlines.*

Not satisfied with life on a newspaper, Sprang quit and secured work as a pulp artist for Street and Smith and other pulp magazine publishers. Although he primarily illustrated Western stories,

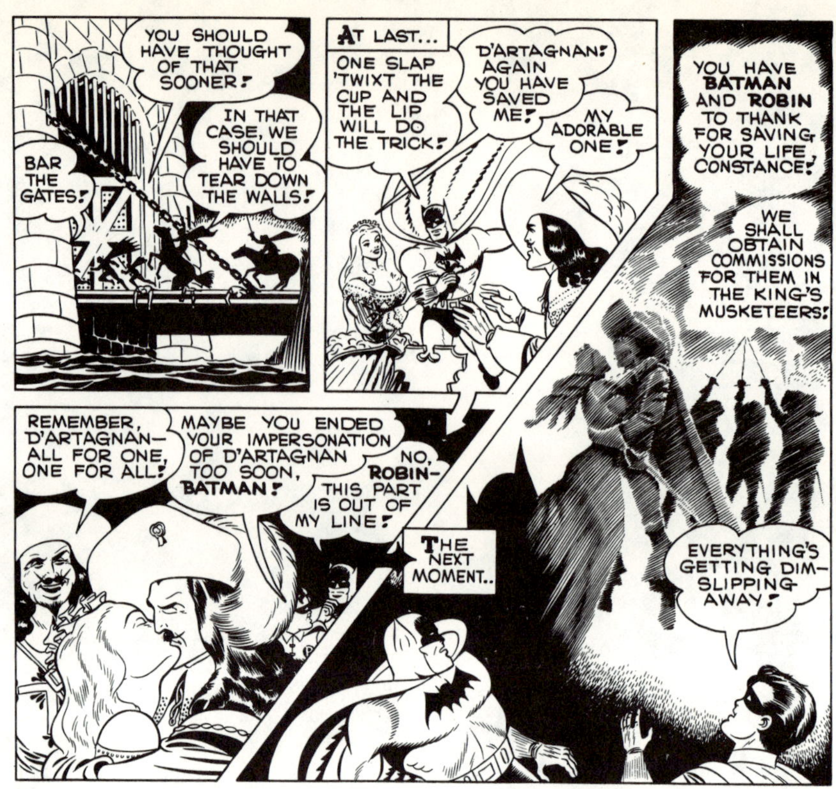

From Batman #83: note the elaborate linework

Sprang had definite ideas as to the best tools for an artist to use, "The best way is to try them all. Experiment with them on the drawing surface you will select to use professionally—hot press, smooth, or cold press, slightly textured. Practice extensively and decide which surface suits you best. Having decided, then determine if brush or pen will be your inking tool. You must gain proficiency with one or the other to make this decision, stroking every kind of line and curve. Render curves by rotating the drawing surface to its most comfortable position, then ink the curve. Unless you are left-handed, you will find that stroking from right to left is awkward.

"As to the tool that offers the best control of an ink line, the brush is by far the best for me, perhaps because I never gained true proficiency with pens. The brush is said to be more difficult to control. I found it more versatile than pens in its ability to render thin to thick lines in one stroke; energetic lines which create variegated form in drapery and figure drawing.

"On Batman and Superman, I used the finest sable No. 2 brush, and on occasion a No. 1. Today we do not have the excellent quality of brush manufacture I used in the '40s and '50s. I've recently discovered a brush made in West Germany that works, and lasts, quite well: A. Langnickel pure red sable, No. 1 and No. 2 spotting brush, series 621. It's far better than the British product.

"As to ink, Higgins Black Magic gives the blackest line, although it drys with a slight sheen, and drys thick on a pen. Higgins No. 4415 drys flat, but unless you load your brush fully, its line will fade to grey and thus not reproduce well.

he also did work for ***The Shadow****.*
Sprang formed an agency with two partners, Ed Kressey and Normal Fallon, creating advertising illustration and pulp art, but by the mid-Thirties he closed up shop to work for Prize Comics.
Then came his long stint at DC drawing stories for ***Batman*** *and* ***World's Finest*** *from the Forties up to his retirement from comics in 1962.*
Sprang drew as an anonymous artist whose work was either published under the "Bob Kane" signature or under no signature at all.
Today he's doing licensed recreations of the covers he drew for DC, in full color, and has a three year waiting list .

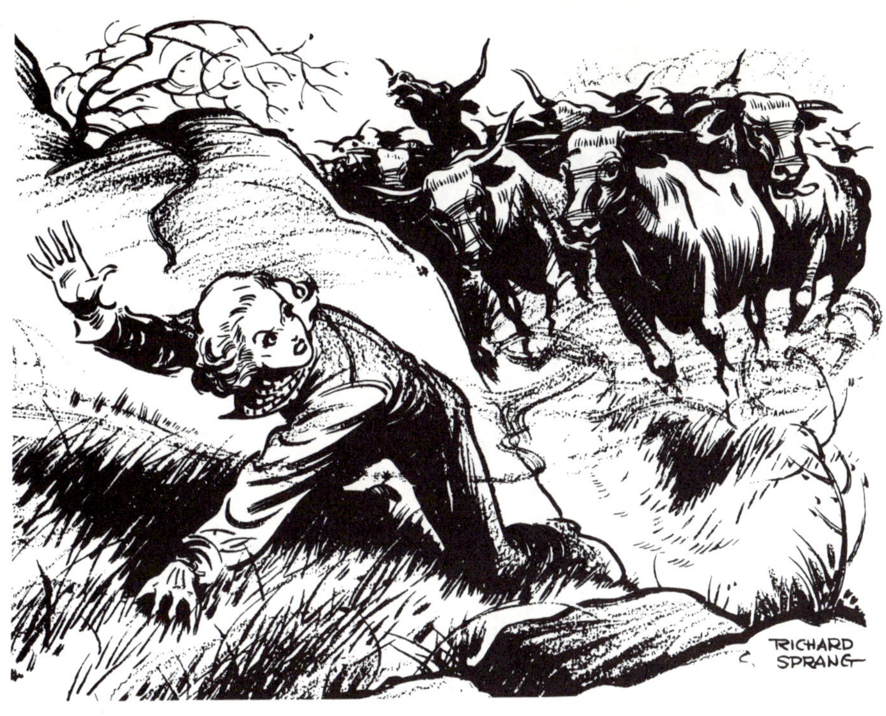

A Western pulp illustration typical of Sprang's early work

"For ruling panel borders, I use a Speedball B-6 or B-5. For ruling lines on buildings, curbings, and tightly parallel shading, I use a pointed pen, its stiffness, weight and flexibility determined by the quality of line desired. Only much experimentation can inform you of how the many various pen nibs and forms can serve your purposes. As to favoring a Gillot steel nib or a Crowquill, I use them all as occasion demands.

"I cannot overemphasize the value of continual practice with brush or pen. Because I prefer the brush for my figure and face inking, and for clouds, ocean waves, curved speed lines, rocks, mud, trees, horses, etc., I begin each day of inking by covering a practice sheet with every sort of brush line. And while doing the actual inking, I keep a sheet of 20 lb canary bond under my hand, and after filling the brush, stroke it out to a fine point on the bond, then attack the rendering. You should keep a sheet of scratch paper under your hand at all times for this purpose, and to prevent skin oils from being transferred to your working surface and cause faulty adherence of the ink to the paper."

Sprang always worked from a full script, and never from anything such as what we call the "Marvel Style" of scripting today.

"I never worked with a script that did not break the pages down into individual panels. I don't know how balloons and captions can be assigned without the writer fulfilling his obligation to provide a scene-by-scene script.

"As to my guide for figure composition in individual panels, you are asking for a treatise on the whole art of graphic design

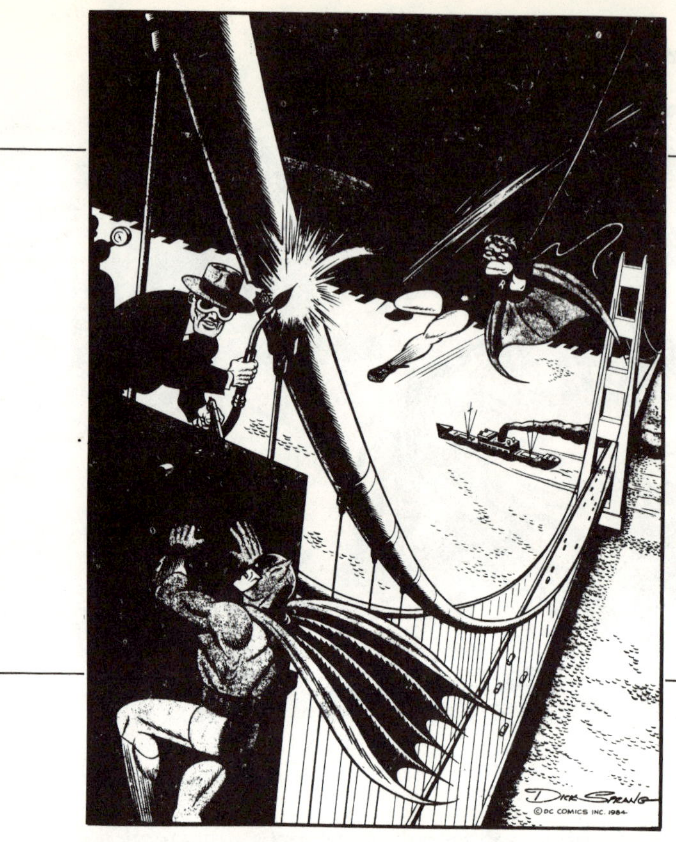

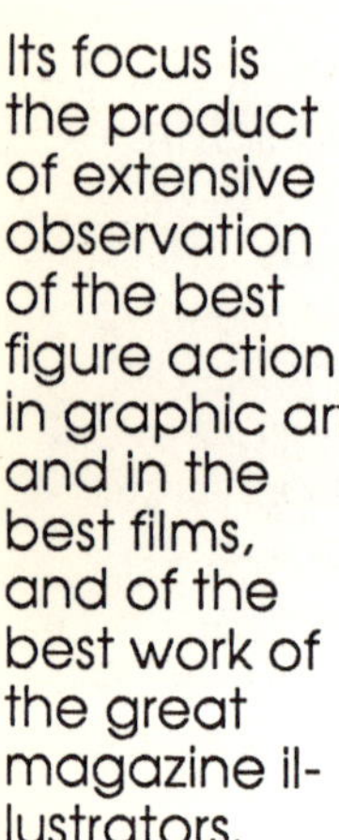
Its focus is the product of extensive observation of the best figure action in graphic art and in the best films, and of the best work of the great magazine illustrators.

in an action, adventure comic book or script. The process is highly subjective. Its focus is the product of extensive observation of the best figure action in graphic art and in the best films, and of the best work of the great magazine illustrators who predated the advent of the comic books, and of those exemplary masters: Alex Raymond, Roy Crane, Hal Foster and Milton Caniff. This observation will create a matrix of information that your subconscious will call forth to suggest the ideal *dramatic* figure composition for the scene at hand. Your treatment has much to do with your feelings and much to do with your developing sense of what the public (and editors) want. The rules of composition are well documented and should be learned by the beginning artist to the point of their becoming instinctive in their application."

So far as the kinds of breakdowns Sprang does when working from a script, he explains his technique in the following way:

"When I received a script, I would read it straight through. Then I would let it cook in my mind overnight. Next morning, I'd attack the splash page, which by then I'd fairly well figured out. If not, I would do a thumbnail sketch, then start my pencil on the illustration board. As a veteran in the medium, my succeeding pages needed no layout prior to the actual pencils. I would read, of course, the following page to establish the flow of continuity to come, and continue that way throughout the story, tying everything together in transitions of facing pages and overleafs, establishing a cadence and a tempo and a clarity of progression. It's wise, however, for a beginning comic book artist to design his layouts in the manner

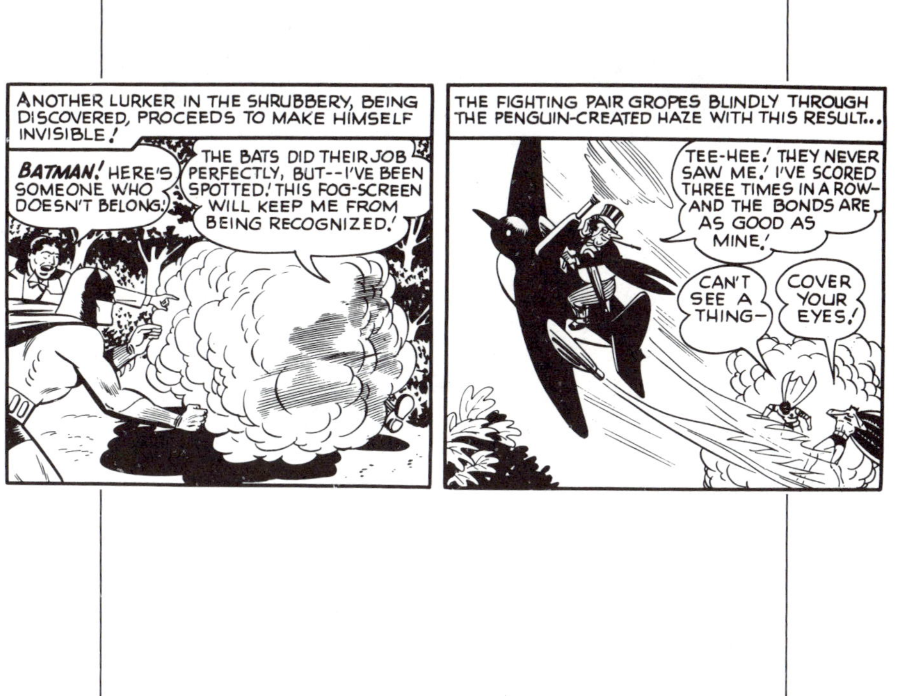

There should be a synthesis of words and pictures, an harmonious blending of illustration and words. Rarely can a sequence be told in pictures alone.

Here we see two panels from Batman #56.

of a story board; small rough sketches which will inform him of the authenticity of his continuity. He should analyze these layouts for the inclusion of the above elements, and revise his sketches as his growing sense of fitness dictates. He should be his harshest critic. Soon he will find that his experience, combined with intense study of other artists' work, will inform his design and compositional aptitude enough to eliminate the rough sketches, although after ten or twenty years of such direct drawing, he will find that on occasion he will be confronted with a problem of illustration that can best be solved by several thumbnail sketches. Trust your first sketch; it's almost always the best."

When it comes to drawing pretty pictures instead of following the primary needs of the script, Sprang explains, "The thrust of the storytelling needs should be put ahead of everything else. Your job is to interpret the script, to interpret the story in illustrations designed to convey not just surface style,

'but also considers the composition of panels and of pages and renderings as leading the reader to *read* the story, considering the above as elements in a unified whole.'

(Quotation from David Bachman supplied by Sprang)

Anything else is extra baggage, especially renderings that employ precious art for art's sake, which by its divergence from the story line impede the flow of the story.

"There should be a synthesis of words and pictures, an harmonious blending of illustration and words. Rarely can a sequence be told in pictures alone, but words preceding it are needed to plant

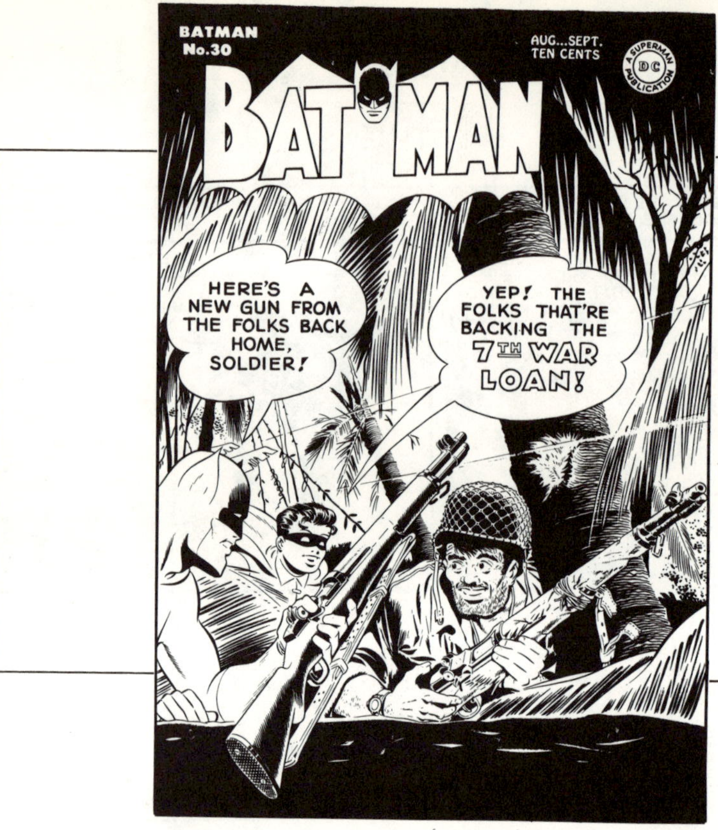

Observe in good film, such as ***Citizen Kane,*** how an actor's body language creates mood, suspense, humor, fear and all manner of interpretive elements that advance the flow of the story by calling signals of what is to come, and reaction of what has just occurred. Facial expression is extremely important.

The earliest of Sprang's cover originals known to exist, from 1946—from the collection of Joe Desris

the scenes. Milton Caniff was marvelously adept in creating this particular technique. In the general run of comic strip or comic book production, however, the simultaneous conjunction of words and pictures are primary in enhancing the telling of the story."

Part of telling the story, of course, is how the artist communicates feelings and events through the characters, which is accomplished, to a large degree, via body language, something that Dick Sprang considers to be very important.

"Observe in good film, such as ***Citizen Kane***, how an actor's body language creates mood, suspense, humor, fear and all manner of interpretive elements that advance the flow of the story by calling signals of what is to come, and reaction of what has just occurred. Facial expression is extremely important."

Sprang has tips on learning how to do this, and how to expand on the four basic expressions of joy, thoughtfulness, anger and sorrow that some artists fall back on to stand in for others.

"The best way for me is to assume these expressions while looking in a mirror. Also, to collect prime examples of them from magazine and newspapers, and make notes of observations of movie actors. The four basic expressions serve most purposes, but I would expand them to include the expressions of humorous disgust, intense disgust, questioning, greed, hatred, envy, sympathy, cynicism, and satiric response (taking the form of a smilingly arch expression). Some of these can be emphasized by the placement of the hand, or hands, to the face, as: two fingers to the cheek along with pursed lips when expressing doubt, and fingers to the fore-

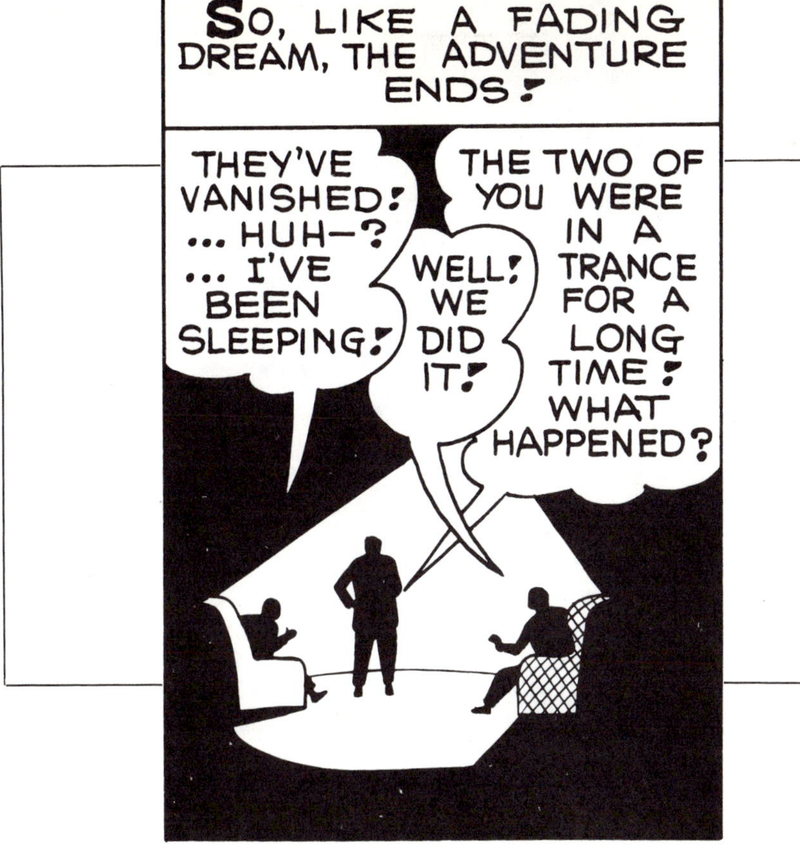

In action scenes you visualize your grouping of characters as on a theatre stage. You can compose from the angle of view from the orchestra pit, or from looking down from the top of the proscenium, from right or left stage, looking straight on in a long shot. Variation.

head when expressing weariness."

Explaining how to choose the most interesting angles within a panel, Sprang once again refers to what we learn by watching films.

"Yes, precisely as in a movie or on the legitimate stage." Sprang felt he best described this in an interview with him conducted by Ike Wilson which was published by the Comic and Fantasy Art Amateur Press Association (CFA-APA) in its journal No. 13, September, 1988: "In action scenes you visualize your grouping of characters as on a theatre stage. You can compose from the angle of view from the orchestra pit, or from looking down from the top of the proscenium, from right or left stage, looking straight on in a long shot. Variation. Never repeat the same scene, never the same degree of sequential medium shot or closeup or long shot. Always vary it. Then, in all this moving around, try to bring a rhythm into the way you draw the continuity of action and setting—the slant of a building in exaggerated perspective leading into the opposite slant of a bridge in the next panel. Something that always keeps the reader interested and alive visually. He is supposed to read the story, but to keep him reading you must not bore him with repetitious panels. That is the trick. After all, it's a graphically flowing medium. We learn this from good films. Good film-makers do this kind of thing all the time. The camera moves and that's what you are, the camera, and you are probing constantly for the interesting shot. Now remember, we are drawing dramatic action stuff, not pretty pictures. So the camera probes trying to get the best effect of movement and suspense. When you study the top continuity il-

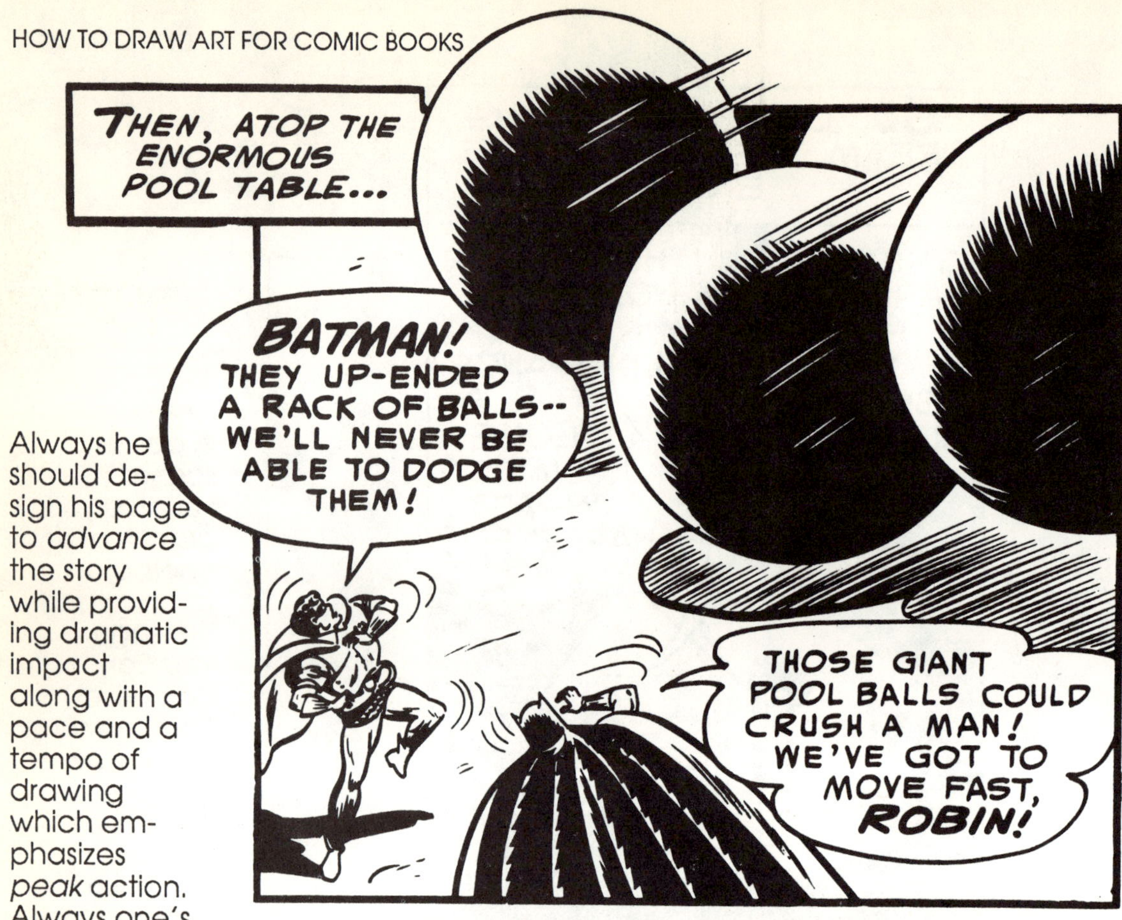

Always he should design his page to *advance* the story while providing dramatic impact along with a pace and a tempo of drawing which emphasizes *peak* action. Always one's illustrative intent must be *clear*.

lustrators, like Caniff, you'll see them doing this all the time. It's a great tool. As to evoking mood, the composition of panels establish danger, serenity, suspense, fear, humor—all by the arrangement of the panel components. The direction of lighting is always important. Learn how, for heaven's sake, to project a situation with impact and to interpret a script with gusto, liveliness, vigor, vitality, and authentic substance. That's tough. It's either a self-learning process or a native instinct."

When an artist has to design a page because he isn't working from a full script, there are ways which are best to approach the creative decisions.

"Here again, as in figure composition, the artist's subjective creativity provides the decision. But always he should design his page to *advance* the story while providing dramatic impact along with a pace and a tempo of drawing which emphasizes *peak* action. Always one's illustrative intent must be *clear*. I've seen pages so cluttered with outsize panels which dominate a bunch of oddly placed small ones, that the viewer needs a road map to figure out what the devil is going on.

"All types of drama and settings can benefit from a dramatic use of different shaped panels, provided that panel shapes, small or outsize, are designed to provide dramatic impact, but are also designed with a restraint that enhances clarity and does not create visual confusion. Study the work of the best artists, but be aware that even some of them go overboard. Train your eye to recognize the interpretation of a script that advances the story with an easy progression, and does not get so complicated in panel arrangement as to destroy

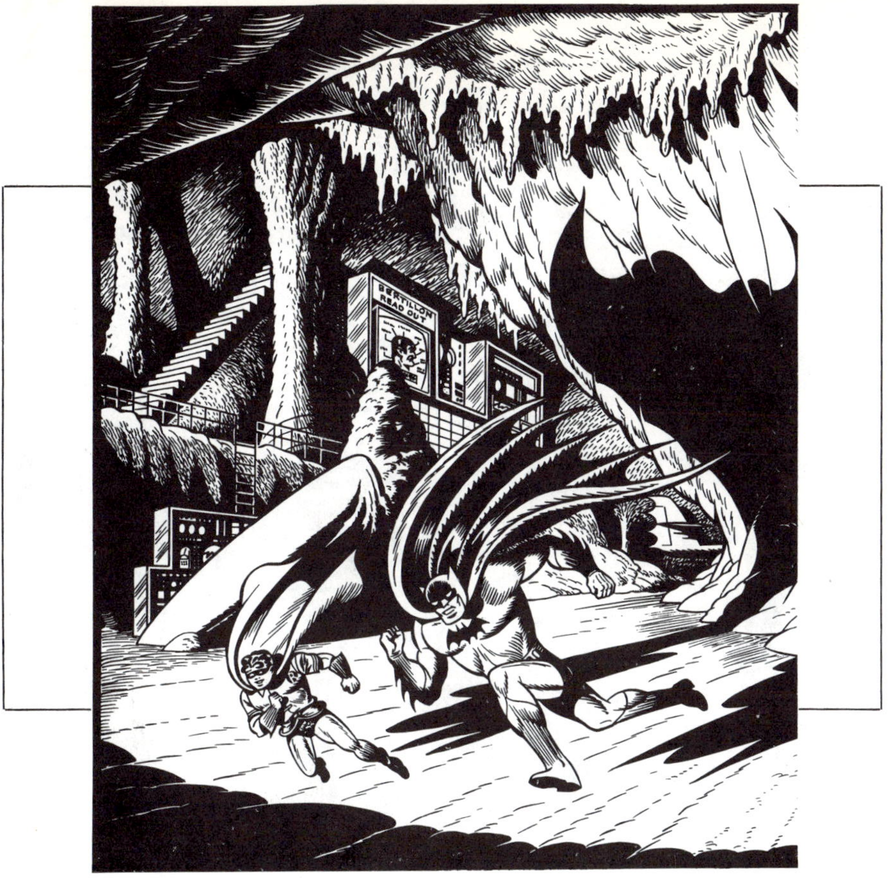

"Black areas are important for dramatic effect in color or black and white," Sprang observes. "A comic story, can be just as interesting when viewed in black and white as when seen in color.

A conceptual drawing of Batman and Robin running through the Batcave from the collection of Steve Leialoha

the immediately recognizable flow of the story."

A skill often ignored by modern comics artists is the use of black areas to achieve dramatic impact. Many artists are so aware that their work will be published in color that they draw for the color and ignore a vital element in the effectiveness of their technique.

"Black areas are important for dramatic effect in color or black and white," Sprang observes. "A comic story, can be just as interesting when viewed in black and white as when seen in color. My Batman work was *designed* for color, and when my inked pages are viewed in their original form, they lack the unified compositional integrity that the addition of color provides. Many areas are left open. These areas, if color were not to be used, would be rendered more fully in black and white."

Although Dick Sprang started out inking his own work, he soon had collaborators, and when pencilling for another artist one often approaches the final pencil work differently since to communicate the full intent to the inker.

"I draw all the details for the inker," Sprang explains, "draw them cleanly, not sketchy. My splendid inkers, Gene McDonald, Stan Kaye, and Charley Paris —the master— were thus always fully informed of my intentions, and they appreciated it. Areas that are to be solid black, I indicate with an X within the area; no need to 'scrumble' in the black with pencil. If I'm doing my own inking, I pencil all the details I will ink."

Those details involve how much or how little is drawn into the background.

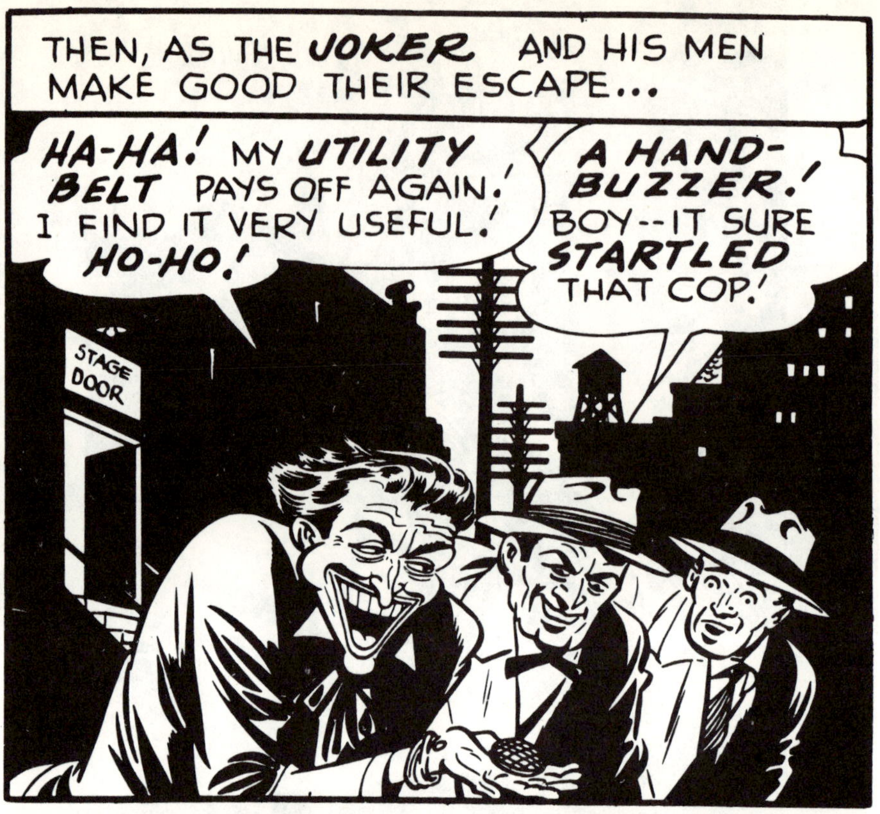

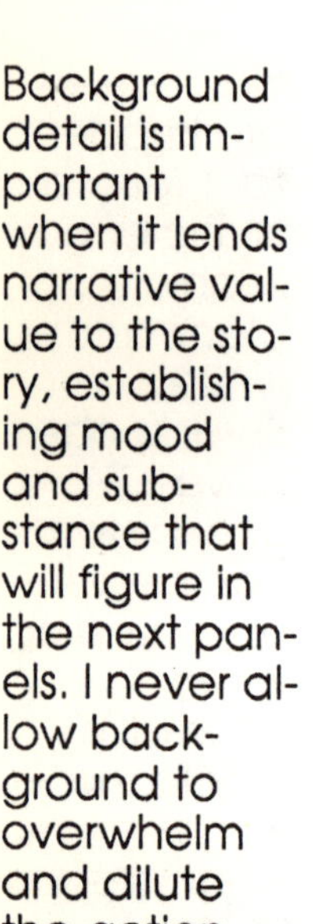
Background detail is important when it lends narrative value to the story, establishing mood and substance that will figure in the next panels. I never allow background to overwhelm and dilute the action..

"Background detail is important when it lends narrative value to the story, establishing mood and substance that will figure in the next panels. I never allow background to overwhelm and dilute the action.."

Dick Sprang's Batman stories are grounded in a type of reality sustained by drawing recognizable commonplace objects, which is where an artist's swipe file can come into play. Sprang says the swipe file is, "Extremely important because this resource will guarantee the accuracy of your depiction of these objects. My scrap file occupies two file cabinets."

Sprang had this advice to offer to an artist who wants to learn more about drawing comics and wishes to improve their skills:

"Draw, draw, draw. Draw continually, using the best examples of graphic art you can find to guide you. There's nothing wrong with copying when you are learning, for thus you discover the intense discipline employed by the copied artist. Then go on from there to develop your *own* unique style. *Master* perspective; learn to draw hands and feet. Once I worked as an art editor. When shown samples by an aspiring artist, I first looked at his depiction of hands and feet. If they were well done, I knew I had a prospect. Because, if you can draw the hand in any position—pointing, pushing, the fist, the calm grace of the hand in repose—you can draw anything, for the hand embodies almost all forms, plus foreshortening. Make a claw of your hand and look at it, palm toward you. Learn to draw those foreshortened fingers. It's tough.

"There are many instruction books available in public and university libraries, in large art

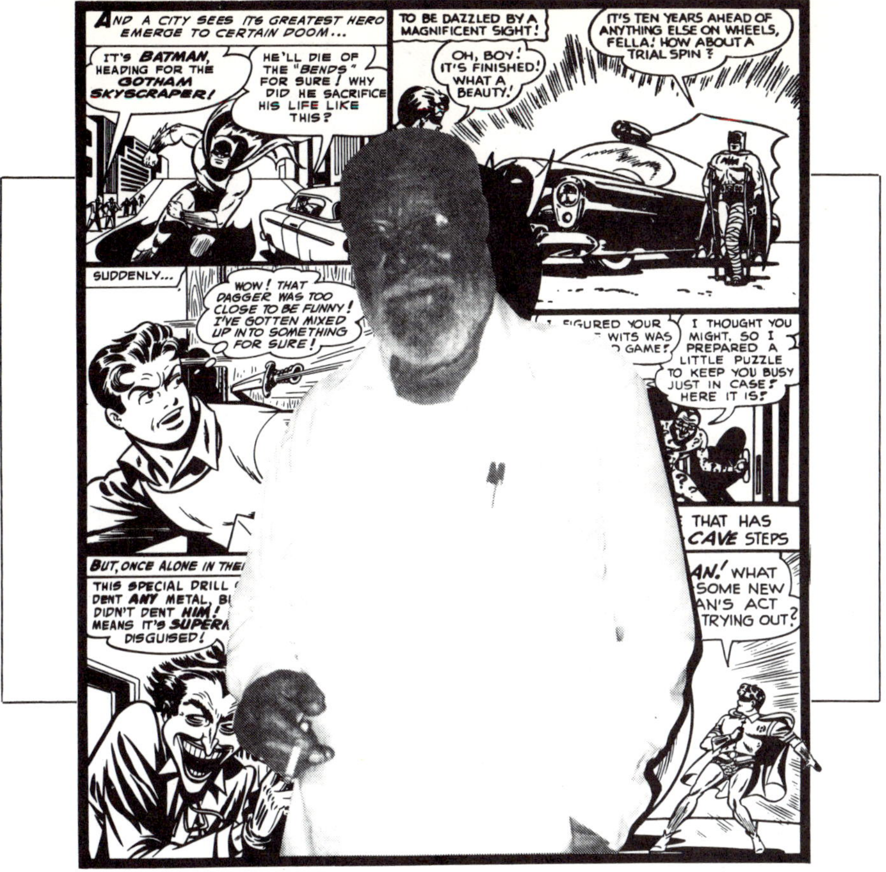

supply stores, and in large general bookstores. Some are far out arty stuff designed to encourage people to mess around with charcoal and paint who can't draw and never will learn to draw because they don't work *hard*. Ignore those books and focus on the literal manuals. Marvel Comics published **How to Draw Comics the Marvel Way**. It's an excellent manual, softbound, large format. It is written by Stan Lee, who knows what he's talking about, and illustrated by John Buscema, who knows how to draw.

"I don't know of any correspondence schools. There was one, now defunct, called Famous Artists Course. Their lessons in very large looseleaf format concentrated on realistic illustration. If ever you can find a set of these lessons, you will have a prime source of self-instruction.

"Learning to draw anything and everything well is hard work, damned hard work. There is nothing simple about it and never will be. You'll always be learning, or should be. Occasionally, you'll meet some genius who can draw everything with no training. Salute him and go your difficult way. I went my difficult way for damn near half a century, and I am still learning, cussing myself, trying to get just the right effect. I achieved facility in the eyes of others, but to me I'm still a kid in school, learning, learning, learning. It pays. I've had a wonderfully independent life drawing Batman and Superman. You too can draw them and a myriad other characters if you're willing to dedicate your life expending the energy of a longshoreman loading all alone the biggest freighter that ever docked."

Learning to draw anything and everything well is hard work, damned hard work. There is nothing simple about it and never will be. You'll always be learning, or should be. Occasionally, you'll meet some genius who can draw everything with no training. Salute him and go your difficult way. I went my difficult way for damn near half a century, and I am still learning, cussing myself, trying to get just the right effect.

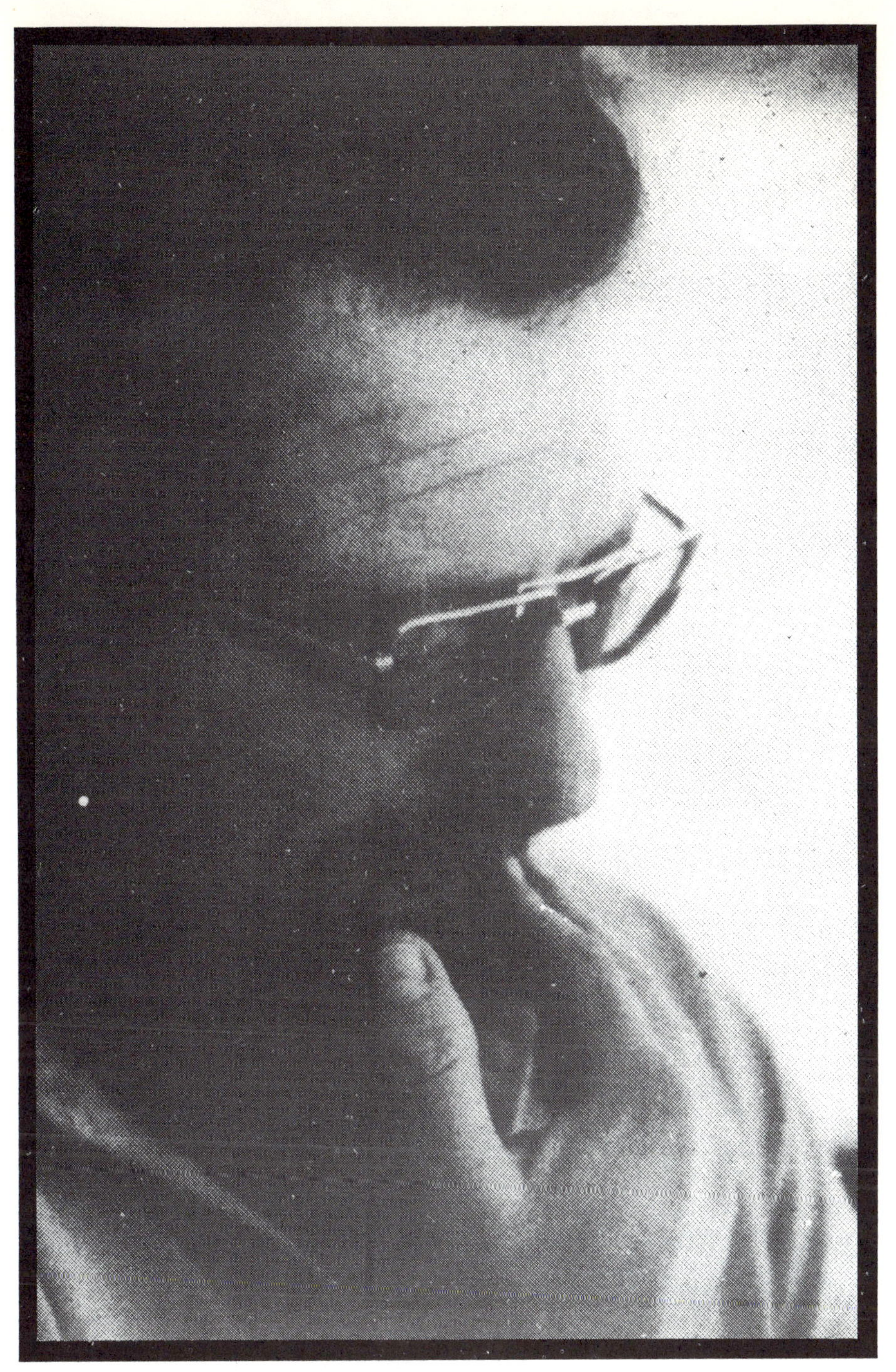

Chapter Two
JOE KUBERT

Joe Kubert began drawing comics in his early teens, in the early 1940s. At that time, there were twenty-five or thirty comic book publishers. While Kubert was attending the High School of Music and Art and living in Brooklyn, he would play hooky from school and go with his friend, Norman Maurer, to make the rounds of the publishers looking for work. While trying to find work, Harry Chesler, who ran a studio, invited the young Joe Kubert to come by and do some drawing which the artists would critique, an experience Kubert found invaluable. Kubert then secured work with Timely, Avon, M.L.J., Quality, Biro and Wood. At Avon Kubert worked

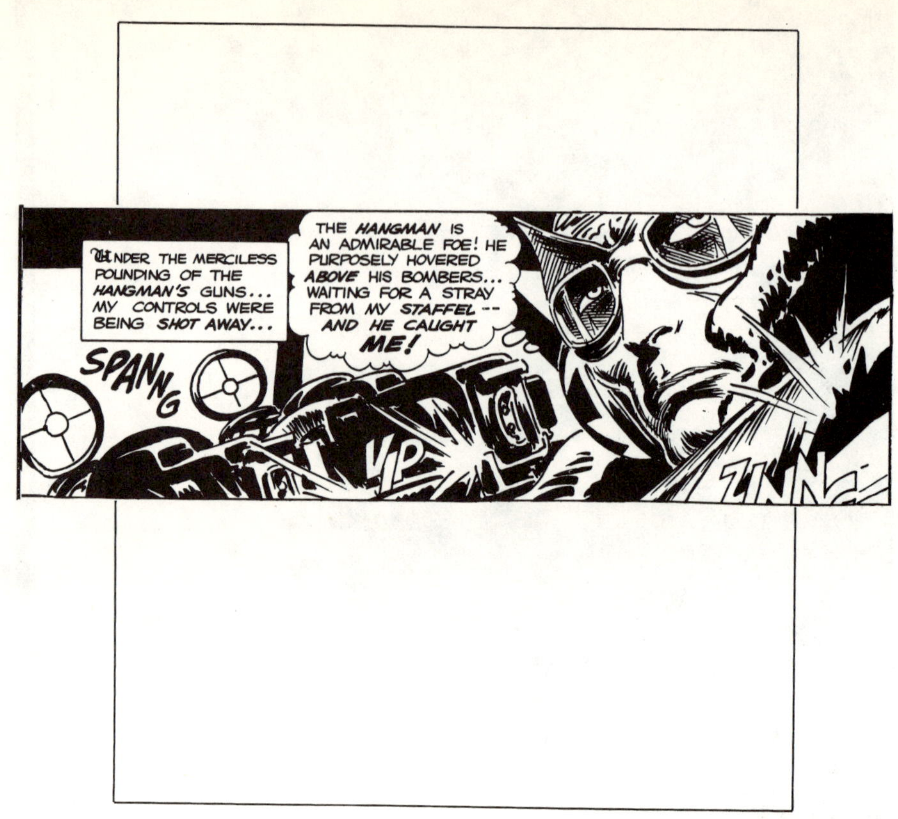

Note the emotion in captured in this panel from an Enemy Ace story

"As far as the tool is concerned, my preferences are the same tools that have been used for decades in this particular profession," explains Joe Kubert, "and that is: India ink, brush and pen, and combinations there of. I've tried almost every tool you could think of; every other kind of marker that you could think of, or combinations of grease pencil, ink and pen and so on and so forth. I feel that for this particular medium, and I must underline that this is personal, the determination for which tool each person really goes for is very subjective. For me the brush, the pen and the India ink do the best job for the textures, for the rendering, for the kind of line and for the reproduction that's involved.

"Now, I don't use just *a* brush or *a* pen. I may have three or four different brushes which I use for the same job, and I may be using half a dozen different pens for the same job. The reason is that I want one particular kind of line, for instance, for one particular kind of texture. If I really pushed on it, in all probability I could perhaps use the same two to get the kind of texture that I'm looking for. But if I want a thick, coarse line, it's a lot easier to resort to either a pen that will give me that coarse line, or a brush which perhaps doesn't have the fine kind of point that I would otherwise use for rendering hair or rendering the texture of skin, which is a softer tone.

"In the main, what I would do is utilize the pen and brush for the whole job, but with variations of those pens and brushes, depending on the particular texture I'm looking for. I'll go way beyond that. If I want, for instance, the texture of stone on a flat surface, I may take a piece of rough cloth and flatten out a small section of

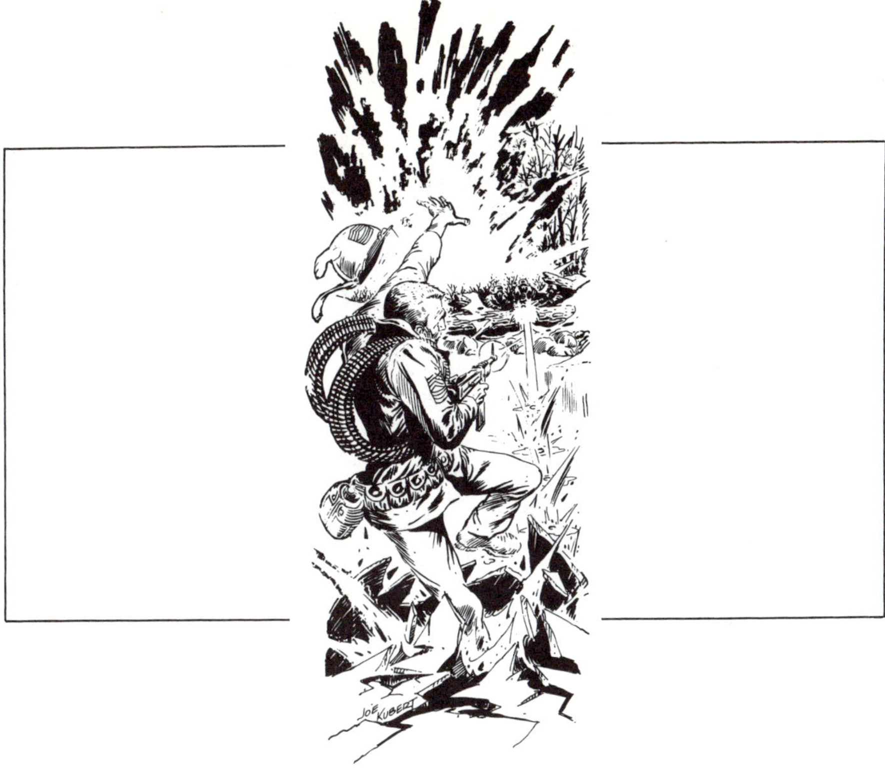

An explosive scene from a Sergeant Rock story

it to work as a stamper. I may ink in that portion of that cloth, depending on the texture that I can get with it. With a cloth you can get almost any kind of a texture you can dream of: wool, or varieties of nubby cloth, and so on. If you ink that in you can almost use it as a stamp and get a complete and total texture of a stone wall instead of having to depend on rendering those things, each and every mark, with a pen or a brush. Sometimes, if it's for an overall effect, I would use that. In fact, if I were doing smoke for an explosion, in war scenes, and I want a soft edge on the cloud of smoke that occurs, I can do that soft effect by just pushing my finger onto the ink, getting a little bit on my finger and using my fingerprints to give those little soft whirls at the end of the smoke effect to soften that up. This is something that's been used by many artists that I know."

Regarding specific pens, Kubert states, "I use a crowquill, a steel nib and what they call a school pen. I will maintain my tools for a long time because one pen may start out giving me a fine line, but in its usage and its spread, it will eventually give me a coarser line. Well, that coarser line I can use for something else so that until and unless a pen actually falls apart, or a brush falls apart as a result of use, I can use my tools. There are, however, tools which have a finite life. If I want a really fine line, those are tools which have the shortest life span for me. Because in the use of a brush against paper, there's almost a sandpaper effect. The same thing with a pen. You're filing that instrument every time you're using it, and eventually the brush will lose its fine line and a pen will lose its fine line. You can use it for something else, but that's the time you've got to get new material.

with Carmine Infantino. Kubert started working for D.C. in the Forties, drawing the Hawkman strip. When a new version was revived twenty years later, Kubert was the first artist to draw it due to the impression he had made in the Forties.

During the Fifties Kubert spent two years in the Army, still drawing short strips for DC At St. John, Kubert and his old friend Norman Maurer produced the first 3-D comics. Later he collaborated with writer Robert Kanigher on Sgt. Rock. Kubert continued working for D.C. and drew the fondly remembered Viking Prince, Enemy Ace and Tarzan. Kubert also drew the syndicated ***he Green Berets*** *and acted as an editor for DC .*

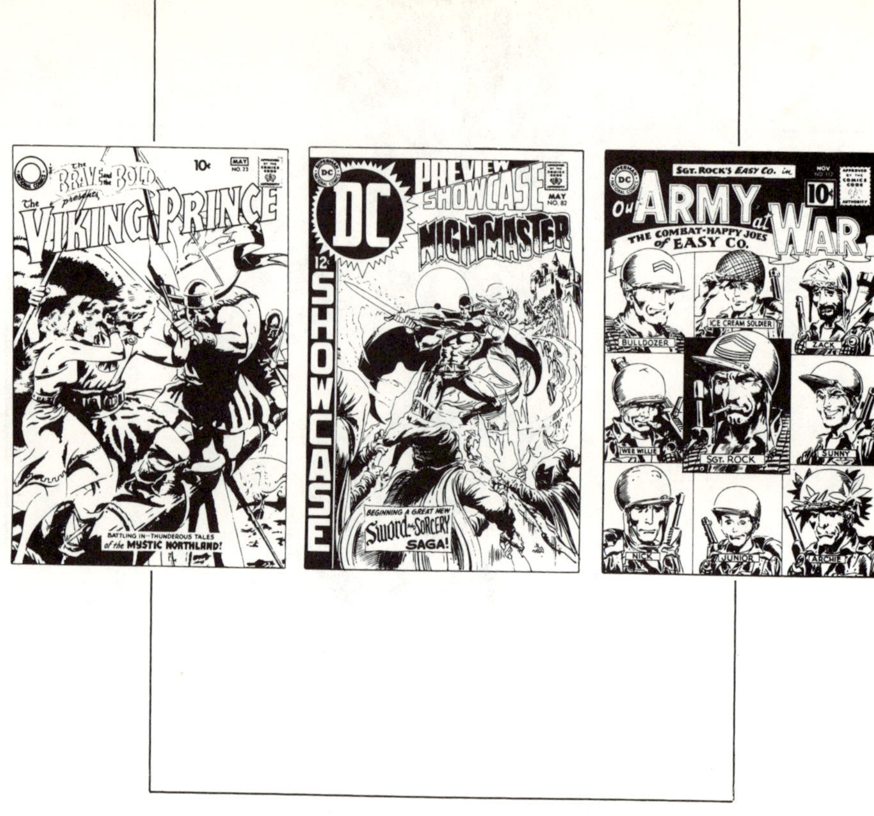

One reason most people do not use a pen and brush when they start to do this kind of work is because ballpoints and markers are a hell of a lot easier to use. They'll try the pen and brush and say: 'I can't use these tools. They just don't do for me. I can't get the same kind of effect with a ballpoint or a marker.'

On the other hand Kubert has obviously mastered the tools well as these covers illustrate.

"I have found that in particular areas the materials over the years seem to have lost a certain quality, and this is testified to by most of the guys who have been in the business for a long time. For instance, Strathmore makes a terrific paper, probably the best available. The surface of it is terrific, a lot of rag content and so on. But it seems the paper I used twenty or thirty years ago had more quality, resiliency and surface than that which I'm getting today. Also, I find that the brushes don't last as long. They've lost the consistent quality that they had. I find myself constantly testing other brushes when I go into an art store. When I was in Europe, when I got together with a guy like Will Eisner, what did we do in our spare time? In Paris we would go to art stores to see what new material was there that wasn't available to us domestically, to see what kind of new materials could be used to take the place of the stuff that we had been using but which seemed to have deteriorated over the years."

Not everyone starts out using the more elaborate pens and brushes which are available. Kubert explains why one should not restrict oneself to a certain tool just because it's easier to handle.

"One reason most people do not use a pen and brush when they start to do this kind of work is because ballpoints and markers are a hell of a lot easier to use. They'll try the pen and brush and say: 'I can't use these tools. They just don't do for me. I can't get the same kind of effect with a ballpoint or a marker.' In fact, they take it a step further: 'I can work more easily with pencil than I can with ink.' The reason for that is everybody starts with the pencil first, and as a result of practice it becomes easier to use. The same thing applies to the

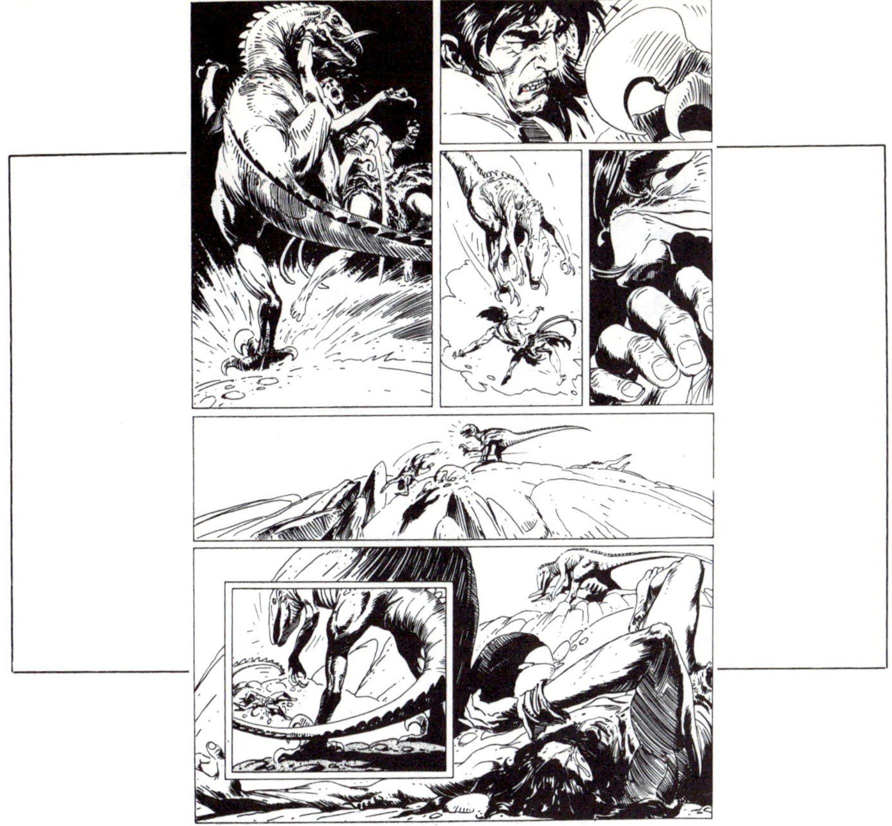

brush and ink. It takes a little more doing to really be able to control those particular tools, but once you've got it you find those tools will do everything plus for you. But you've got to learn how to use them first. You've got to have the *patience* to learn. A ball point or a marker, most markers, don't have any flexibility at all, so that in those areas the tools lack those things that I think are important to drawing."

Moving on from the tools to the work those tools are used on, Kubert has very specific recommendations for breaking down a comic strip script into pages and panels.

"The cartoonist has to be able to tell a story graphically, tactfully and effectively, but most importantly, to be legible. If you design a page that's really attractive looking, but the reader can't make heads or tails out of what the story's about, then you've really defeated your own purpose. It's important for people to realize that the cartoonist is essentially a storyteller. If he doesn't successfully put across those elements then he's not doing his job. In the case of art designers who put wall paper together, that doesn't have to be read and doesn't have to make any sense. If the color is nice, and the design is nice, that's what sells it. But in our particular case, the strength of the cartoonist is his ability to tell a story graphically, effectively and recognizably. So when I'm working out a script, I apply perhaps the same elements that a movie producer or a movie director does. He wants to make sure his story is recognizable, easily followed and as dramatic and as effective as he can possibly do it. And in all of those cases, composition, placing the figure in the proper setting, the sense of space and depth and de-

The cartoonist has to be able to tell a story graphically, tactfully and effectively, but most importantly, to be legible. If you design a page that's really attractive looking, but the reader can't make heads or tails out of what the story's about, then you've really defeated your own purpose. It's important for people to realize that the cartoonist is essentially a storyteller.

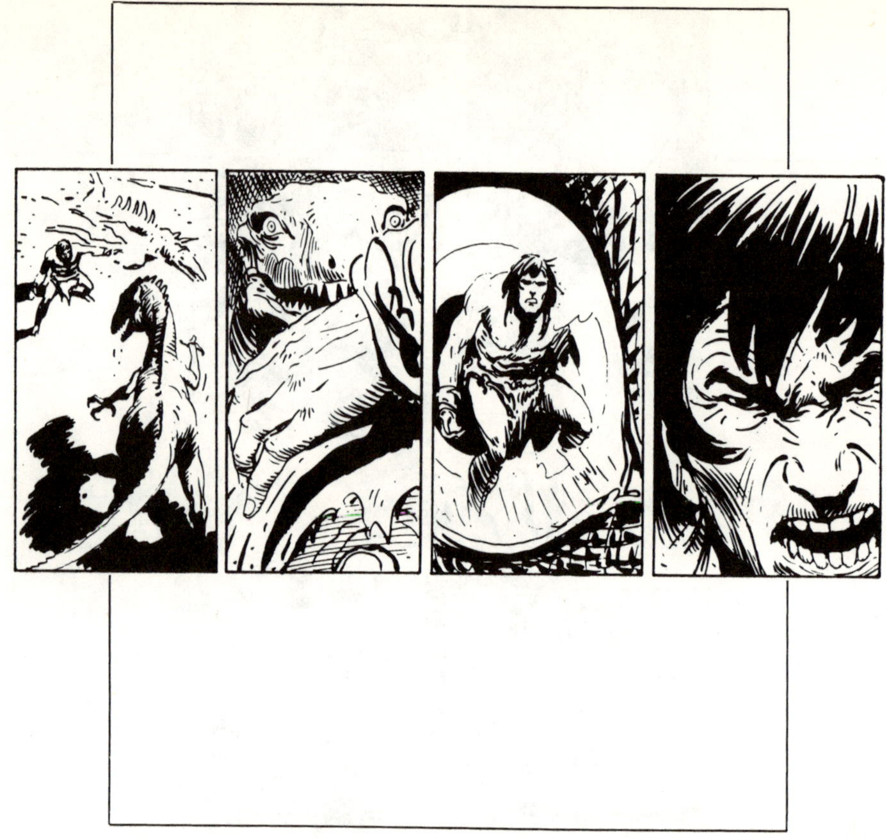

As far as breaking the action down into panels, that really depends on how long the story is, how many pages are involved, and how many panels per page.

This wordless sequence of panels progresses the action.

sign, are all contributory to the full effect of the story that you're telling. Clarity of storytelling is the most important factor.

"As far as breaking the action down into panels, that really depends on how long the story is, how many pages are involved, and how many panels per page. Most of the time, the stories that I've done were not along the Marvel script style of story. That is, Marvel gives the story a broad breakdown where perhaps one sentence in each paragraph describes a panel and then it's left up to the artist to make his selection and put the whole page together, after which the text is added.

"My preference, maybe because that's the way I started out, is to work from a full script which, coming from the writer, tells me how many panels he wants on that page and what's supposed to be going on in each one of the panels as well as what text or dialogue is involved in each panel. The reason that I prefer that is because I feel very strongly that the composition not only involves the figures and the action that's going on, but also how much dialogue is in that panel and where it's going to be placed, which is as much the job of the artist as creating the figures. To put together a page of illustration without knowing where the dialogue is going to go, or what dialogue is going to be there or how it might change the character is not doing my job. So given a finite number of pages and a finite number of panels that go into the page, I still want to know that I have the freedom to combine two panels into one, or do a three panel sequence if that works better than one panel. And with every writer I've worked, that's the way it pans out. It presents a workable challenge, and that challenge to

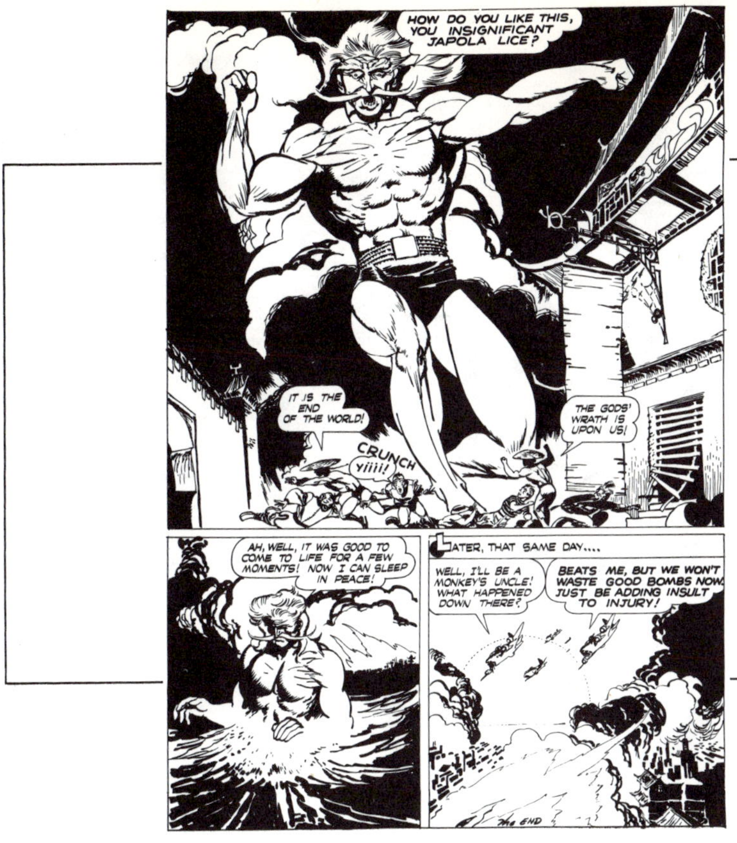

You use space to generate a more effective illustration. I usually try to do that at those points where I feel the story is most effective and can utilize that space most effectively.

me is that the writer has a concept, an idea for a story in his mind, and he's described that to me in the form of a script. What I'm going to try to do in making this graphic story is to to push what that writer has done perhaps one or two steps beyond what the writer himself has in terms of a good story.

"The number of panels on a page, for instance, relates to the storytelling mechanism that you're using. I don't care if there are twenty panels on a page, or two. It depends on what you need to tell the story legibly. I've seen artists who put two panels on a page, but they've made the illustrations so complicated that you can't read what the hell is going on. One of the guys who's outstanding in storytelling is Will Eisner, and I don't care how many panels he puts on a page, it's still legible, readable and effective. So the number of panels is far less important than what those panels are supposed to be doing in terms of telling the story."

The size and shape of panels used in breaking down a page is also an outgrowth of the needs of the individual story.

"You use space to generate a more effective illustration. I usually try to do that at those points where I feel the story is most effective and can utilize that space most effectively. One of the people I learned that from was Mort Meskin. He created the Vigilante character and a lot of others a long time ago. Mort was a very good friend, and to my mind an outstanding artist. In fact, early in my working for comic books I had a job inking in a lot of his work on Johnny Quick and a lot of other strips. Mort would look over a page of script and decide which panel or panels were the most effective and dramatic in

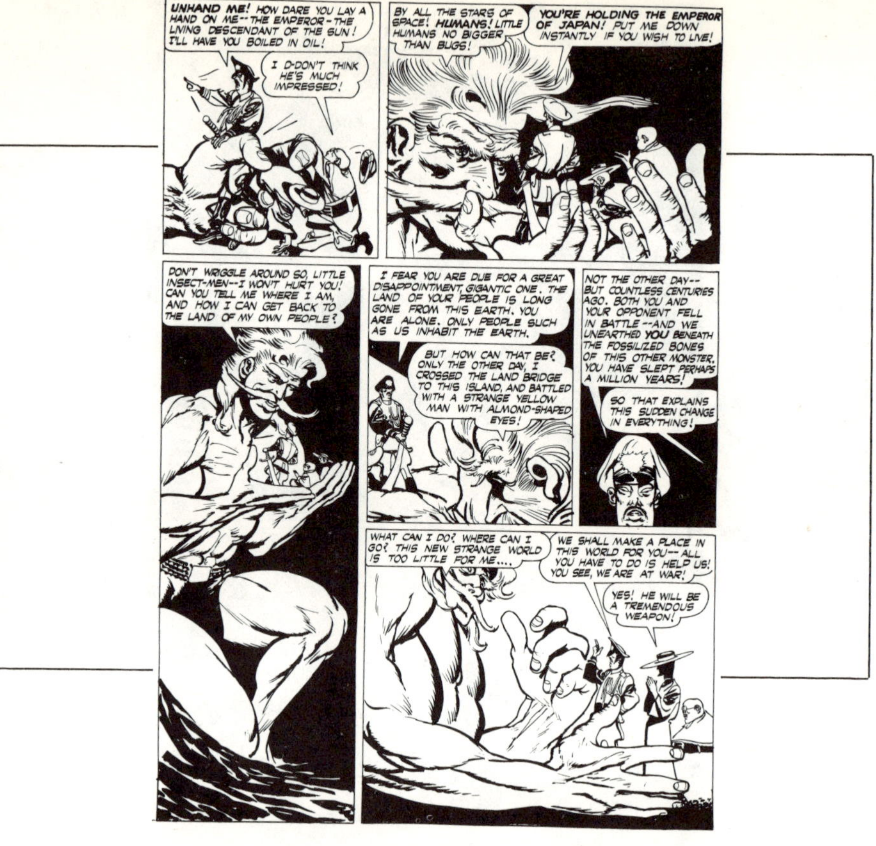

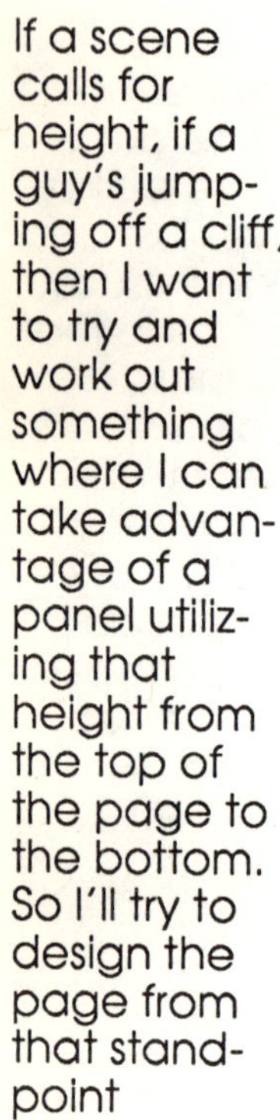
If a scene calls for height, if a guy's jumping off a cliff, then I want to try and work out something where I can take advantage of a panel utilizing that height from the top of the page to the bottom. So I'll try to design the page from that standpoint

terms of action, drama or whatever it might be. And he would design his page so that particular sequence took the largest space. For instance, if you have a fight scene and you have six panels of action and you devote equal sizes to each one of the panels, then you're not really taking full advantage of the battle scene. If the guy just discovered that he killed somebody inadvertently, and that is just one of the six panels, I'd feel the lack of utilization of space takes away from the impact that the illustration would otherwise have. So when I designed the page, I purposely tried to utilize the largest space for the most dramatic or effective action, just like Mort told me."

When breaking down a story into art, Kubert designs the layouts on another sheet and does thumbnail sketches of the pages.

"Those thumbnails can be the size of one by one inch. What I'm looking for is really not so much how I'm going to design what's going on inside the panels, but the overall design of the page. For instance, where I want a closeup. Where I want a long shot. Where, perhaps, I want a vertical panel as opposed to a horizontal panel and so on. If a scene calls for height, if a guy's jumping off a cliff, then I want to try and work out something where I can take advantage of a panel utilizing that height from the top of the page to the bottom. So I'll try to design the page from that standpoint."

Some artists become too concerned with rendering an interesting picture, and ignore how it advances the story, something Kubert finds unnecessary. He believes the art and story must work together and serve each other's purposes.

"Storytelling is *absolutely* critical. That doesn't demean or less-

SGT. ROCK

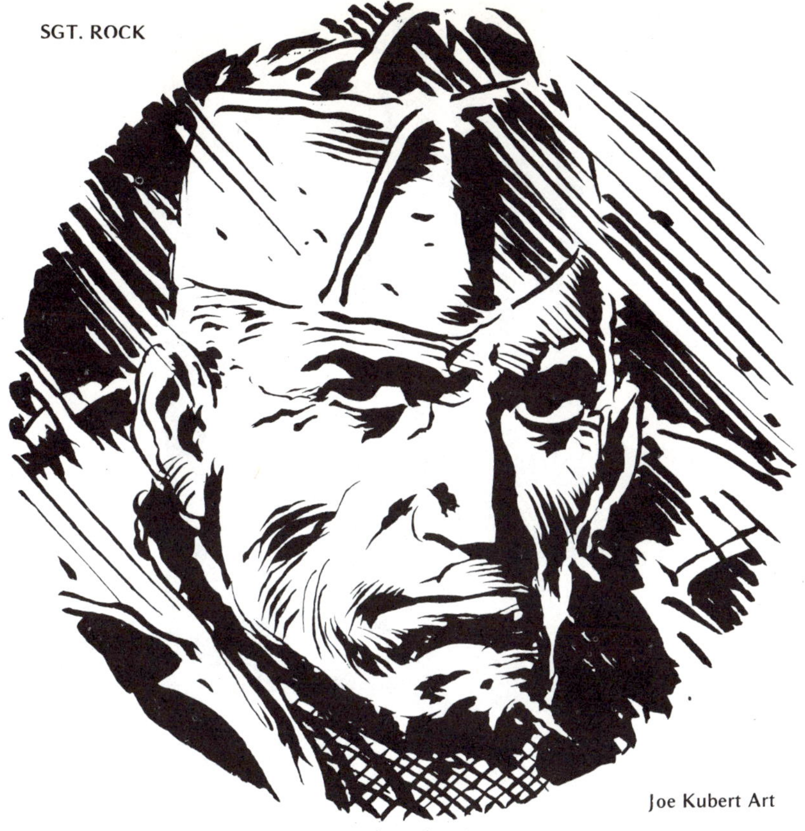

Joe Kubert Art

en the effect of a good, vivid, exciting picture, but that's part of the whole. An interesting picture involves the excitement that is lent to the page as the result of making an exciting picture in that space that you can devote to each one of the pictures. Still, the most important factor is storytelling. To be able to tell a story, to have a continuity in that story. What the artist is trying to do, consciously or subconsciously, is create still images which will give the impression of movement, and of validity. And if the reader loses track of the story, then he's looking at pretty pictures, and that's only a small part of the cartoonist's job. Drawing is the easy part. The tough part is putting those drawings in a fascinating, exciting and, most importantly, legible context. Storytelling is the most important aspect."

Part of creating storytelling which is legible and communicates involves using body language and facial expression.

"If you're describing a situation in a story where a guy has his back up against the wall and his life is being threatened and he's smiling while this is being told, well, forget about it. The person who's reading this says what the hell is going on here? Here's a guy who's being threatened, who's just about to die, and he's smiling. The artist must be sensitive enough to see what is going on in the world about him and has to sensitize himself to actions. When somebody gets frightened, he has to notice in his mind's eye what occurs when a person gets frightened, or angry, or sad or humiliated and variations on each one of these actions. The cartoonist really has to sensitize himself to everything that's going on around him and

The artist must be sensitive enough to see what is going on in the world about him and has to sensitize himself to actions. When somebody gets frightened, he has to notice in his mind's eye what occurs when a person gets frightened, or angry, or sad or humiliated and variations on each one of those actions.

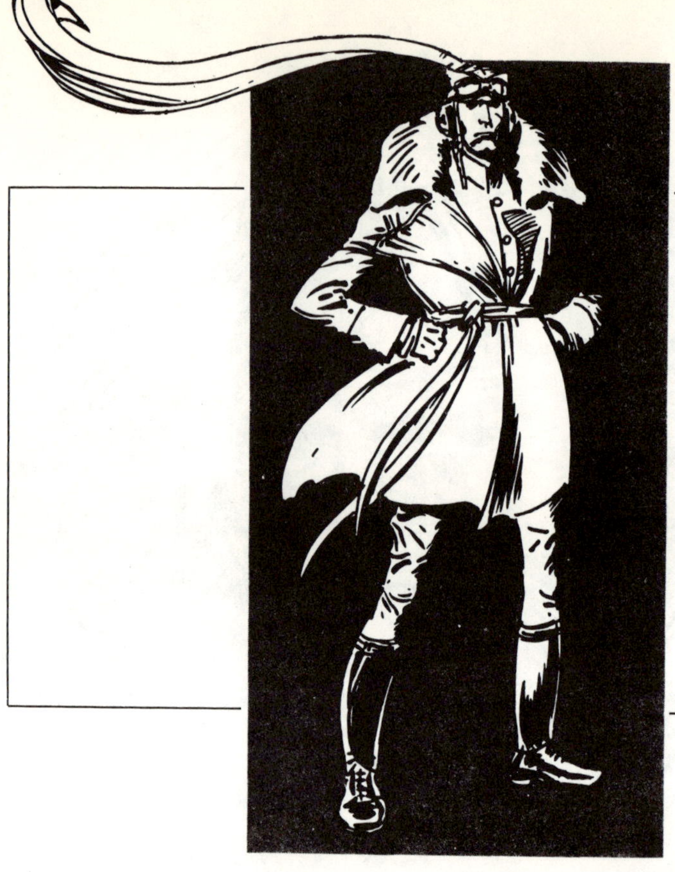

Body language is important enough so that when I was doing Sgt. Rock, I felt that it was important to be able to illustrate that character so that he would be recognizable without a tag hanging from his helmet. So that he'd be recognizable from the back walking away. For that the artist really has to get to know that character.

then transpose all of these things, filter all of these feelings and things that he knows and feels through himself and into his illustrations. It's up to him to get those essential feelings and emotions into an illustration and to communicate that to the reader. That's also part of storytelling.

"Body language is important enough so that when I was doing Sgt. Rock, I felt that it was important to be able to illustrate that character so that he would be recognizable without a tag hanging from his helmet. So that he'd be recognizable from the back walking away. For that the artist really has to get to know that character and give that character a history and a life so that he can feel how that character should move, how he should lean and what his body language would be.

"Some things should be avoided, though. For instance, a character constantly walking around with his chest thrust out, his legs parted, and hands on hips is all rather one dimensional. There should be variations of characters in order to make a story interesting."

There are many ways of making story and art work together, including the rare exceptions of stories told with no text at all.

"Successful strips have been done without dialogue, but that's very unusual. If we can do that successfully, that's great. I don't know if we could do that consistently. That would be a tough row to hoe if we had to do that with every story because some stories are so intricate it's totally impossible to describe every nuance of what's going on. It would be like trying to do a movie without dialogue. The most successful comic strips are a perfect union, a perfect marriage of word and picture so that the pic-

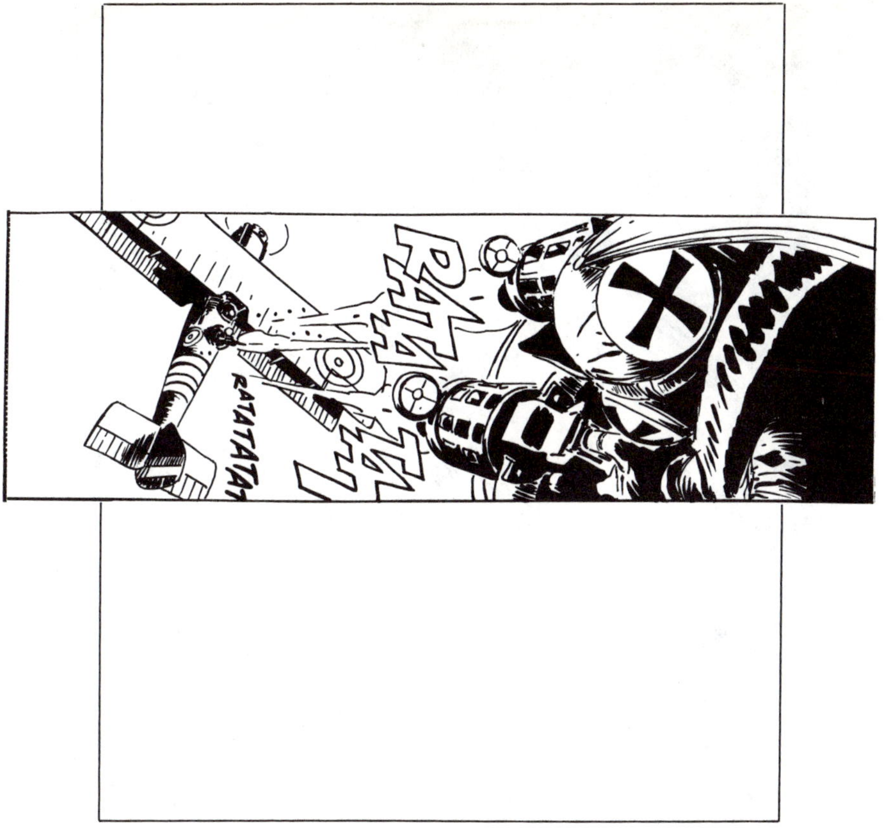

I think in terms of a camera. I also think of myself as the person to whom the story is being told. As an artist I create images to put the reader in positions that otherwise he would not be privy to.

ture isn't substituting for the words and the words aren't substituting for the picture but they work together as an amalgam. The person reading the story doesn't feel as if they're reading a story or just looking at pictures. There's a flow that occurs and the ability to be able to draw that does not come easily."

In deciding how to compose a panel, Kubert explains his personal approach.

"I think in terms of a camera. I also think of myself as the person to whom the story is being told. As an artist I create images to put the reader in positions that otherwise he would not be privy to. I can place them on the shoulder behind the ear of a person, making him almost part of the action that's taking place. In fact, point of view is a device used to pull the reader into the story. If you can do that, then the story becomes effective. Then it's touching that reader so that if you're reading a science fiction story and the artist has created a milieu where you feel you're on an alien planet and you feel you're in a position where you're privy to certain things happening, then you almost sense it, feel it, taste it, smell it and you become a part of the story. The artist and writer have enabled you to become a part of that story and that's when it's most effective."

Although most comics appear in color, some are still printed in black and white. Each method has its strong and weak points, and these, too, effect how a reader interacts with it.

"We've seen comic strips done in dull color and and those which in black and white were terribly lacking; they needed the effect of color to really make it a complete illustration. Other jobs done just in black and white are

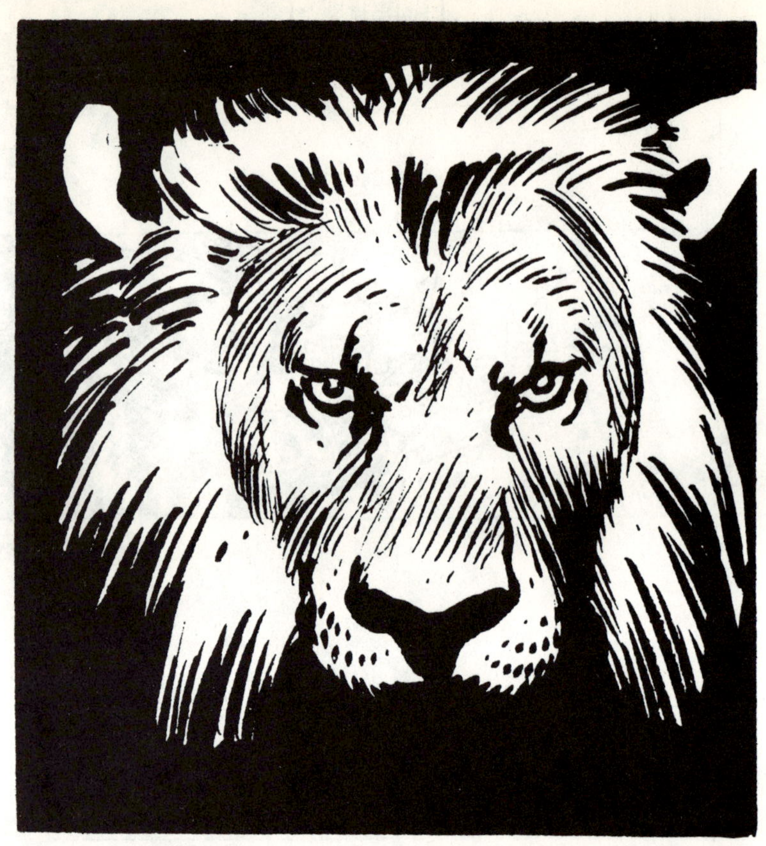

I tried to create an image in black and white which could stand up by itself. I think more in terms of the color being a tinting mechanism rather than a coloring mechanism.

extremely effective because the whole job is complete. An artist like Milton Caniff, who did **Terry and the Pirates** on a daily basis, utilized black to its most effective advantage. His drawings were finished and they were complete black and white illustrations, and most effectively done. In the main, when he did a Sunday page, he still utilized the blacks because Caniff realized black is as effective, if not more effective, as any other color that he's got on the page."

How artists utilize black in their work varies from artist to artist depending on their individual style and experience.

"Most of the coloring that was done on my art was not done by me. I've always tried to eliminate the possibility of change the color might cause on my artwork; I tried to create an image in black and white which could stand up by itself. I think more in terms of the color being a tinting mechanism rather than a coloring mechanism, and it's been my experience that under those circumstances the colorist has an easier job than just putting the color down. He can't read my mind as far as what I had in mind when I was doing the drawing. There's no way unless I put a color note down, and even at that there would be variations. But if this is a night scene and I put the sky in crosshatch or make it dark in whatever way I want in terms of that black and white, then any color that he puts down on that black would work, even a yellow. So I find that it has eliminated a lot of problems in trying to make that illustration and that story as complete as possible in terms of black and white. So if somebody else is coloring it they're not hampered by having to read my mind to know what colors I wanted to put down."

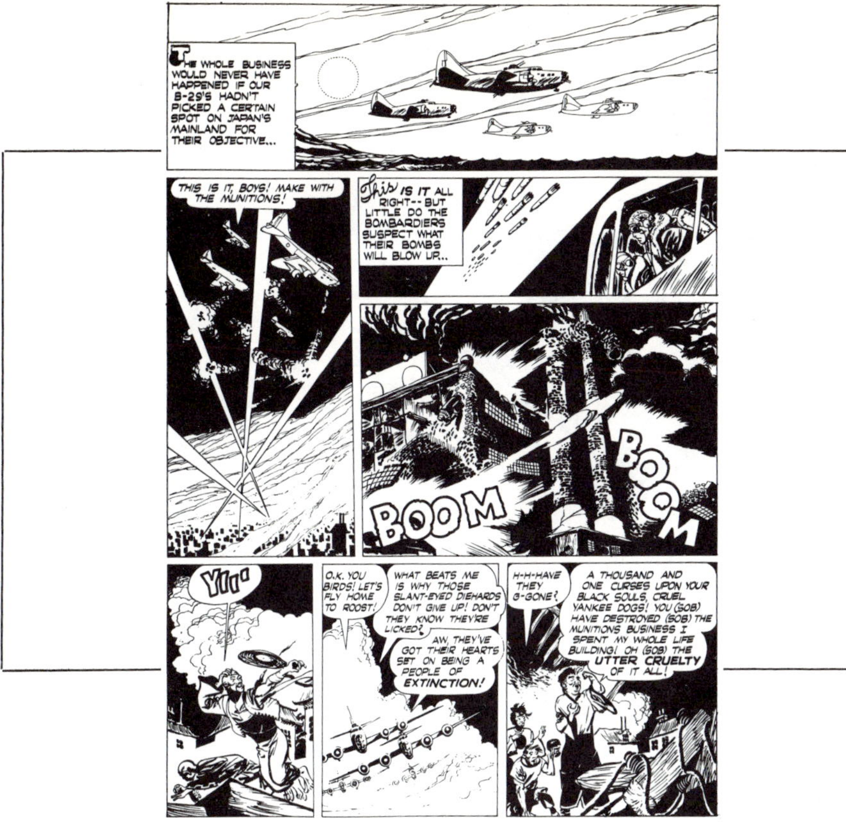

I don't like anybody else inking my work. It's not because I think it denigrates the work, or somebody else's inking is better or worse than mine. It's just different. I feel that, as an artist, I'm making a statement with the work I'm doing and it's not my statement if that work is broken or splintered up into different groups.

Although many artists are hired as pencillers only and other hands ink their work, Kubert has avoided this as much as possible. Thus when he pencils a page he's not concerned with someone adding to his work or putting in details his pencils didn't suggest.

"I don't like anybody else inking my work. It's not because I think it denigrates the work, or somebody else's inking is better or worse than mine. It's just different. I feel that, as an artist, I'm making a statement with the work I'm doing and it's not my statement if that work is broken or splintered up into different groups. What I'm looking for is to do the entire job. In fact, the work I'm doing right now not only includes the pencilling and inking, but also the lettering, the coloring and the storytelling. That, to me, is the ultimate of what a cartoonist could and should be doing. And since I don't have anybody else inking my stuff, I pencil it to the degree where I can add work to it when I'm inking. To me, to do a pencil job that is so tight that all it takes is just re-inking the pencils becomes a little bit boring. It's almost like duplicating that same illustration. So what I do is, in my pencils, allow myself enough latitude to impart, in my inking, another phase or another sector of what the whole illustration is going to be.

"That is something, incidentally, that novices should consider very carefully before they try because good drawing is not a matter of luck. People should know that a professional can't afford to base his career on luck. The way a good drawing works out is that the artist applies all the basics that he's learned throughout his life, and he doesn't even do that consciously. Those basics have

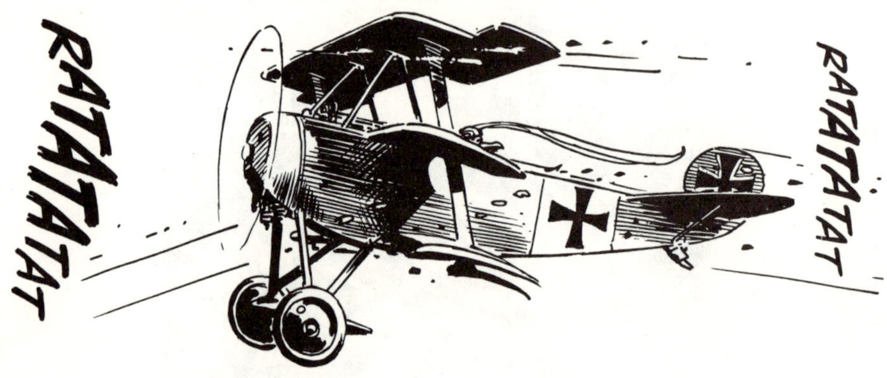

If you give a sense of unbelievability when it comes to objects then that refutes the validity of the entire story. We try to make what we do utterly believable, regardless of how outrageously imaginative it is.

become such an integrated part of him that whenever he draws, whenever he picks up that pencil, almost automatically, intuitively, he applies everything that he knows.

"I've been at this for so long, I can leave a lot out of my pencils that perhaps others would have a problem in inking. But when I first started, as with most people, I didn't do that and I wouldn't recommend that approach for novices. A lot of young people starting out have a tendency to put less into their pencils than they should because they're anxious to get the drawing done. You have to learn how to pace yourself to do this kind of work. You can't be going a hundred miles an hour all the time and finish what you set out to do. If the person is just starting out, they should have enough information in their pencils to know clearly what the drawing is going to look like when they're finished."

Part of knowing what a drawing is going to look like when it's finished is dependant on good research, such as when the artist has to draw actual cars, planes and weapons. This is where the artist's swipe file comes into play.

"It's absolutely critical. If you give a sense of unbelievability when it comes to any of those objects then that refutes the validity of the entire story. We try to make what we do utterly believable, regardless of how outrageously imaginative it is. Alex Raymond, who created Flash Gordon, was able to create a world that seemed believable fifty years ago when the idea of leaving the Earth was strictly Jules Verne stuff. He had enough knowledge of mechanical objects to put together a rocketship, or the buildings on the planet

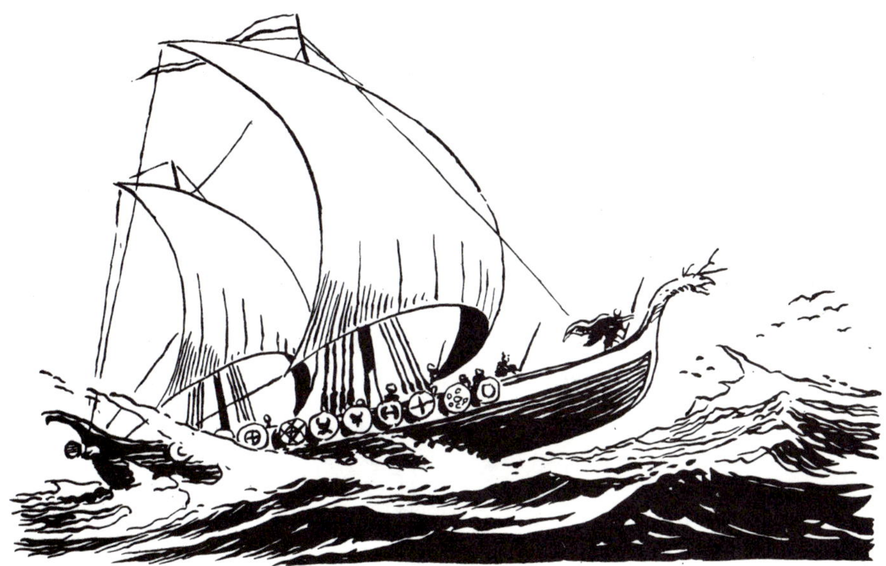

VIKING PRINCE Joe Kubert Art

Mongo, so that it seemed reasonable these things would work. And because of that believability and that credible kind of set up that he had in his illustrations, the whole story was credible. And if the whole story is credible, then the people who read it are concerned with what happens to the characters. But if the story is not credible, you don't care what happens to the characters. They don't mean anything.

"The swipe file gives you the knowledge. If anybody asks me to draw a car, well, I guess I can get away with that. But if anybody asks me to draw a Cadillac, I'm going to need reference because I don't remember the details. I can draw a building, but if anybody asks me to do the Empire State Building, I'd have to use reference. I can draw airplanes, but to do a tri-winged Fokker I'm going to have to have reference. Not only that, but when I did Enemy Ace I got every kind of reference I could, inside and out. I read about how the things were put together, how it was laced together and how the pilot would sit inside the cockpit and how he would feel in flying so that I could get a feel of that airplane in flight. Then when I drew it, I tried to get that feeling of cloth and wire and wood slapped together across to the readers."

Kubert feels that a firm background in reading the comics form is far from enough for an artist to learn.

"A cartoonist learns his craft by learning how to draw, and you don't learn how to draw from watching other comic book artists. You learn to draw by going to base one, which is learning about anatomy, properly, from looking at artists like Michaelangelo, Rubens, DaVinci and from every anatomy book you can get

When I did Enemy Ace I got every kind of reference I could, inside and out. I read about how the things were put together, how it was laced together and how the pilot would sit inside the cockpit and how he would feel in flying so that I could get a feel of that airplane in flight. Then when I drew it, I tried to get that feeling of cloth and wire and wood slapped together across to the readers.

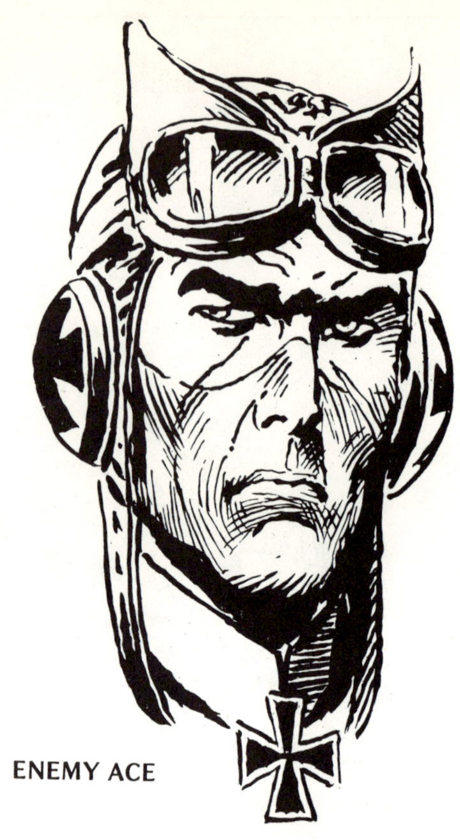

ENEMY ACE

To me the ability to draw is to sit down, take a piece of paper and a pencil, and if somebody says: 'I want you to draw a figure of somebody running straight at you, a man, not a superhero character, not somebody whose muscles are bulging all over the place. I want you to draw an anatomically correct human figure with the proper foreshortening in the torso and the proper proportion and balance without any reference at all.

in addition to life drawing classes, composition classes, color classes. You learn how to draw well first, and by that I don't mean learning how to ink or learning how to render or learning how to use an airbrush or how to put color so that it blends beautifully from one to another. Coloring and applying those kinds of things to a piece of artwork is part of drawing, but it's not drawing. To me the ability to draw is to sit down, take a piece of paper and a pencil, and if somebody says: 'I want you to draw a figure of somebody running straight at you, a man, not a superhero character, not somebody whose muscles are bulging all over the place. I want you to draw an anatomically correct human figure with the proper foreshortening in the torso and the proper proportion and balance without any reference at all. I want the fingers to look like fingers, the hands to look like hands and so forth. Do that without any reference at all. Do that right now. I don't care if you use a pencil or a pen or if you dip your finger in the ink and use it. Just do that drawing for me.'

"Every guy in this business, like Jack Kirby, Neal Adams, John Severin, Russ Heath or any of the people, can do that without a second's hesitation. That's knowing how to draw, and that's one of the requisites of what we do as cartoonists. Why? Because we don't have the luxury of using reference and setting up photographs for every drawing that we do. It's just not in the nature of the business. One of the most important things is to be able to tell a story clearly, concisely and effectively. The other, equally important, is to know how to draw."

An artist learns by studying the work of other artists, but the artist must know what to look for.

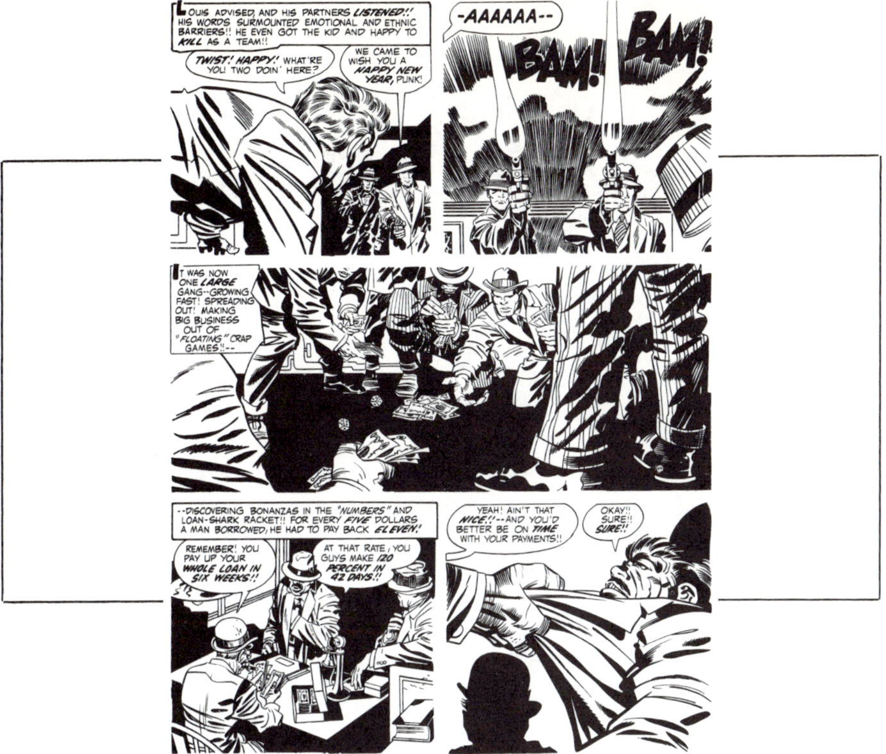

From "Murder Inc." by Jack Kirby

"Every cartoonist is showing you his interpretation. So a guy like Jack Kirby, doing the exaggerated poses and the tremendous foreshortening and the square fists and square knees and all that, is showing his interpretation. It's his rendering, his pulling together an illustration so that it comes across with the effect and force that he's looking for. Jack Kirby is one of the most outstanding anatomists I know. He knows anatomy backwards and forwards. That's the only way he can gain a consistency with the exaggerated work that he does. But a novice will come along, take a look at Jack's stuff and say, 'Look at the dynamism in that character! Look at the dynamism in the drawing that he's doing,' and attempt to do those drawings without the background and knowledge Jack Kirby has. He may even do one drawing very successfully. One pose. But when he tries to turn that drawing around or move that fist in another direction, or move the leg in another direction other than the trite, hackneyed poses this young novice may use all the time, he finds himself falling flat on his face. Why? Because he doesn't have the knowledge of the basics like Jack Kirby does, or like Neal Adams or any of these other people. You *can* learn from other artists. You analyze what it is in their work you admire."

Kubert doesn't think it's a mistake to be influenced by another artist, as one can see in his own work.

"Every one of us, as an artist, is affected by anything good that we see. We are all affected by everything that we see around us. If an artist does see another artist's work who he likes very much, what they should do is analyze it and see what it is in that work that looks good. And if

Jack Kirby is one of the most outstanding anatomists I know. He knows anatomy backwards and forwards. That's the only way he can gain a consistency with the exaggerated work that he does. But a novice will come along, take a look at Jack's stuff and say, 'Look at the dynamism in that character! Look at the dynamism in the drawing he's doing,' and attempt to do those drawings without the background and knowledge Jack Kirby has. He may even do one drawing very successfully.

There's nobody who starts out from scratch. Thank God, we all start out being influenced by work which gives us the impetus to go ahead and do this in the first place. And to be fearful that your work looks too much like somebody else's is rather foolish.

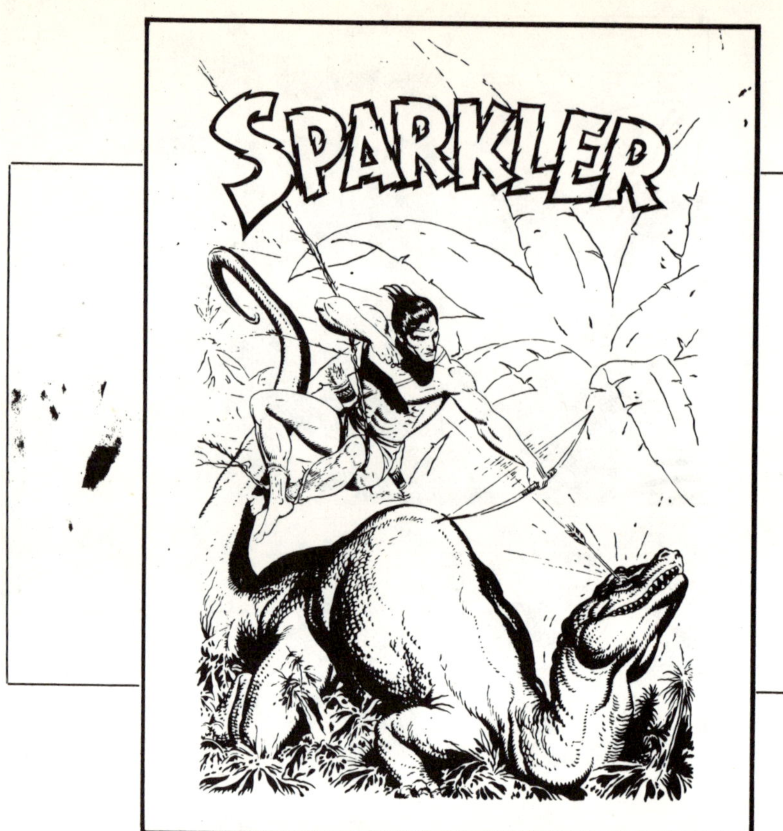

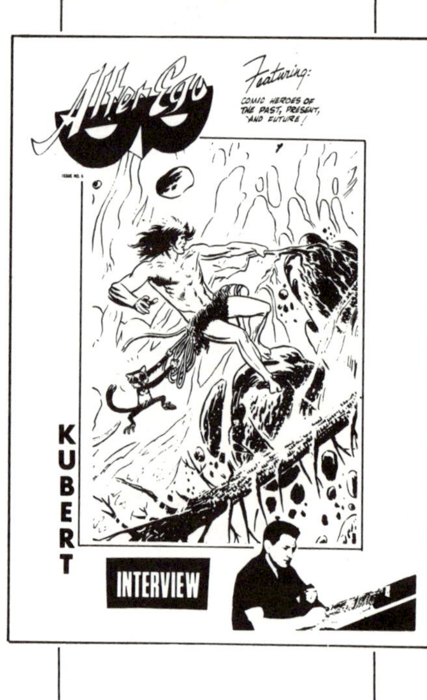

While Kubert began his career strongly influenced by artists such as Burne Hogarth he clearly made the techniques his own.

he's affected by it and his work looks like he's patterning it after somebody else's work, well, so be it. Eventually those elements that he likes and enjoys will slowly become his own. Another artist may recognize that influence in his work, but there's no question that, at that point, it will be totally that artist's own work. That's occurred with people like Alex Raymond, Hal Foster or Milt Caniff. Every one of those guys had been influenced by artists before them. There's nobody who starts out from scratch. Thank God, we all start out being influenced by work which gives us the impetus to go ahead and do this in the first place. And to be fearful that your work looks too much like somebody else's is rather foolish.

"One of the reasons I came into this business was because of the admiration I held for guys like Foster, Raymond and Caniff."

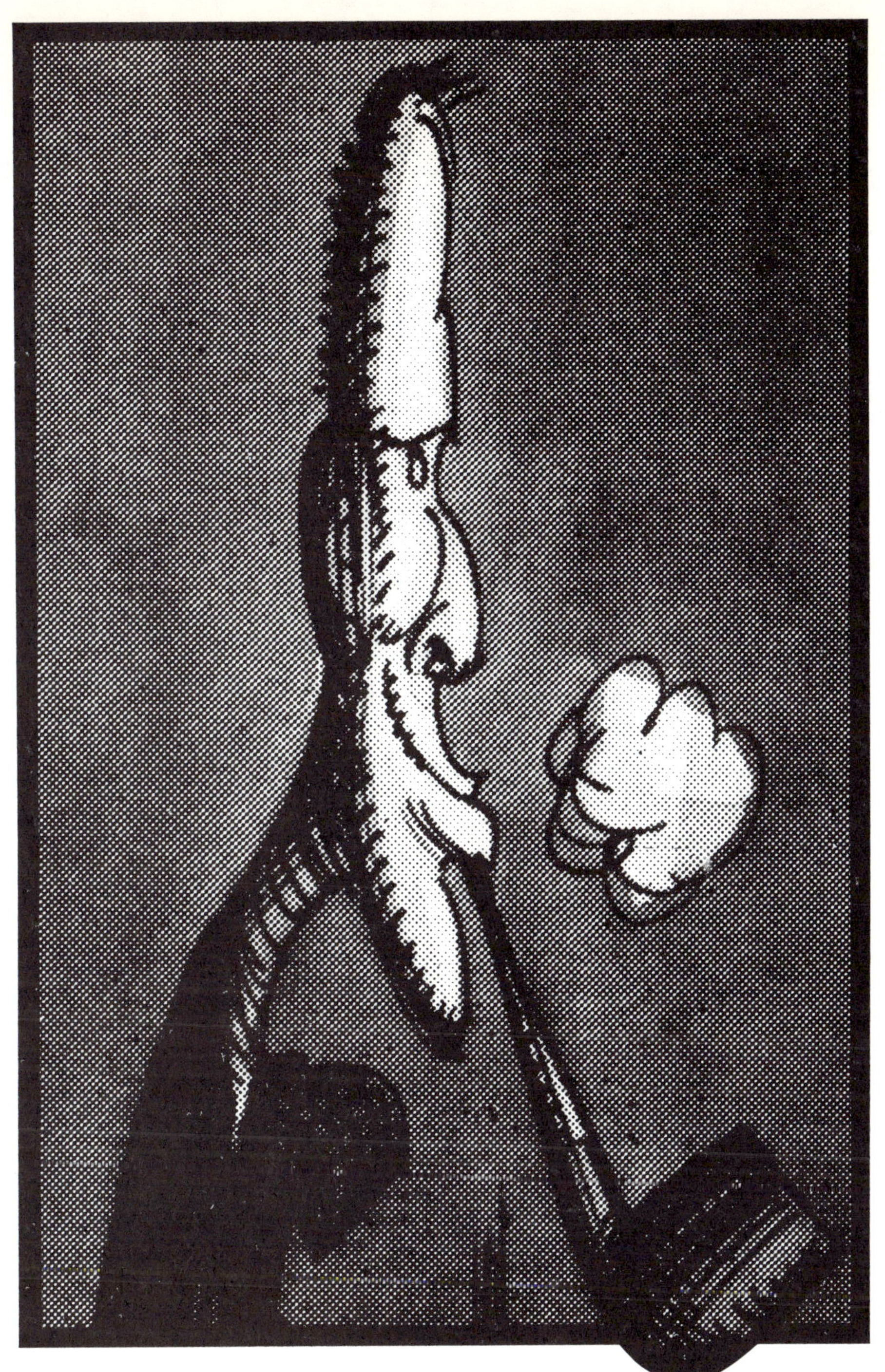

Chapter Three
HARVEY KURTZMAN

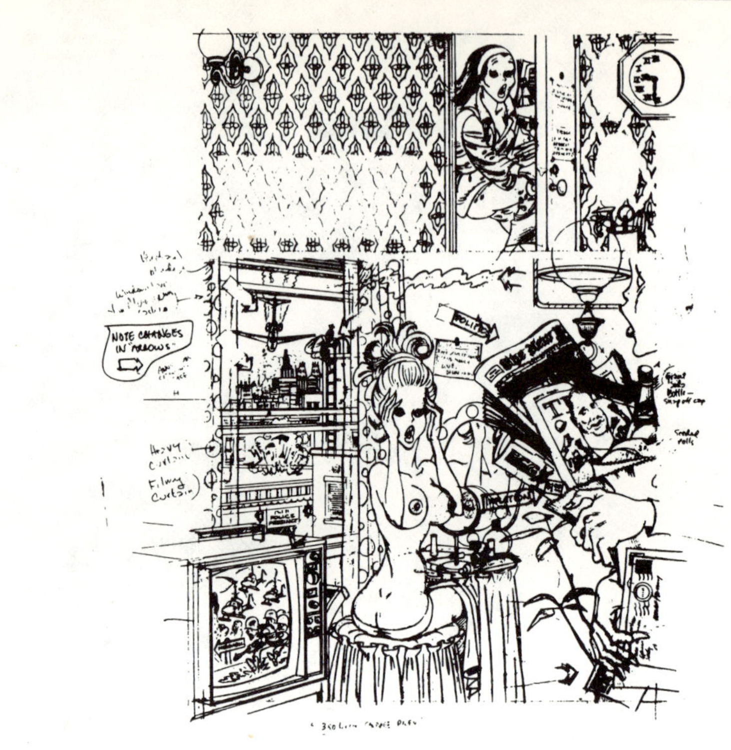

Preliminary art prepared prior to finished piece, also on opposite

The types of pens, brushes, etc. used by artists are generally arrived at after years of experimenting with different types. The one used by an artist this year might be abandoned in favor of a different kind a year from now. The fact that artists are rarely completely satisfied with the tools available to them is evidenced by the fact that when traveling in Europe, artists often visit shops to see what kinds of pens and brushes are available there which haven't yet made it to the United States. Knowing this, one might overemphasize the importance of these tools because artists always seem to be in search of that elusive perfect point. But if you put it in perspective you'll realize that an artist is always able to manage with what is available to him, while curious to see what else is available to replace it. It may well be that artists are never satisfied with the tools currently available in art supply stores, and keep searching for the instrument which will most completely translate what their talent guides their hand into rendering.

Kurtzman feels that, "the talent of the artist determines the technique." By this he means that even the finest tools cannot render what the artist just plain cannot draw.

Artists who have been drawing for many years tend to agree that the quality of the pens and brushes they buy today do not measure up to what was available to them twenty years ago, and in some cases types of pens they had come to depend on are just no longer available. This has contributed to the continuous search for the modern equivalents of old reliables. Harvey Kurtzman states that, "I like a pen point that you can't buy any more. About fifteen years ago I bought a box of pen points I like.

Born October 3rd, 1924, Harvey Kurtzman is one of the most respected creative artists in comics. An artist and a writer, he worked on a variety of humor and western strips in the 1940s (the Golden Age of comics) including over a hundred of his one-page gag-strips "Hey Look!" In the Fifties he began working for E.C. Comics where he wrote much of what he drew in the horror, science fiction and war comics. Kurtzman edited most issues of E.C.'s ***Two-Fisted Tales*** *and* ***Frontline Combat*** *and wrote most of the scripts himself for the many other contributing artists to those titles. He also created a comic book called* ***Mad****, which became a*

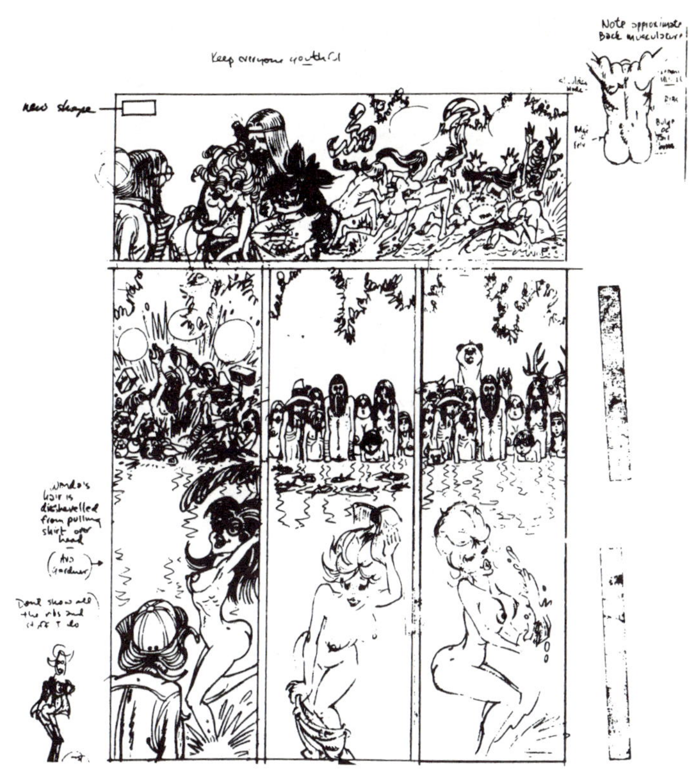

They were Gillot, rigid, and they didn't have a very fine point, and I haven't been able to find that pen since."

This doesn't mean that you won't find a point to suit your needs, as every artist's style is unique and the linework they want to execute might be quite different from what Harvey Kurtzman is looking to achieve for himself.

Tools aside, the comic book artist in drawing a story has to break down a given script into pages. If one is working from a "full script" (in which the story is broken down into pages, and each page is broken down into panels), then the artist doesn't have to concern himself with this so much. Some full scripts even describe how the individual panels should look. But today scripts are commonly more general than that, and even when an artist is given a story which is broken down into pages, the individual pages will only describe the overall action and provide certain key dialogue. While this makes more work for the artist, it also allows him a greater realm in which to be creative as he can then design the look of the page and exactly how he visualizes the action best being translated into art.

When approaching a page of script to break down, Kurtzman states, "You do first things first. Form follows function depending on the situation. By first things first I mean that I decide what's important, and after that, the rest follows." For instance, starting out by deciding the main action and which characters need to be emphasized. "It's a matter of deciding what's most important. You start with that and then you work your way outward. It's like a cartoonist that I know, Bernard Levin. He says that he

*black and white magazine after two-dozen issues. Kurtzman went on to create humor magazines for other publishers, with titles like **Trump, Help** and **Humbug**. While continuing to write other humor work in the Sixties, he created the strip "Little Annie Fanny" for **Playboy** magazine in 1962 which he wrote and pencilled, and which was inked and colored by his long-time friend and collaborator Will Elder. Kurtzman continues to do "Little Annie Fanny" on an irregular basis and also teaches at the School for Visual Arts in New York City.*

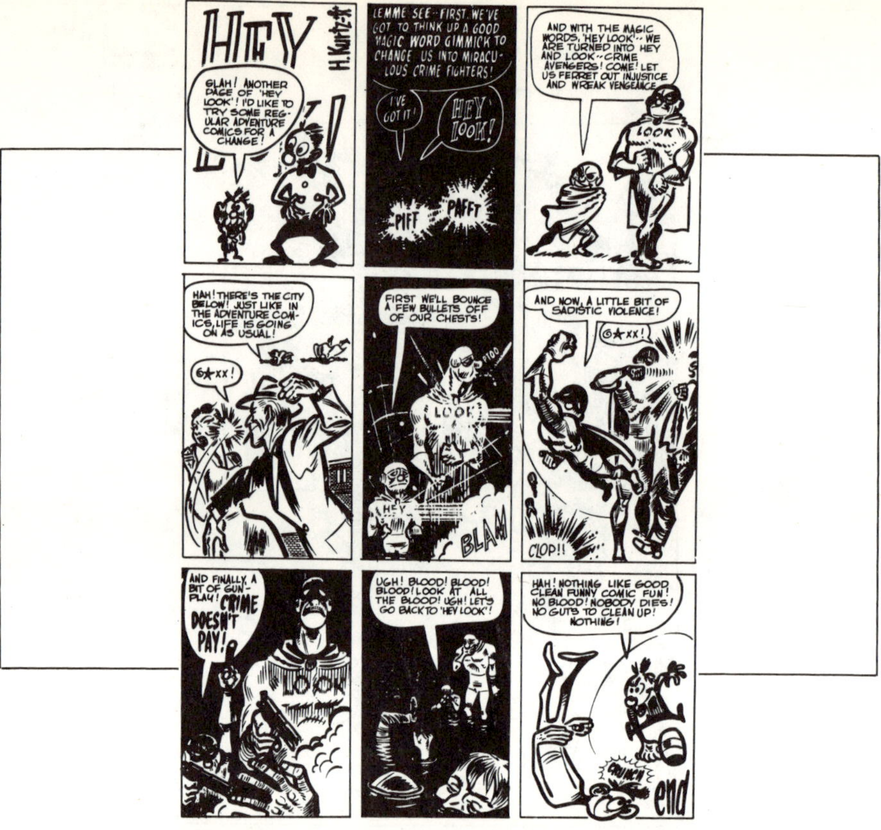

I'm a story man myself. I like to do writing. To me that's the most important thing—the writing.

starts with the nose and then his whole gag cartoon is built around the nose. However you do it, you do what's first in importance to you, and you work your composition outwards.

"I'm a story man myself. I like to do writing. To me that's the most important thing—the writing. Composition should follow the writing. Form should follow function."

Kurtzman is not impressed with overly fancy story breakdowns or unusual effects achieved with strange panel shapes, as sometimes this can inhibit the flow of a story and interfere with understanding what is going on within the confines of the page. "I remember when I used to be in comic books, guys around me would do triangles, circles, squares. They'd do everything except tell the story. I never fell for that."

But the use of panel sizes to achieve various effects in terms of drama and pacing is nonetheless important. "It's a matter of timing. You can speed your action or slow it down through the use of panels. A great big panel does several things at once. It blasts at you and gives you that advantage, but it slows down the action very often. A series of small panels can speed it up, done in the moving picture technique, so that an artist goes bing-bing-bing-bing! That can grease the wheels of the strip. On the other hand, you can have a series of drawings, say, ten drawings the same size and an object the same size sitting in each box. That'll cause a slowdown of sorts, like the ringing of a gong. So six panels per page, nine panels per page or one panel per page, it's all according to what your composition is. You can play with most of these continuities and your panels can give you

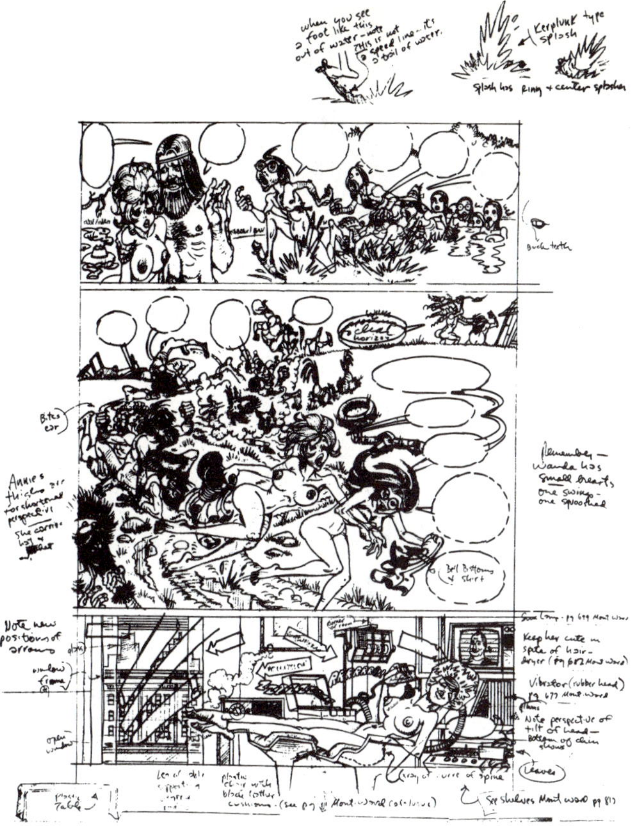

a continuity which you can strengthen by the use of panels. But there's no specific formula. That is, your formula could be in a series of panels or your continuity could be one panel, and it'll all say different things."

When breaking down the script into panels, Kurtzman does his breakdowns on another sheet of paper and works out the basic approach there before drawing the panels themselves on an art board. "When I've got it broken down, then I'll do it over in a separate place. That way I control my compositions."

Kurtzman feels that a synthesis of words and pictures makes for the most successful comic strip as the writing is very important to the effectiveness of the finished art.

"If you can write and draw, you're in luck. That's what my theory is. The best people around are the people who write and draw because that allows you to put a lot more strength into your product. If you have to get a writer, very often it waters down your product. So it's very important to have a synthesis of words and pictures. The strongest people in the business have that talent." But since many artists have to work with writers, the closer the two can work together the better, Kurtzman says. "The closer the writer gets to the artist, the better off the whole operation is. What most often happens is that the writer is visual. Today you have a lot of writers who are visual, and they make storyboards or sketches to get close to that synthesis of words and pictures, of writing and drawing. If the artist doesn't have a writer who thinks visually, then he can anticipate the problems. Writers should think visually, then they can anticipate the problems of having too much

The closer the writer gets to the artist, the better off the whole operation is. What most often happens is that the writer is visual. Today you have a lot of writers who are visual, and they make storyboards or sketches to get close to that synthesis of words and pictures, of writing and drawing.

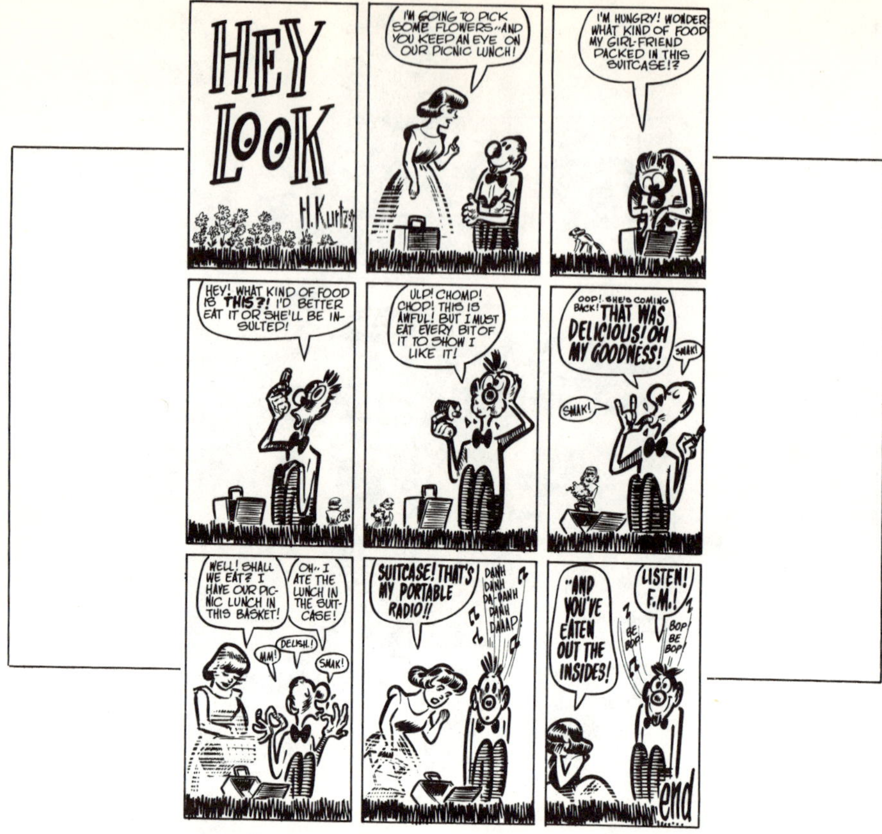

If you're not good at it, then body language and facial expressions don't mean anything. In other words, talent is what everything hinges on. Formula doesn't do anything for you if you don't have talent. You can have all the formulas in the world, but if you're not good, then you've got a problem.

text or too little text. They can anticipate whether there's excitement in the images." The artist should be able to read the script and have it unfold in his mind like a motion picture so that he can visually capture the dynamics that his mind portrays. "Absolutely, positively. It's very important to be visual. If you think pictures, you're ahead of the game. I used to see things like a moving picture myself."

Although body language and facial expression are often important artistic keys in rendering a story, Kurtzman doesn't feel they are the end-all and be-all of storytelling. "It's important if you're good at it. If you're not good at it, then body language and facial expressions don't mean anything. In other words, talent is what everything hinges on. Formula doesn't do anything for you if you don't have talent. You can have all the formulas in the world, but if you're not good, then you've got a problem."

Artists must consciously plan for the addition of color, since most comic strips are published in color. The original art, unless it is painted, is normally black and white, and the impact of black and white drawing and the use of contrasting black and white areas is an art in itself which should not be overlooked or downplayed.

Kurtzman feels each approach has its virtue. "When I teach my class about color, I always make the point that black ink is like a hole. Black is a non-color, actually. Scientifically black is an absence of color. Color is the presence of light and consequently black has a deadness to it that I've never been able to appreciate. It's a very important point.

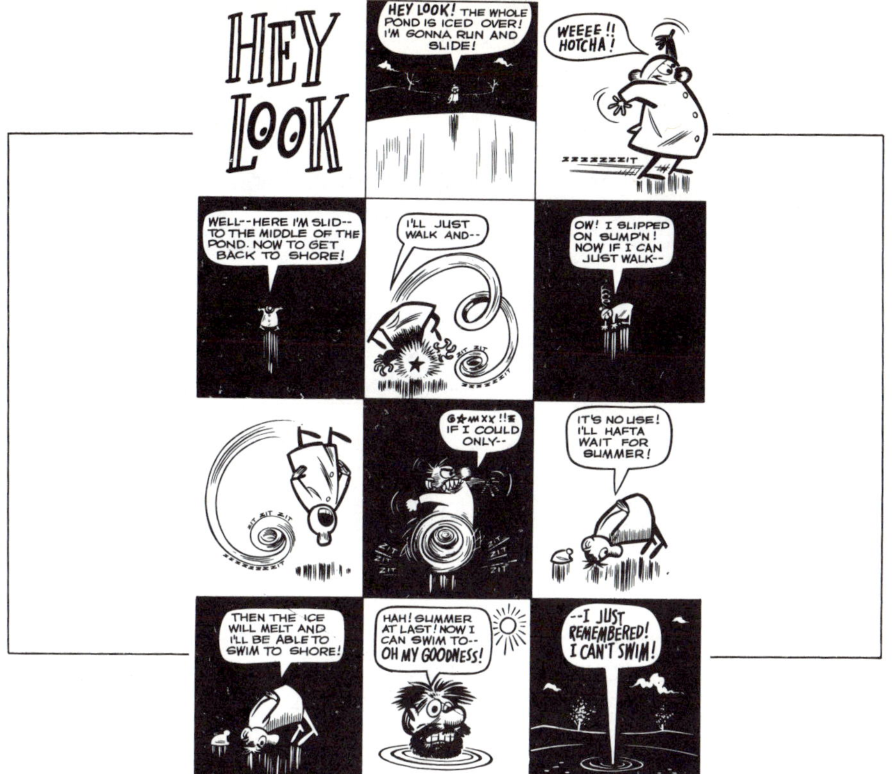

I've come to the conclusion that usually some color is better than no color. People enjoy seeing color. But let me quickly add that drawings *can* be spoiled by color.

"I've come to the conclusion that usually some c olor is better than no color. People enjoy seeing color. But let me quickly add that drawings *can* be spoiled by color. There's a Bob Crumb cartoon that I saw, and it was just beautiful in black and white. But then the publisher overprinted color and it was very bad for the finished effect. It's like the colorized movies. It doesn't necessarily come out well. The intentions are good, and people like color, but sometimes the original black and white is more pleasant and easy on the eye. So a comic strip can be more or less interesting with the use of color."

Different artists take different approaches to penciling, depending on whether they're inking their drawings themselves. In Harvey Kurtzman's case, he's not bothered by an inker adding additional details beyond what he suggests in his pencils.

"Not at all. Will Elder and I have worked that way for years. Will is a good detail man and, as a matter of fact, he started a system of sorts where he would get the laughs in the strip we're doing with the details he adds. The story very often was secondary to this."

This is sometimes done with background details, but Kurtzman doesn't feel this is a formula one can follow or not follow to achieve a desired effect. There are more basic considerations involved, such as whether the artist has the ability to make the basic thrust of the art effective. "Talent is everything. If you're working with talent, then the background detail could be important. If you're working with no talent, then nothing's going to help you." But if you have the ability, it is possible to use background, or its absence, to your artistic advantage. "I re-

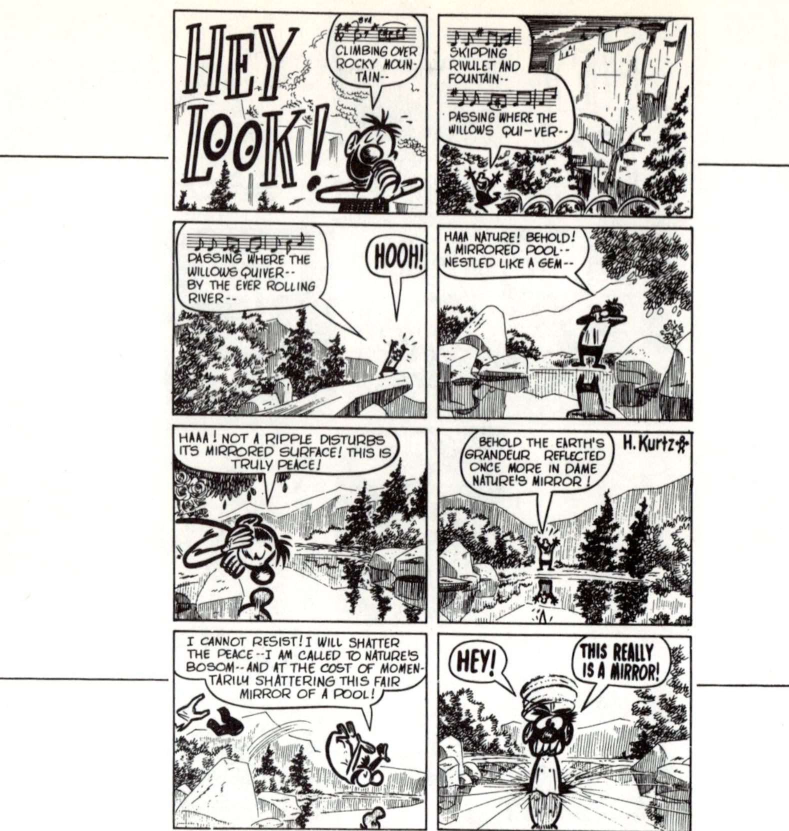

I went through great pains to research my material. Research is most important. It's more important in adventure type cartoons than it is in humor. Humor somehow is collected in your brain automatically. With things like military hardware, airplanes and guns I would have to spend a lot of time looking things up.

member things by Milton Caniff where he had no backgrounds and he did that with action drawings. By just confining the action to a foreground group, he'd be much more effective than if he had panels with a foreground and a background."

Another important basic which an artist must consider is his "swipe file." This is a collection of photos of commonplace items such as cars, airplanes, military hardware, guns, buildings and things which would not look quite right if an artist tried to fake them. Although beginning artists might feel that the old pros draw all this from memory, nothing could be further from the truth. Research is an all important task for any artist.

"I always worked very hard on my swipe file," Kurtzman explains. "I went through great pains to research my material. Research is most important. It's more important in adventure type cartoons than it is in humor. Humor somehow is collected in your brain automatically. With things like military hardware, airplanes and guns I would have to spend a lot of time looking things up. There are guys who do seem to catalogue the stuff in their heads, though. Most remarkable is Moebius (the French artist, Jean Giraud, who draws under the name *Moebius*). He's loaded with innovations. I asked him once how he does it and he said that with him it's like having musical hands. You sit down and you play the piano. People can do it without looking it up. They just have it in their head."

Kurtzman feels an artist should learn to draw facial expressions by studying them and adding them to their artistic repertoire. "That's the best way. That's the way I would do my research. When I had a problem I'd go

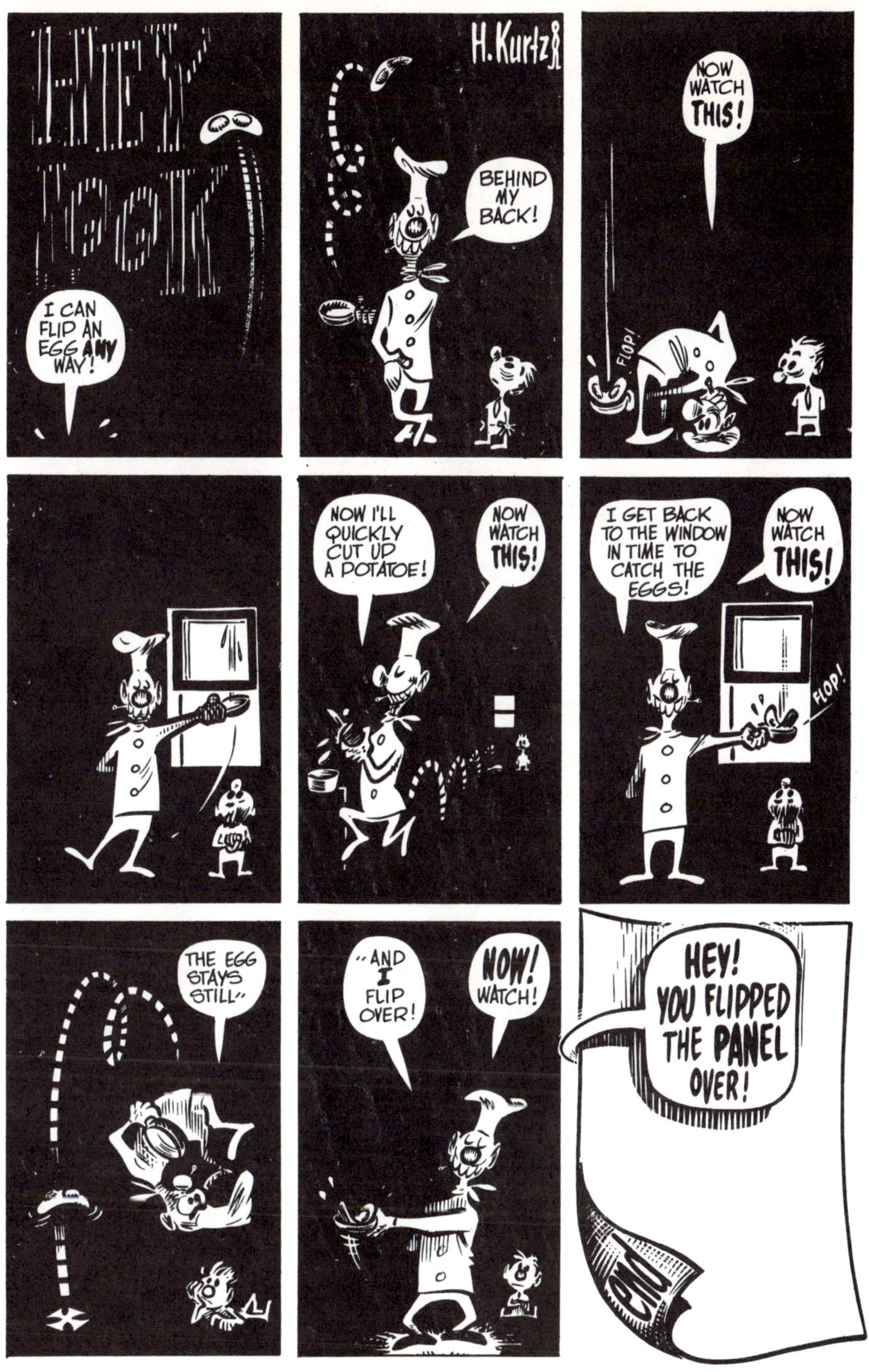

look something up and that would give me my information. I'd computerize the information in my head. That's very important, to collect material in your head. If you're a collector, you ultimately —whether in your head or your index file —have a collection of information and become skillful from that."

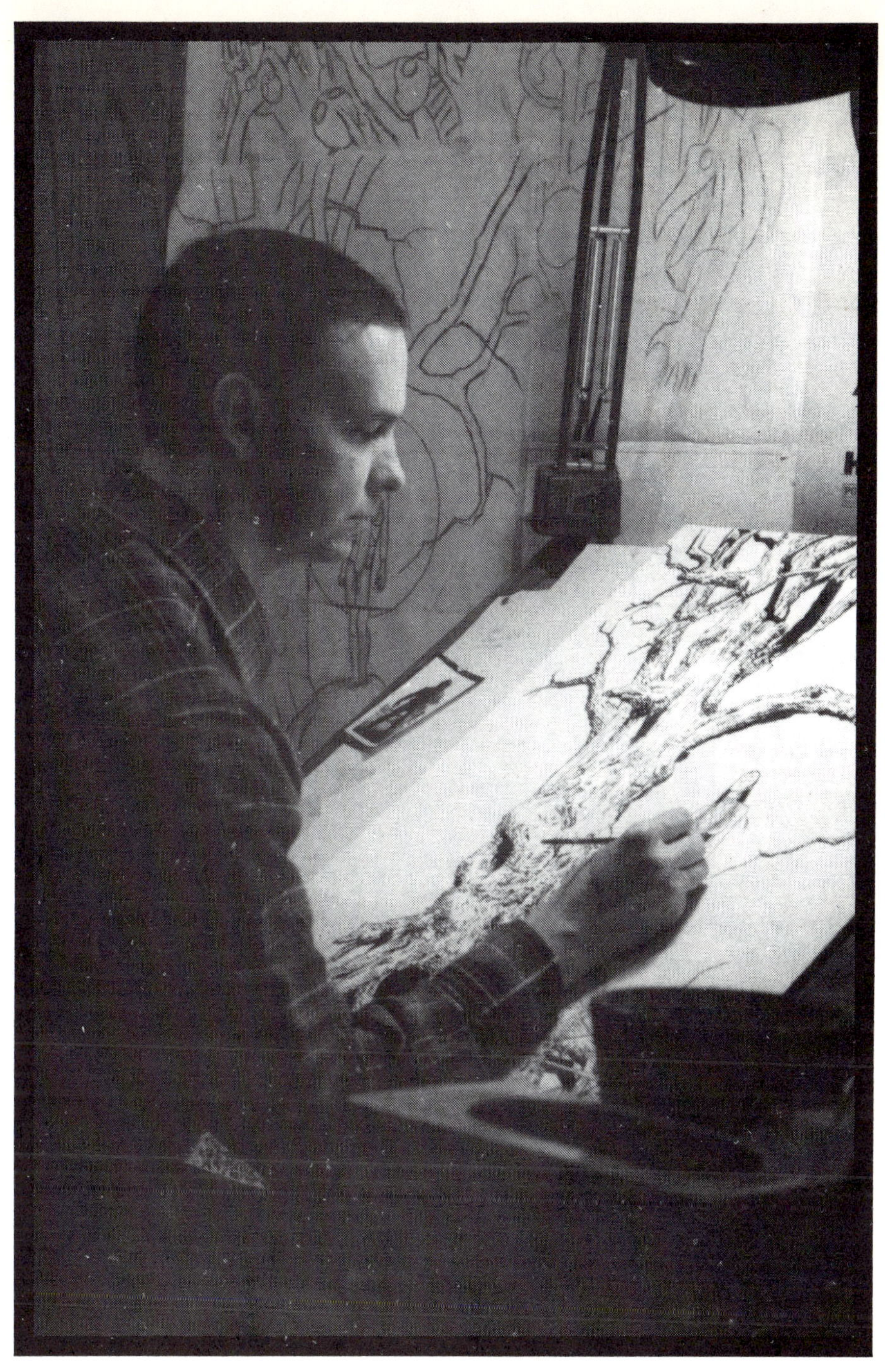

Chapter Four
RICHARD CORBEN

Born in Anderson, Missouri in the early Forties, Richard Corben grew up loving comics. Attending high school and art college in Kansas City, Mo., he acquired a B.A. from the Kansas City Art Institute. Following six months in the Army reserves, he secured a position in the animation department of Calvin Communications Inc. Not finding this a sufficient outlet for his creative energies, he began submitting drawings to comic art fanzines (amateur press publications often printed in quantities of less than a thousand). Finally Corben decided to become a fanzine publisher himself. He printed one thousand copies of ***Fantagor, and*** *with half the run un*

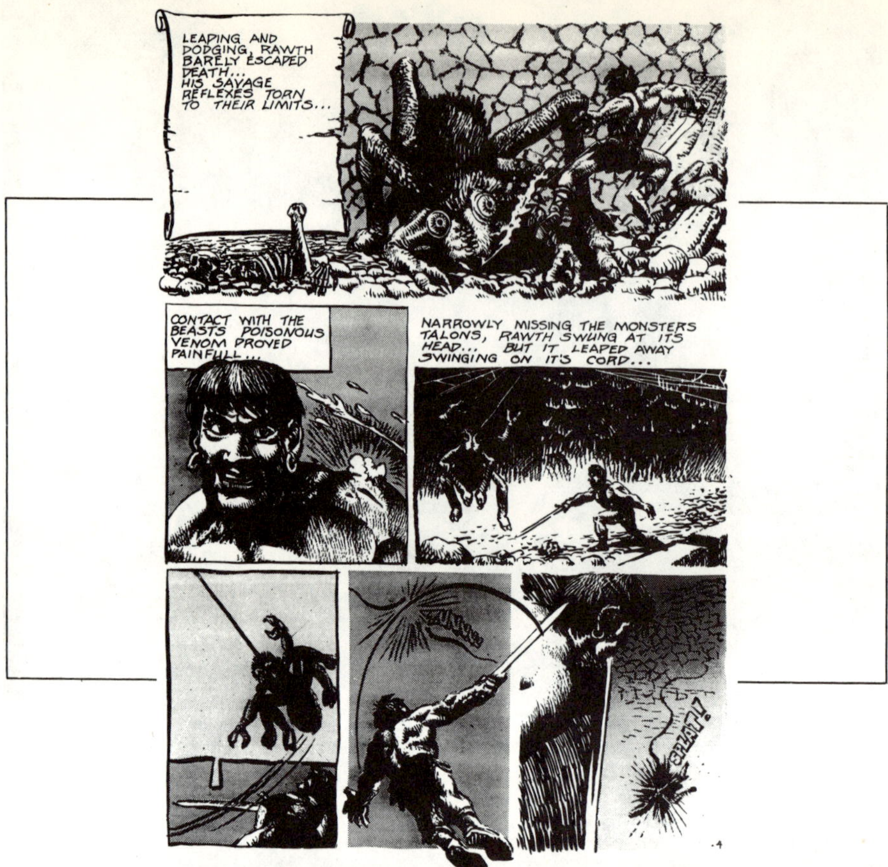

This and opposite page: early fanzine work, note undeveloped style

The tools an artist uses varies during his career as time brings changes in his style and advances in his technique. Richard Corben personifies this tenet as he started out doing pen and ink work and moved on to make extensive use of the air brush, an implement which requires a great deal of practice and patience to master. Discussing his basic pen and ink work, Corben states, "The early work I did was with the old brush line. Then I went directly into the technical pen line, like the Rapidograph. Now I use the fine point art marker with a fine Rapidograph point for a finer line. I'm always looking for different things to use. The amusing thing about the Rapidograph is that after I use them for awhile they have a habit of clogging, so I'll throw them at the wall and look for something else. That's why I like the felt tip marker; it's highly responsive. There's no starting and stopping with it. It goes when you go, and you can fill in areas without it warping the paper like most ink would."

Corben explains that how he breaks a story down depends on who's doing the writing. "The last time I had a real full script was back when I worked for Warren. The writers I work with now are more flexible. We'll talk about the story first and they might do an outline or a synopsis, and I'll do my breakdowns at that point and then they'll look that over and do the final words. How I break the script down is different with each story. It's got to be a certain number of pages with the climactic part towards the end, but still with good movement throughout. I really haven't analyzed it. I'll do it one way and if I don't like it, I'll keep changing it. When I do breakdowns, I take pieces of typing paper, fold them in half and

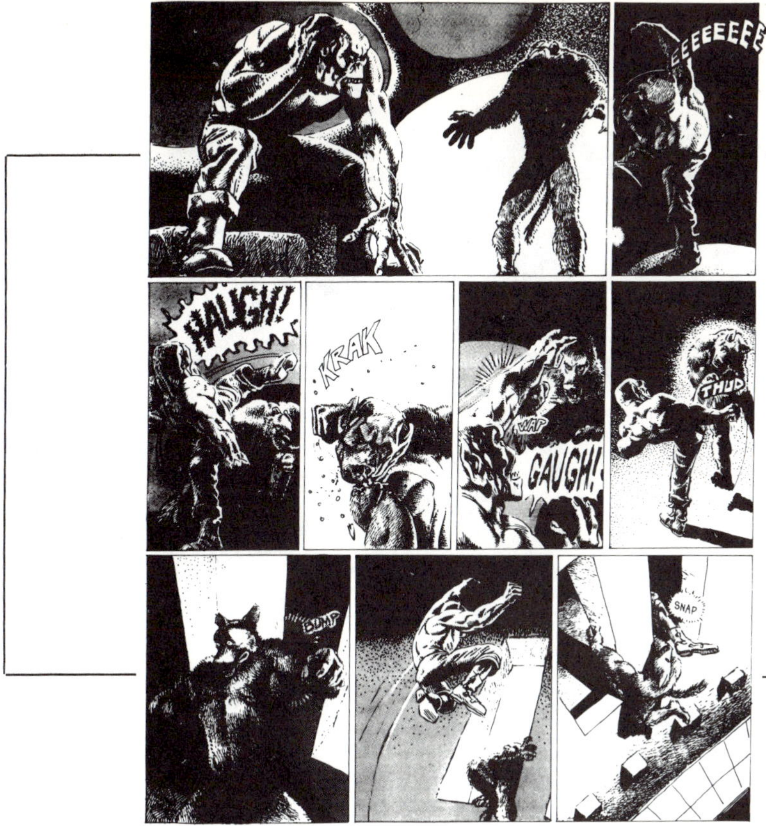

do a thumbnail comic on them. I draw in panels and some stick figures of the characters to see roughly what's going on and what they're saying. This acts like a first draft that I can rewrite."

Corben determines the prominence of figures in the panels and their final composition by usually making the main figure, "the person talking, but not always. I'll figure: What's the most important thing? And that's what I try to emphasize, maybe somebody who's talking or something they're talking about. Or maybe something's going on while they're talking that they don't even know about. It's like I'm watching a movie."

Corben translates into artwork how he sees a character's actions unfolding in his imagination . Their body language. "That's all part of characterization," Corben states. "It's very important, but in some characters maybe you don't want to emphasize it too much. For instance, if you've got a sort of stoic character who's not very demonstrative, the *lack* of body language would be important. Body language is sort of like stage acting versus movie acting."

Part of body language is the facial expression a character portrays. Rendering that expression convincingly so that it communicates a specific emotion and intent to the reader can be crucial. Learning how to do this is therefore also crucial. One way to learn to draw convincing facial expressions is for artists to use themselves as a model, via a mirror. "Yes, probably a mirror would be the main thing because you've got to *feel* it to be able to draw it," says Corben. "If you make a face as if you're scared and look at it in the mirror, then you decide that maybe you can

sold six months later, abandoned his dreams of self-publishing. Uncomfortable with the restrictions imposed by mainstream comics (including the insistence at the time of relocating to New York), Corben found a professional outlet in the then-new underground comics. Corben continued drawing for undergrounds even as the field started slowing down, but he also did a lot of work for ***Creepy*** *and* ***Eerie****. Corben found his work in demand in Europe and was quickly snapped up to be a regular contributor to a new American magazine,* ***Heavy Metal****. In the Eighties, Corben returned to self-publishing.*

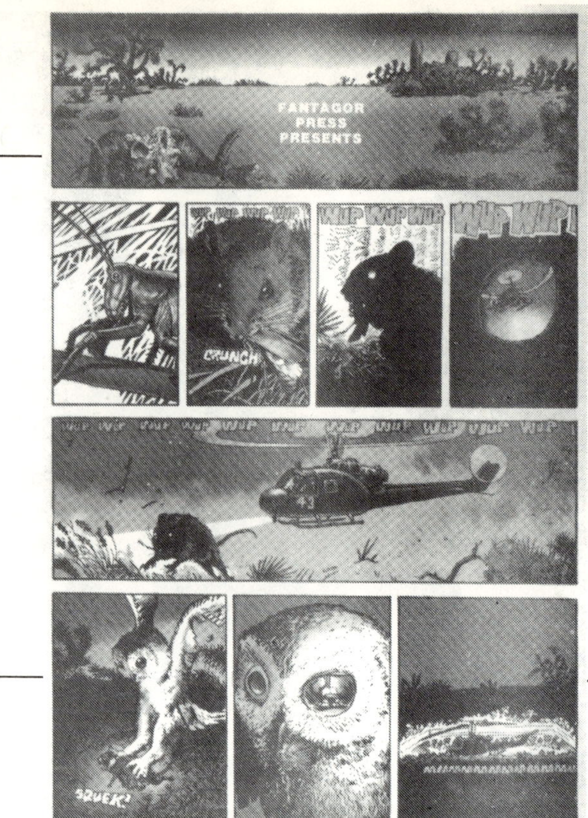

Some artists might feel that the art should be more prominent than the text. "Maybe some writers would object to that, but then the artist might counter, well, the art *is* the story. I believe in some cases that may be true.

improvise something around this in your art."

One of the decisions made in translating a story into art is what the balance will be between text and art. Some artists might feel that the art should be more prominent than the text. "Maybe some writers would object to that, but then the artist might counter, well, the art *is* the story. I believe in some cases that may be true. One thing I like about comics is that it doesn't have to be one thing. It can be many things. Some stories can work well with pictures. And for some stories the words are more important. It depends on the story."

When he's not working from a full script (one which stipulates the exact number of panels per page), Corben has the freedom to let the needs of the story dictate how many and what kinds of panels he'll use to break the page down. "Depending on the mood, sometimes little peripheral actions are important and you need a lot of panels. But sometimes the simplest way is the best and I do it with fewer panels. Say you've got a scene of people talking. Maybe you'd just have it in five or six panels with rather large balloons. Or maybe you can break it into four panels and cut the balloons down so that there's more emphasis on pacing, and that gives you a chance to go from a medium to a close-up to an extreme close-up from panel to panel."

Varying sizes of panels is one way of slowing down and speeding up the action within a scene. "This may be personal, but I feel that when you add more panels it speeds up the pacing and when you have fewer panels it slows the pacing down. If you have just one panel on the page it may be dramatic but it stops everything dead for that one page."

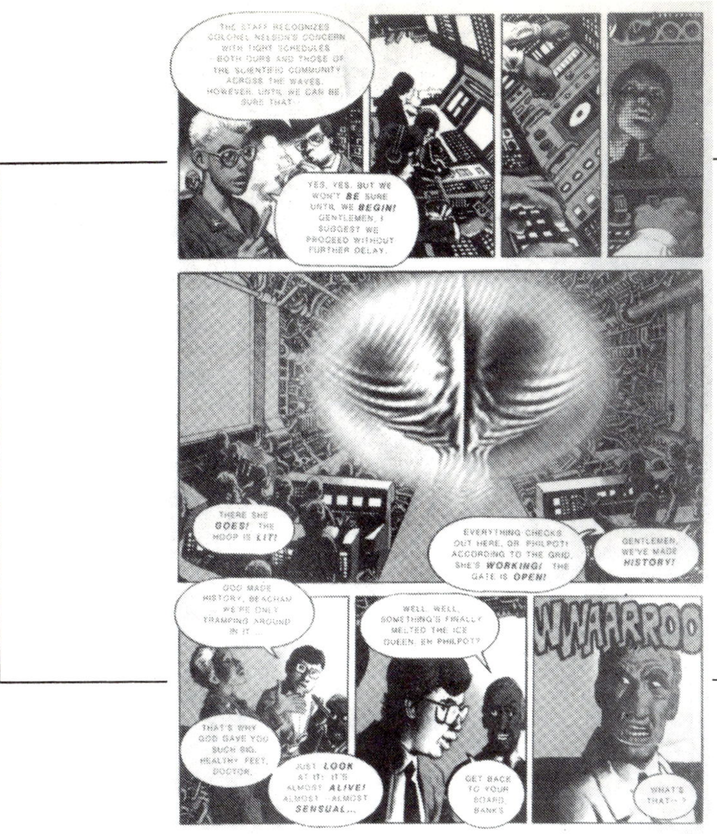

Although most comics are published in color, the use of contrasting black and white areas, of light and shade without the presence of colors (called "chiaroscuro"), remains an important consideration to the artist, and particularly to Richard Corben.

"Strong black and white art is important. There are great artists who use very little black and use contour lines only. Sometimes I try to see the artwork with patterns of black and white running through it, maybe as an abstract way of looking at things, as well as a drawing in that sequence."

At the pencilling stage, the artist decides how many details to include. Some artists include all of the details which the finished art will contain, while others suggest details they will finish later when they ink their work.

"My pencilling is very rough," Corben states. "My thumbnail breakdown is just like stick figures. When I start pencilling, it's slightly advanced from that, but when I start inking I add in more detail and then I may decide I need to work a little more into my pencils. Then I'll go back and put some more work in and then go back to inking again and switch off from one to the other. But the actual pencil stage is very rough because mainly you're breaking the page into panels and placing where the main characters are."

One of the decisions made at this point involves the use of background detail and how important it is to telling the story. "When you've got a lot of background detail it can slow down the pacing of the story and may even detract from what the story is saying. But sometimes it may be an important part of a story, such as the setting and the ambience." Once again, it's the story

Strong black and white art is important. There are great artists who use very little black and use contour lines only. Sometimes I try to see the artwork with patterns of black and white running through it, maybe as an abstract way of looking at things, as well as a drawing in that sequence

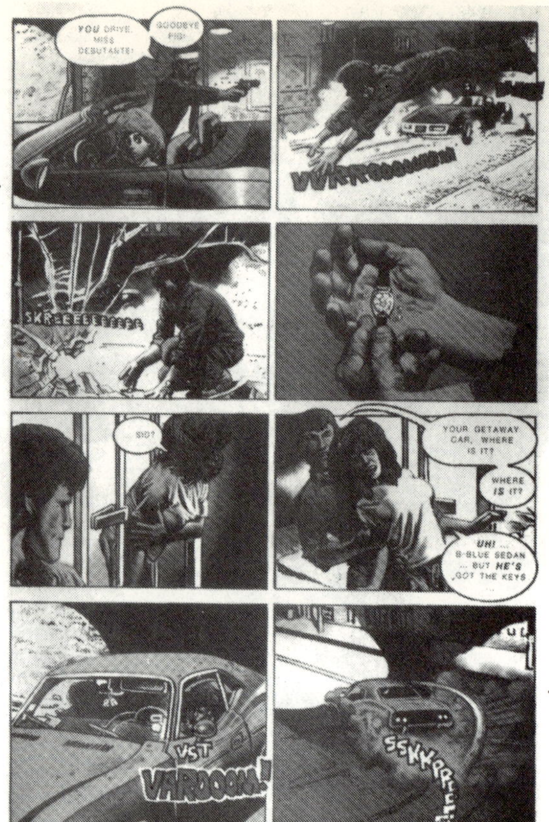

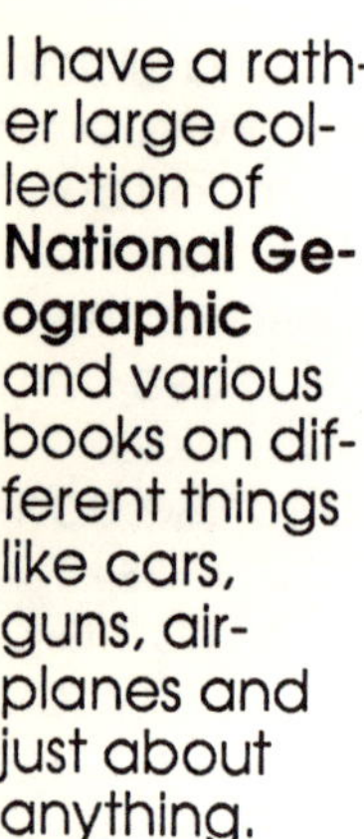
I have a rather large collection of **National Geographic** and various books on different things like cars, guns, airplanes and just about anything.

which dictates what needs to be in the art, and if the setting is incidental and secondary to the plot and the action, then filling up every inch of the panel with exquisite detail is quite unnecessary.

Details can be crucial when the story involves objects and hardware which are either well known to the reader or which require a degree of authenticity in order to make the action believable. This is when research and what artists refer to as their "swipe file" comes into play. "I have a rather large collection of **National Geographic** and various books on different things like cars, guns, airplanes and just about anything," Corben explains. "My assignments may not be specific, but I try to pick them as to what would be logical to the story and try to stick with it."

In conclusion, Richard Corben maintains that in order to draw comics well, the artist much know more than just what he can learn from reading and copying comics. This added knowledge broadens their approaches to what they're drawing and gives them much needed insight into the field.

"I've never taken a course on comics," Corben explains. "I went to an academic drawing course, which is very important. Your interest in comics will be a more specific thing. The problem I commonly see is that if someone is just interested in comics and they draw comics from comics, it becomes convoluted. All they do is swipe from other comics. Taking life drawing classes contributes to how you'll want to express something and you'll continue to have your own expression rather than just copying someone else."

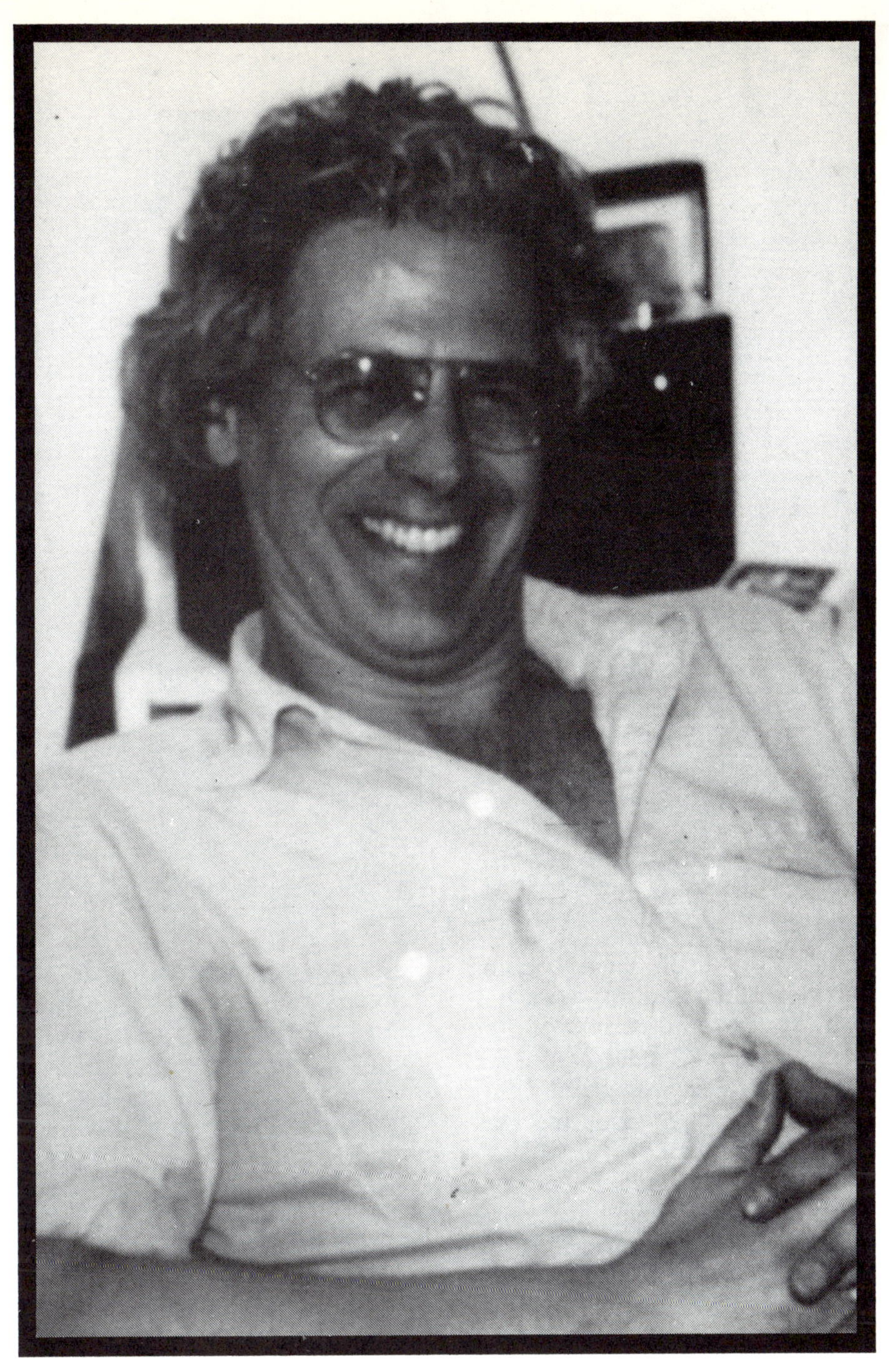

Chapter Five
AL WILLIAMSON

Born in New York in 1931, his family moved to Bogata, Colombia when Williamson was a year old and he lived there until he was twelve. While a child in Colombia, he fell in love with the Flash Gordon comic strip by Alex Raymond and the Universal serials starring Buster Crabbe. After he returned to the United States, he studied drawing and took a class from Burne Hogarth while just fourteen. By the time he was twenty he had started drawing for comic books and landed a job at E.C. Comics just before his 21st birthday. Williamson drew numerous strips for E.C. from 1952 until the company folded their comic book line in 1955. He

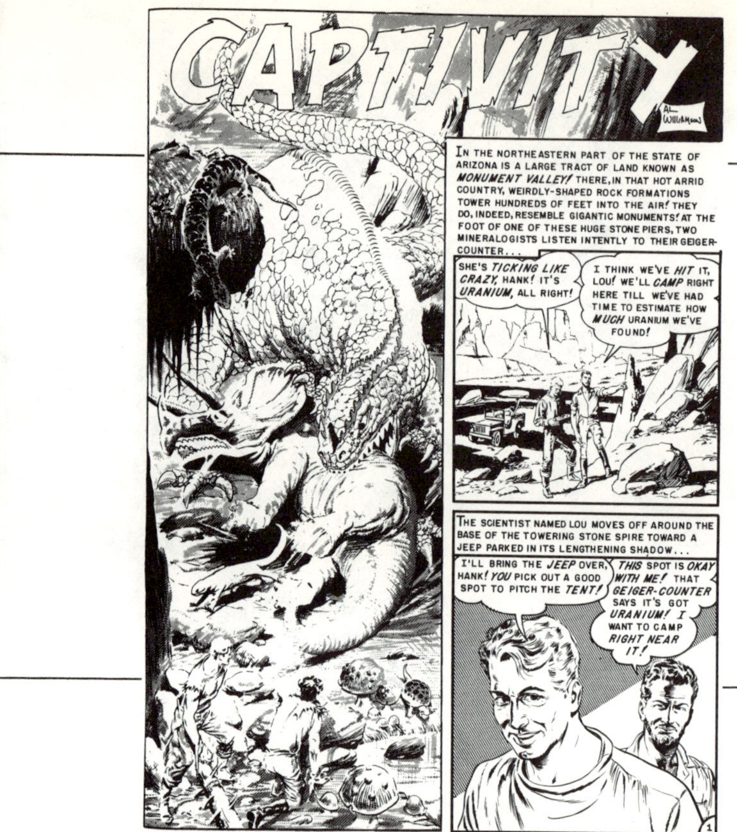

Al Williamson has become known for pen and ink work in a lush style reminiscent of the classic masters of the craft. Although he doesn't do much illustration these days since his stint on the syndicated **Star Wars** newspaper strip ended, his penwork is much in evidence as he inks the work of other artists. So using the right pen to achieve the maximum desired effect remains very much a concern of Williamson.

"The Hunt 108 is a very good pen," the artist firmly states. "And the Lang-Nickel #3-700 is a very good brush. I use that for inking." Although some artists prefer a brush over a pen, Williamson says, "with me it's fifty-fifty. It's the way I feel, or the way the job calls for either pen or brush. It all depends. I have absolutely no set way of working. The way the muse hits me, that's it."

Although the more loose arrangement of a plot broken down into pages by the artist rather than the writer is often the rule these days, Williamson has seldom worked that way. "I worked with a story from the Marvel Style once when it first started back in '58-59, but I didn't like it. I think a full script is better because it's all there. You can incorporate the balloons and the captions into the drawings without doing a picture that's going to be screwed up by having a balloon cut off somebody's leg or eyeball or something like that." With a full script, the artist just has to design the composition within the panels, something Williamson feels should be instinctive to an artist by the time they're working professionally. "If you grow up with comics you absorb that and you make the balloons and captions a part of the picture. The important thing is for the reader to follow the

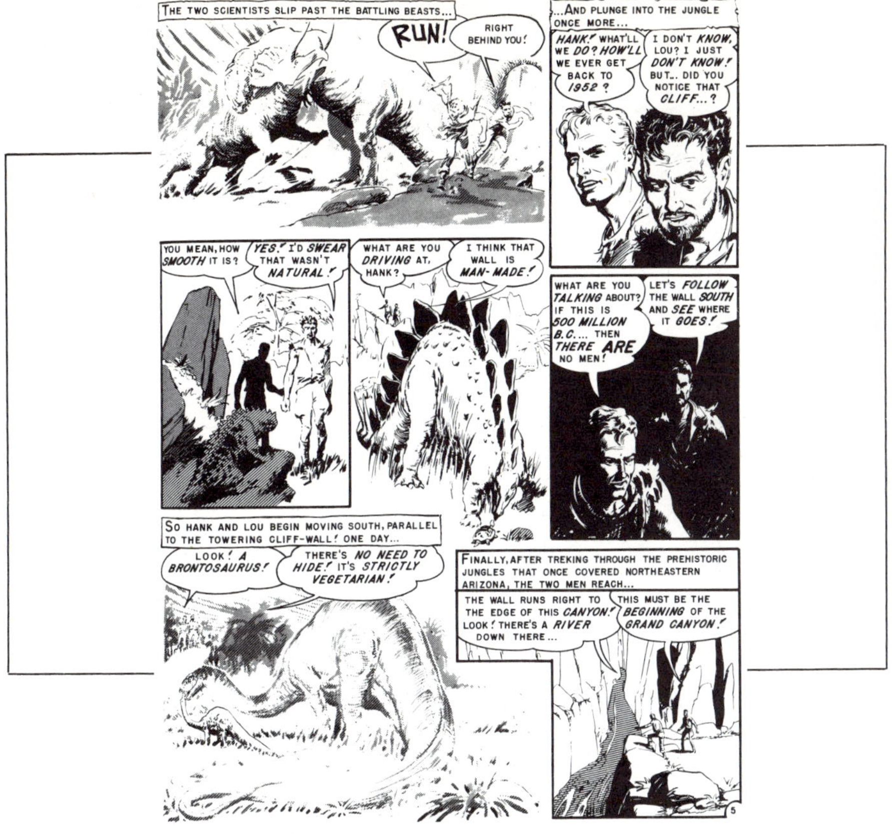

story. So you make sure that balloon #1 is followed by balloon #2 without adding any confusion. You make it easy to read as well as easy to look at as a picture. That's important. It's very important to tell the story. I sometimes get carried away, but I always try to tell the story. Some of the stories that Warren Publications used to print had beautiful pictures, but you couldn't read the darn thing or know what the hell was going on or who was talking or who was saying what or what balloon you had to read first! Beautiful pictures but no story, and what the hell good is that?"

An important way of communicating the feelings which are in the story, and present in the writer's words, is through body language. This involves the position the figure is in, the expression on a character's face, what his hands are doing, and all of the signs that we notice in others when we're talking to them in order to read their response. An artist must incorporate these gestures, which can be subtle as well as obvious, into his work to achieve the best possible communication.

"That's the way an artist can tell the story," Williamson states. "Hal Foster could do that. Roy Crane could do that, and a guy named R.B. Fuller could do that better than just about anybody. I think those are the most important storytellers in comics, although nobody knows R.B. Fuller and they hardly know Roy Crane. It's hard to explain the importance of these guys to comics artists because they don't have access to the work to study it."

Storytelling is generally accepted as being a synthesis of words and pictures where one does not overbalance the other. How this balance is achieved depends on

continued working for many publishers throughout the Fifties and in the Sixties drew three issues of a Flash Gordon comic book for King Features as well as worked on newspaper strips with artists like John Prentice. He even drew the revival of the **Secret Agent X-9** *strip, which was soon retitled* **Secret Agent Corrigan**, *from 1967 to 1980. In the Seventies, Williamson drew black and white science fiction strips for* **Creepy** *and* **Eerie**, *among other things. In the Eighties he aptated* **The Empire Strikes Back**, **Return of the Jedi**, **Blade Runner** *and* **Flash Gordon**. *Williamson also drew the* **Star Wars** *newspaper strip.*

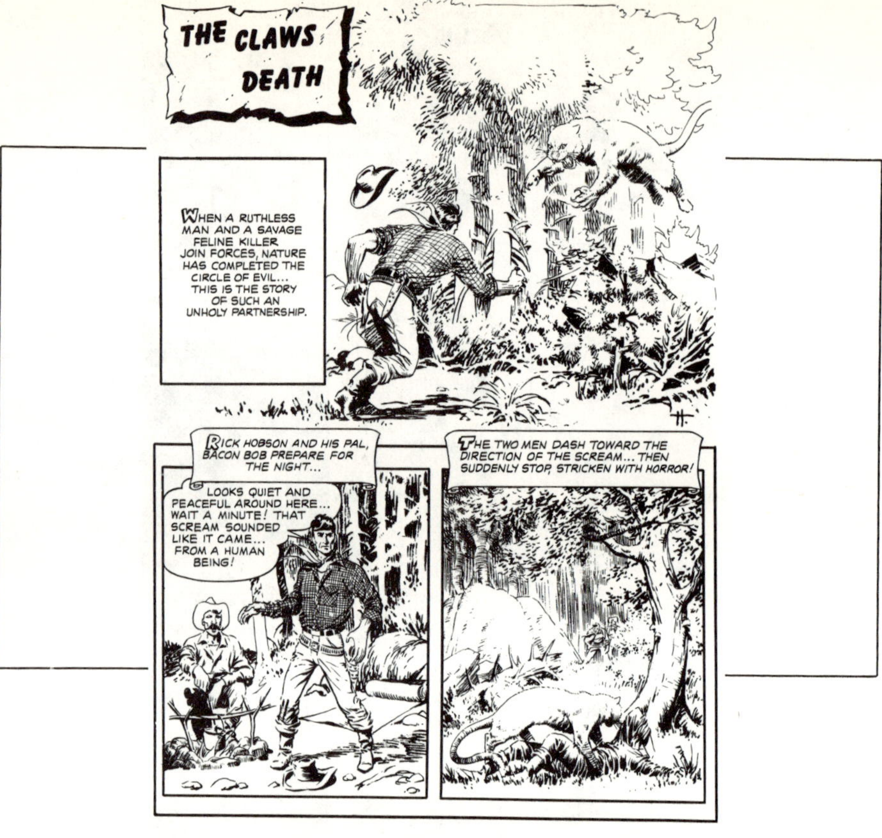

I never really thought a lot consciously about how to tell the story. I grew up with comics and so it's a part of me to tell the story. I think you absorb a lot of that when you're a kid. And if you really love it and want to be in it, then it's second nature to tell that story.

Artwork from John Wayne Comics by Al Williamson and Frank Frazetta

the internal demands of the story itself, and how many or how few words are needed to convey the message being illustrated with the art.

"It all depends on the story. You can actually tell a story without any dialogue. There's no question about it. It's been done several times and done well, but those were tailor-made. You could see what was going on, but as a rule it's difficult to do every story like that. I don't see how you could do every story like that."

The composition of a scene within a panel communicates the thrust of the story, but as Williamson said earlier, he feels that such composition is more instinctive to an artist by the time they're an adult. They absorb the ability by reading hundreds of stories over the years. Williamson feels it cannot be explained through any easy theory or approach which is easily taught.

"It's very hard to answer that question. I never really thought a lot consciously about how to tell the story. I grew up with comics and so it's a part of me to tell the story. I think you absorb a lot of that when you're a kid. And if you really love it and want to be in it, then it's second nature to tell that story. It's the way you feel and the way you see the picture. After all, that's our business, to tell the story, so we try to do it to the best of our ability."

That ability includes deciding how to use the panels on a page, choosing which shapes and sizes accentuate the drama and the action. But again, different stories require different panel shapes for an effect within the story. "It all depends," Williamson explains. "If the story calls for it, I'll use it. If it doesn't then I don't. It all depends on the action. You just can't have a formula for this

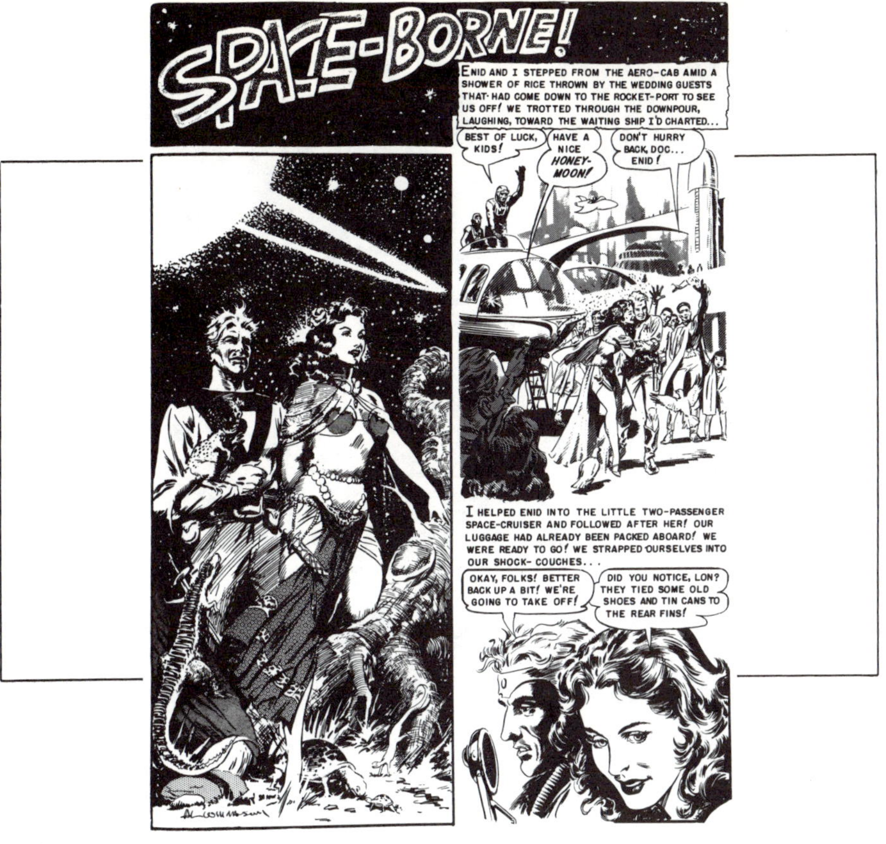

stuff. I don't. I look at it and try to tell the story to the best of my ability. I try to make it as simple as possible for the reader. You can sometimes do an action scene in a little panel in silhouettes and it will read better than a double-page spread with a bunch of figures fighting. It all depends on how you're doing it. There's no set ways. When you're sitting there you try to do the stuff differently. Although it's very hard to do things differently from what you did before, if you don't you could fall into a rut and just keep doing the same drawing all the time. It can happen, especially doing a newspaper strip. Then you start getting into the rut of doing close-ups and semi-close-ups and cut everybody off at the waist. You could fall into a bad habit and not even realize you're doing it, so you have to be aware of what you're doing. Sometimes you could do a comic book page like that, too, and then realize, 'My God, I've got all heads here!' So it's usually best to read the script and as you read it put in the lettering in pencil and place the balloons more or less where you think they might be to get an idea of the size of the panel you're working in and what should go in there. Then as you do that you also think of a picture at the same time and you try to accommodate a quick sketch where you're going to put the drawing as well as showing where the balloons are going. Sometimes they work out and sometimes you have to do it over again and do a different view of it. You *have* to make sure those balloons are in a place where you can read them and the reader doesn't have to guess which one he's going to have to read next. They should follow through very clearly."

I look at it and try to tell the story to the best of my ability. I try to make it as simple as possible for the reader. You can sometimes do an action scene in a little panel in silhouettes and it will read better than a double-page spread with a bunch of figures fighting.

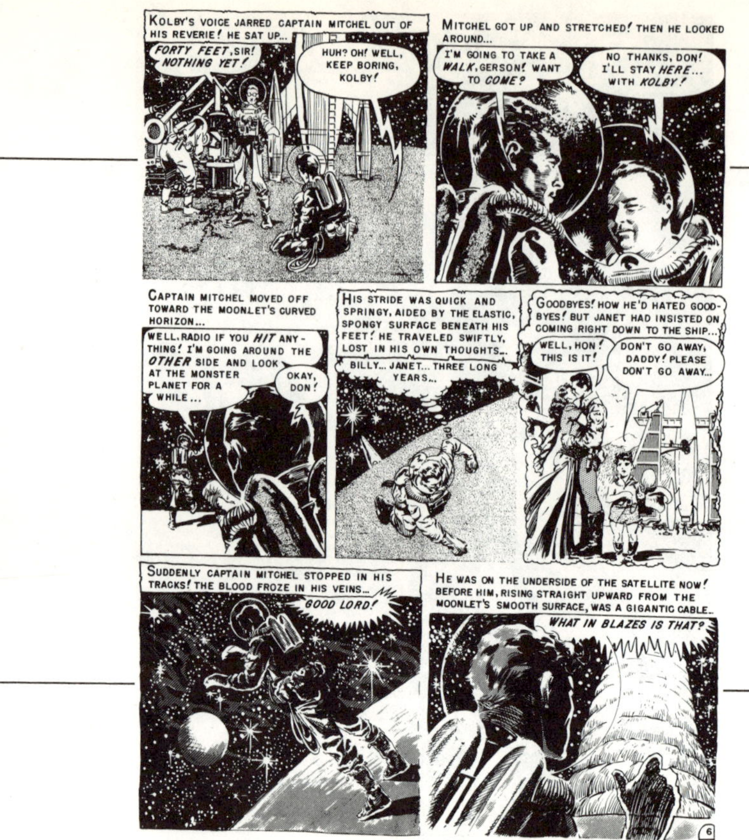

Wally Wood used to do a lot of background work —though with him it worked— while other artists would put very little in the background. Johnny Craig was a very good storyteller who did not crowd his panels, and yet everything was there.

When doing the actual drawing, Williamson pencils tight, finished art. "When you warm up and you're meeting a deadline, you can just sort of suggest it and then ink it. It all depends. But most of the time it's pretty well pencilled." It's at this stage that he decides what kind of and how much detail to put in the background, and again this is dictated by the needs of the story. "Some artists put a lot of stuff in there just to put it in. Wally Wood used to do a lot of background work —though with him it worked— while other artists would put very little in the background. Johnny Craig was a very good storyteller who did not crowd his panels, and yet everything was there. It all depends on the artist and how he feels about it."

Then there's the question of characterization in the art, such as facial expressions and even just recognizable characters. "I think the question cartoonists are most often asked is: How do you keep everybody looking the same from different angles? I could never answer that myself because it's part of being an artist. You just do it. You can use mirrors to learn expressions. I think every artist has done that. I sometimes use (people in) photos as well as my friends as characters in a strip. There're different ways of doing it. Sometimes you just have to fall back on talent and make it up!"

Although the vast majority of comic strips are printed in color, Williamson feels artwork should work equally well in black and white. Williamson believes this must be kept in mind when drawing the art, even though the artist knows that color will be added later.

"I always liked black and white so I would say that in my case I

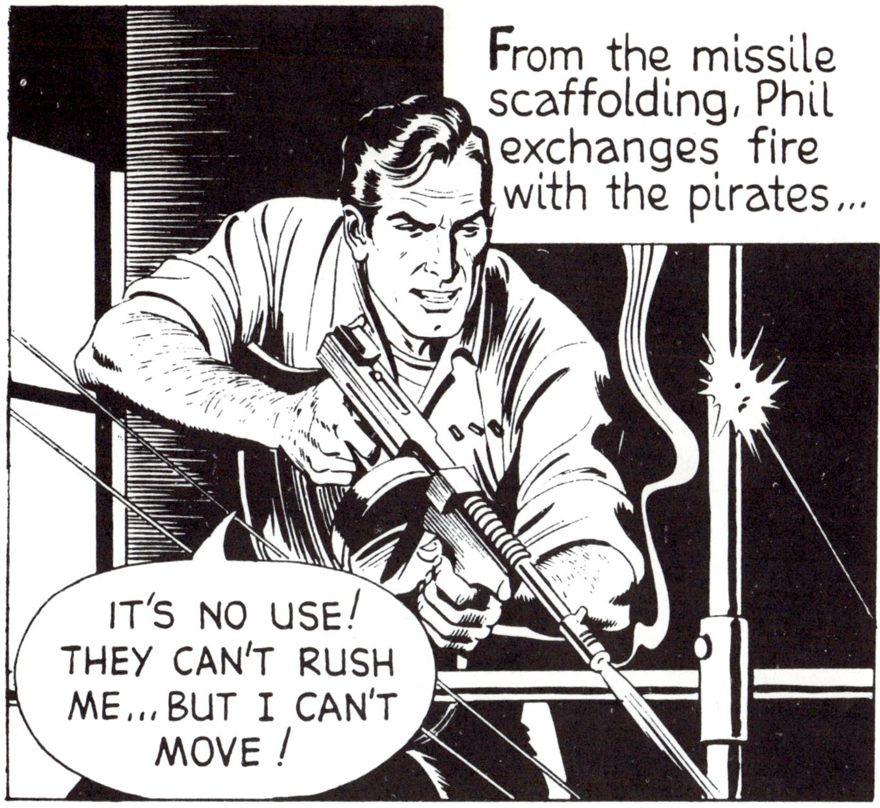

I prefer to see a comic that's been originally drawn in black and white and then colored as opposed to a painted comic. The painted comic has never been done right as far as I can see, and has never grabbed me. There have been some very good artists doing it with very loving pictures, but it doesn't impress me.

definitely prefer to see a comic that's been originally drawn in black and white and then colored as opposed to a painted comic. The painted comic has never been done right as far as I can see, and has never grabbed me. There have been some very good artists doing it with very loving pictures, but it doesn't impress me the way the work of someone contemporary like Dave Stevens or Mark Schultz does. Their work is done in black and white and then color is put over it and it's damn good stuff. Mark's (work) is primarily published in black and white and isn't colored, except for the covers. But I guess most people would rather see everything in color."

Another important "tool" of the comic artist is the "swipe file," a reference file used to draw realistic hardware such as cars, planes and sometimes even buildings. "If you're doing a civilian strip, you need reference for everything around you, and a swipe file is a big help. But doing comics today, there's very little of that. John Romita Jr. is doing an incredible job pencilling **Daredevil**. He's very aware of his storytelling. It's excellent. If someone is in a certain house, he has reference or he makes up this house and draws it from all the different angles, and you *know* they're in that house. He has it all worked out very carefully. He's probably the best storyteller in comics today."

Williamson feels the best way for an artist to learn what he needs to know is to attend basic drawing classes. Although they may seem to have more to do with other types of art than comics it is still the best approach to learning craft.

"Most comic book artists today have never done any real serious studying of art and composition;

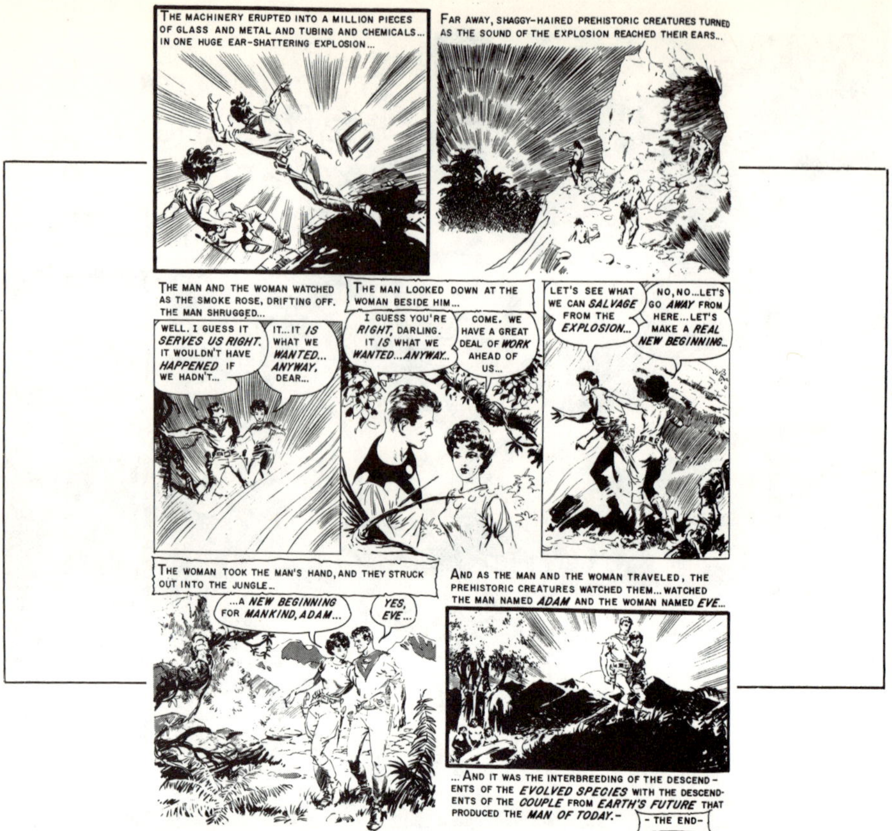

they just jump right into comics. I'm sure there's the exception to the rule, but most seem to just hit eighteen or nineteen and go into comics. They've never really learned how to compose, how to shade in black and white, or how to spot their blacks. And that's a shame. Every artist should try to learn something that has nothing to do with comics but with layout, illustration and composition. Maybe he'll feel that, 'Well, that's not comics. . . ' but that's not true. You learn a lot by going to a sketching class or an art class; learning from teachers who can explain what makes a picture good, and why it reads the way it does. The artist then picks up on that, sees something differently and learns from it. They can become a better artist. You can't learn to be a good artist just by doing comic books and not studying."

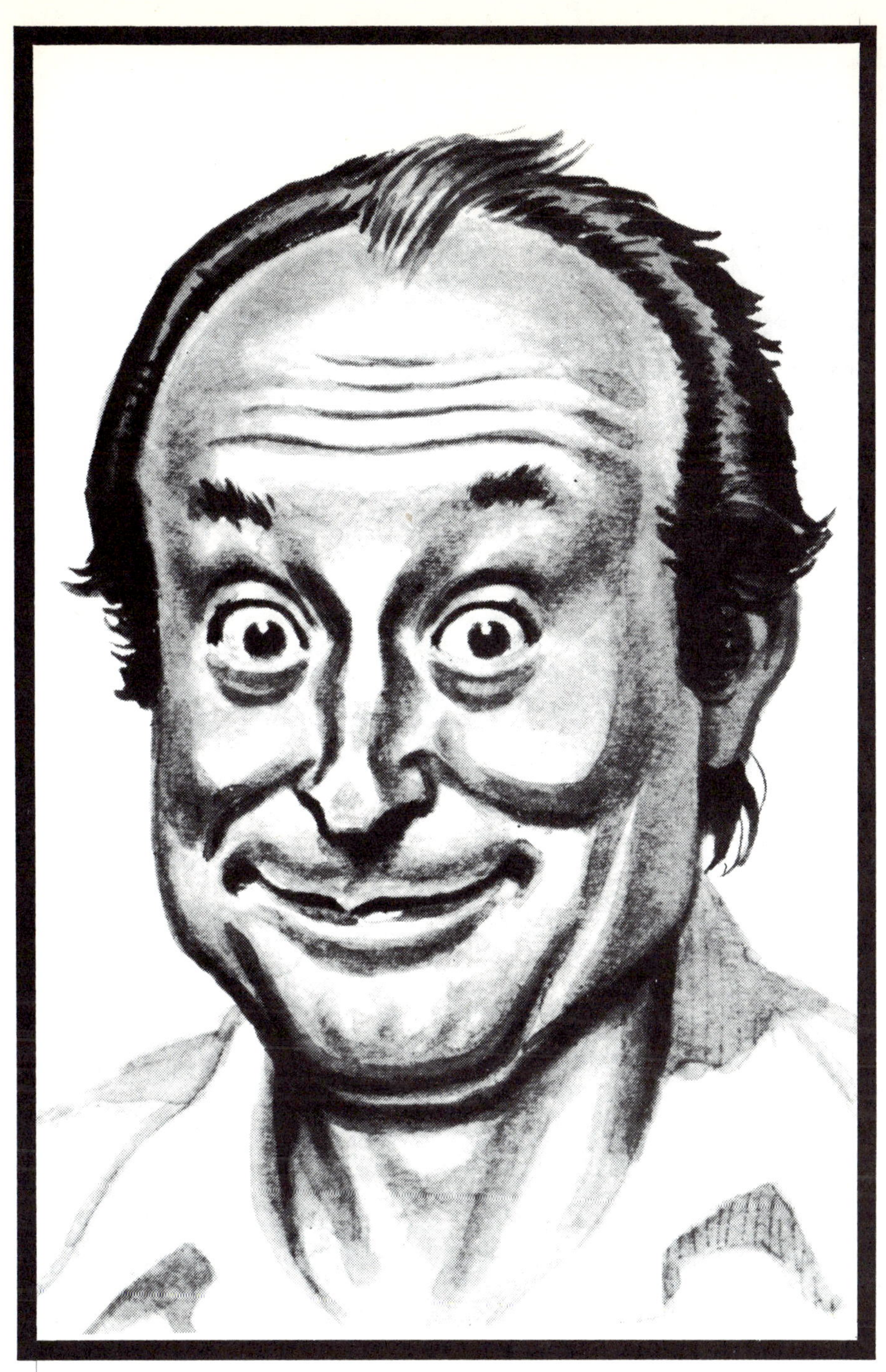

Chapter Six
WILL
ELDER

*Will Elder, the long time collaborator of writer/ artist Harvey Kurtzman, was born in 1922 in the Bronx. Elder demonstrated artistic abilities early in life and received a scholarship to the High School of Music and Art, where he met such future collaborators as John Severin. Elder was drafted into the Army in 1942, and upon discharge at the end of World War Two he entered the field of commercial art. He soon teamed up with John Severin as his inker and inked numerous stories with him for **Prize Comics Western** beginning in the late Forties, as well as a few at E.C. Comics in the early Fifties. Elder began doing art solo for Harvey Kurtz-*

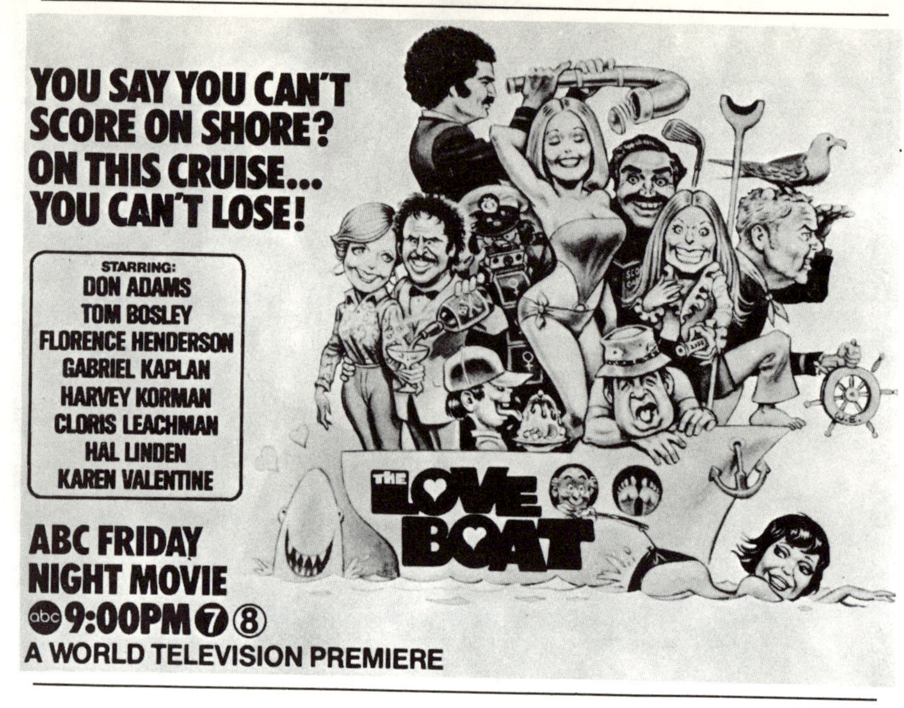

The tools that Will Elder works with are whatever enables him to use the medium to its best effect, which often means vastly different approaches for different strips.

"Generally I love satirizing anything and everything," Elder explains, "I was always kind of a closet comedian and through the art world I've found my niche. That depends on what future generations think. Depending on the satire that I intend to illuminate, I would use the technique that I find apropos. If I'm doing a satire of a fine art piece, or an illustration, such as the Norman Rockwell piece (which I consider one of my finest and most satisfying pieces of work, as I was always an admirer of Rockwell), I naturally used watercolor. Of course, he painted in oils, but I didn't want to make it complicated, so I used the colors simulating an oil painting, which is not an easy thing to do. I used the medium of watercolor and tempura to satirize Rockwell, or to flatter him if he needed any at all.

"Then when it came to doing some of the other satires of commercials Madison Avenue would naturally prefer, I would use pen and ink or black and white illustrations done in gouache. There's a variety of techniques I use, depending on my approach.

"Pen and line usually work best for me most of the time, such as in the 'Goodman Beaver' story. I thought that using that technique would best enhance that kind of satire. It's a matter of personal choice, but I believe it worked. Tools, really, are an addendum to what's in my mind. It depends on the effect I'm trying to achieve. I'm always trying to achieve an effect, and certain tools, certain instruments are appropriate for each particular ren-

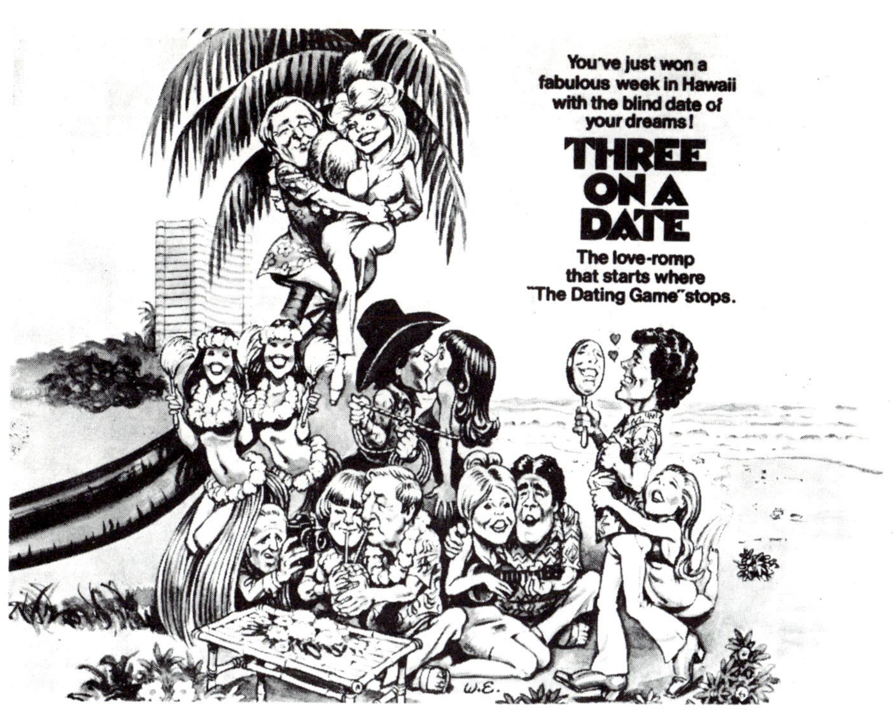

*man on **Mad** beginning with the very first issue. Elder also drew for E.C.'s **Panic** as well as the war and science fiction titles. He accompanied his friend when Kurtzman left **Mad** and worked with Harvey on his subsequent humor magazines **Trump**, **Humbug** and **Help!**. After **Help!**, Elder returned to advertising work until Harvey Kurtzman began the long-running strip "Little Annie Fanny" for **Playboy** for which Elder did the full color finished art over Kurtzman's roughs, and has drawn that feature for some 25 years.*

dition. I don't know how it would work for anyone else, but it seems to work for me. People began to label me as a very versatile artist, because of that, so maybe I was versatile only because I use so many mediums in my work. I never paint in any particular one."

In describing how he works from a script to break a story down into artwork, Elder explains that he's usually worked from someone else's layouts. One of the times he didn't is when he first started out in comics back in 1946.

"When I first started in the comics, I worked for Raye Herman. I think she was the only female publisher in the comic book business at that particular time. That was in the Forties. I had an idea of something I was playing with which was a satire of Cervantes' Don Quixote, which was of course a satire to begin with, and a very biting and trenchant satire. I thought about coming up with a cartoon which would also be suitable for children, because I thought that would be a way to break into comics. It was a medium that would suit my abilities.

"Being just out of the service after World War Two, with nowhere to turn, the comics seemed to be an easy target. So I came up with a comic strip called 'Rufus Debri'. He was a garbage man and it was a kind of truncated refuse and debris. He was a garbage man out sweeping the streets and some truck would come along and this mechanical arm would stick out, making a right hand turn, and would hit this Rufus on the head, knocking him cold, and he would get up in a strange land. Of course that's what happened in **A Connecticut Yankee in King Arthur's Court**. So Rufus is wearing the garbage can as his suit of armor.

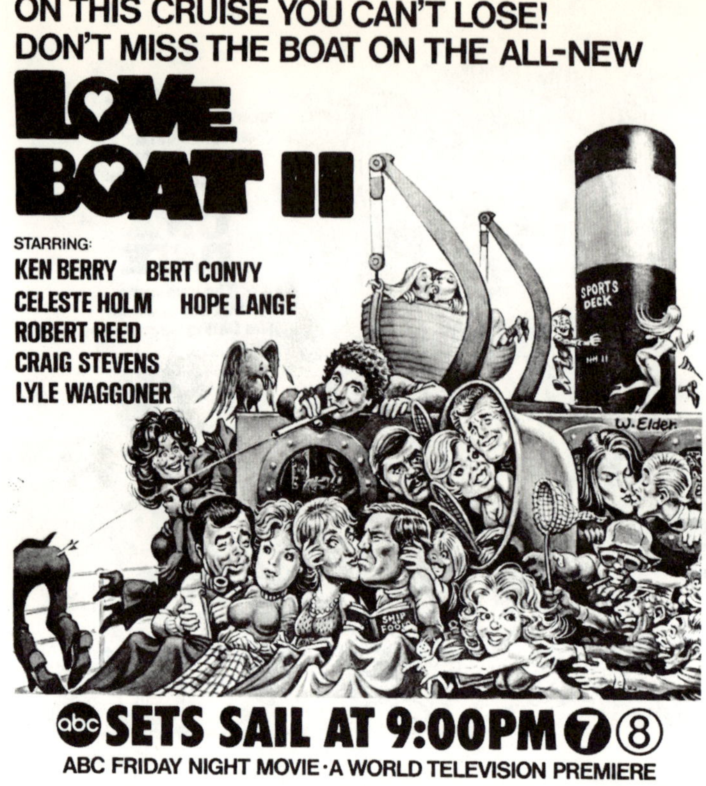

The truck driver would be his sidekick, a short, stocky little man, and they would go into various adventures. And that's how I broke into the comic book business, doing my own stories and approaching a publisher with them. It appeared in **Toy Town** comics."

Then years later, after working as an inker for John Severin for some time, Elder became acquainted with a very interesting approach to breaking down a comic book script into art.

"That came later with Harvey Kurtzman, who is one of the finest artists and comic writers in the world. He came up with this device of writing a story, making thumbnail sketches (tiny little illustrations). He would go over that until he finally got what he wanted, and then enlarge it and break it down into panels. He would go over the storyline with the artist that he'd chosen for a particular story, breaking down the story panel for panel like a coach going over plays with an athletic team, telling the artist to do it this way or that way which would best suit the story. Harvey was very unique that way. It was a remarkable way to approach an artist and break down a story panel by panel so that the artist has a visual picture as to what Harvey would like him to do. And if the artist thought that he could enhance a story by throwing in a little bit of his own particular idiosyncrasies, he would. In fact, that was the way that I worked. I would take Harvey's story, after he broke it down, and I would either embellish, enhance, or sometimes lightly change it, but he was such a wonderful editor that he never minded one bit whether I changed the story slightly or not. As long as it turned out to be funny, direct and made a very strong point. And that's how we

He came up with this device of writing a story, making thumbnail sketches (tiny little illustrations). He would go over that until he finally got what he wanted, and then enlarge it and break it down into panels. He would go over the storyline with the artist that he'd chosen for a particular story, breaking down the story panel for panel like a coach going over plays with an athletic team, telling the artist to do it this way or that way which would best suit the story.

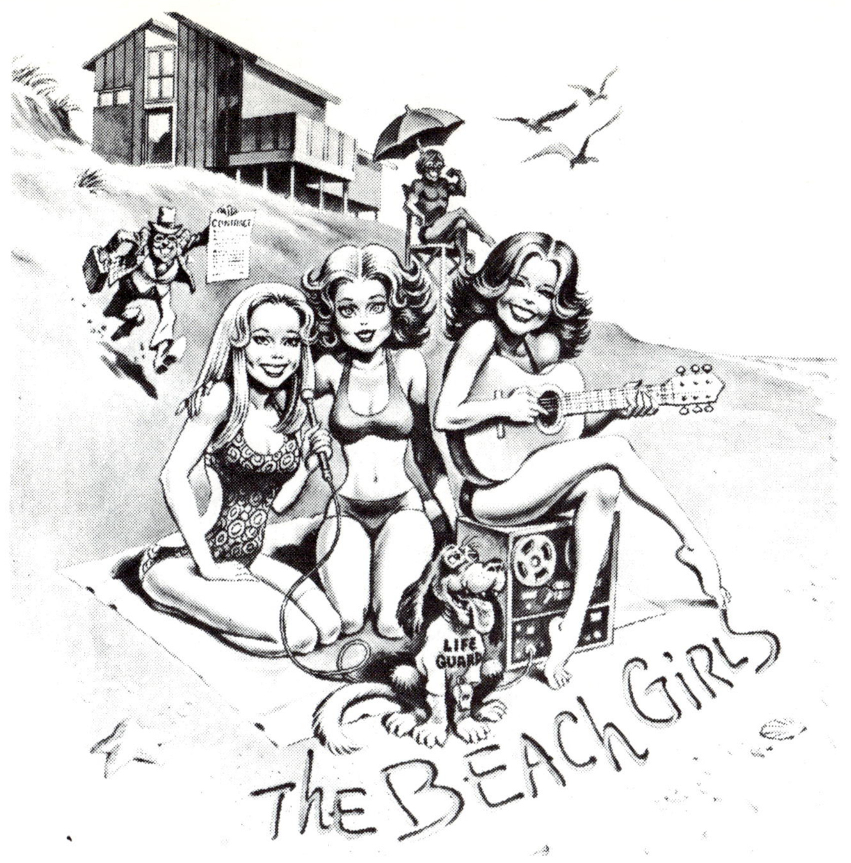

It was a rough layout, for us to play with and work in our own creative abilities. We more or less did that, and broke out in our own individual styles. I had my style. Jack Davis had his style. And Wally Wood, another great artist, would do it his way. Apparently it worked for all of us.

worked. It was a rough layout, for us to play with and work in our own creative abilities. We more or less did that, and broke out in our own individual styles. I had my style. Jack Davis had his style. And Wally Wood, another great artist, would do it his way. Apparently it worked for all of us. We all worked for Harvey at **Mad** and I think it set **Mad** off on a wonderful pace and created a very original type of magazine, as far as comics are concerned."

When Elder worked from a script which didn't have the kind of detailed layouts that Harvey Kurtzman gave him, it allowed Elder to approach the art in still a different way, up to and including generating the plot himself.

"Sometimes it would be a story that was more or less straight (serious as opposed to humorous). It was something that would be a filler for me at E.C., if I wasn't doing something else for **Mad** that month. There were some stories I would make up myself. One story I originated, and then Harvey took it from there and broke it down because he knew how to handle a story editorially better than most. That was the story of Melvin the Mole ('Mole!' in **Mad** #2 - Dec. 1952). That's an original that I created. Harvey broke it down and presented it in a certain way that he thought would enhance the story. So I more or less started my own idea and carried it out through Harvey Kurtzman."

Some artists feel that the artwork is the main point of a comic strip and that an interesting picture comes first and the storytelling second, a point which Elder understands and agrees with, up to a point.

"I would go along with that. I think there's something to be said for that. In the comic world

Abandoned by the husband she loved,
Joyce is finding herself a whole new life.
She's heading for the top in a world
of million dollar mansions and power-mad men.
Now the sky's the limit!
But is that where she really wants to go?

H.K. & W.E.

SOLD

SUSAN BLAKELY in "MAKE ME AN OFFER"

Starring PATRICK O'NEAL With JOHN RUBINSTEIN EDIE ADAMS STELLA STEVENS

abc ABC FRIDAY NIGHT MOVIE 9:00PM 7 8

A WORLD TELEVISION PREMIERE

You can tell a complete story with just pictures and illustrations by themselves. But adding another facet to it by having a written story, by having words involved, adds another dimension

we should be presenting the proper category when we mention art. Comic art is very fancy, high-toned art because it's not only illustration that we're talking about. We're talking about an illustration that moves. It's a vivid, living illustration that sometimes is just a humorous cartoon, but it moves. It tells a story within itself such as an illustration would, but it goes a step further. There's a continuity that's involved here and I think it tells it very well. Comics are a marvelous blend of words and pictures that enhance whatever idea one has. That's one of the great advantages of comic art. Illustrations can enhance and emphasize story."

There are artists who go one step further and feel that in comics the artwork is the story.

"Yes, in more ways than one. I would say, in general, the artwork is the story, but it has to have direction. I'm sure we take that for granted. We can't emphasize that enough. I think it has to have direction. There has to be some kind of control involved. To use another medium as an example, drama on the stage is interpreted and made into a motion picture. Something is lost in the interpretation unless the director is well versed in drama and he can see the transition a lot clearer than the average human being. It all depends on the direction that you're making."

Whether a comic strip should work just on the basis of the art or whether art and story should work in tandem is of great interest to Elder. He states, "You can tell a complete story with just pictures and illustrations by themselves. But adding another facet to it by having a written story, by having words involved, adds another dimension."

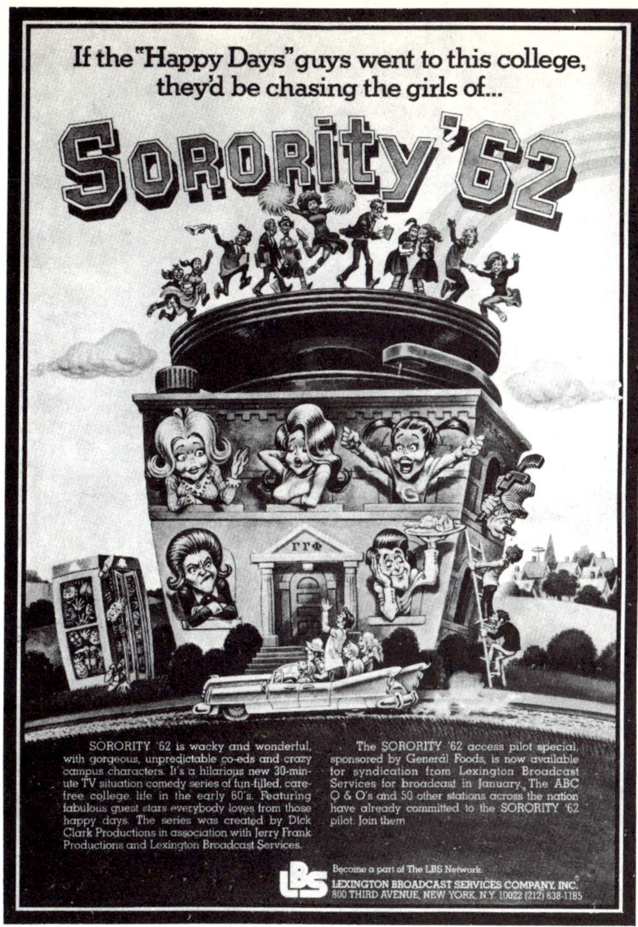

Like many other comics artists, Elder sees the parallel between comics and film. He, in fact, sees stories in his mind like movies before he draws them.

"I see it as a script or a film in my mind. I draw my own pictures and use a vital energy I feel within me. I can either draw upon certain thoughts I've had in the past that would be appropriate in a story I'm working on, such as from my experiences, or from some of the people I've looked at and studied. In other words, it's something that one draws upon from either childhood or experiences one has that one can place in a drawing. I was very much influenced by the movies. There wasn't anything as enlightening as television when I was a child. I would go off to a movie and get lost in the movie theatre, as many others did as a child in the Depression. One's background becomes a part of what they have to say in their illustration. I have the advantage of picturizing, if you can use that expression, some of my earlier thoughts and feelings that I had growing up. If my story will better express what I have to say through pictures drawing on early experience, then I will use it."

The kind of artwork Will Elder has most often done makes great uses of facial expressions and body language to communicate ideas in a theatrical manner.

"I have always been in the habit of showing very exaggerated expressions because, like stage acting, it must emote in the most extravagant way. I was trying to get to the reader, and to get to the reader it's better to exaggerate than to underplay, unless you're dealing with a very mature, adult theme. But I always felt young people were the audience. I'm not saying adolescent people, but high school and col-

I see it as a script or a film in my mind. I draw my own pictures and use a vital energy I feel within me. I can either draw upon certain thoughts I've had in the past that would be appropriate in a story I'm working on, such as from my experiences, or from some of the people I've looked at and studied. In other words, it's something that one draws upon from either childhood or experiences one has that one can place in a drawing.

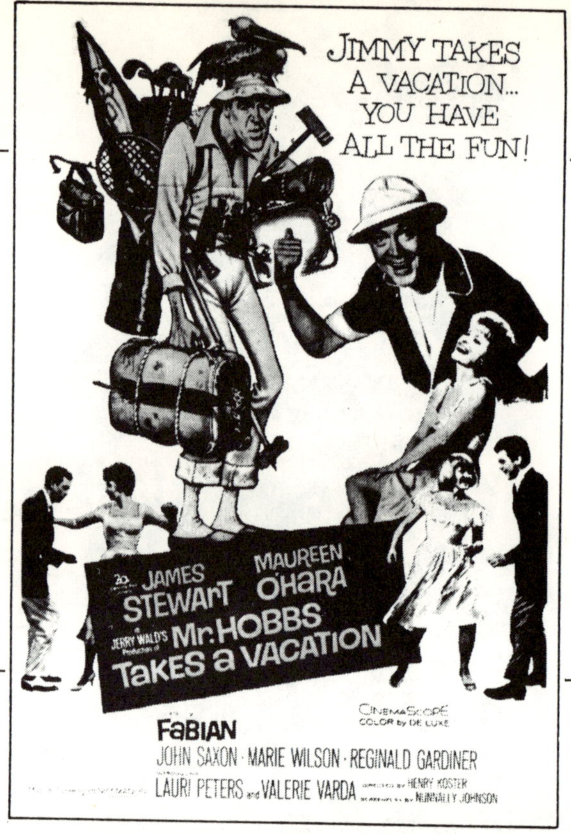

We have to designate who and what the artist represents. Artists are like actors, in a sense. Each one brings his own technique and his own background to express his own ideas. We're all influenced by something in life that comes to the surface when we illustrate.

lege students were generally the people we were reaching, and they were intelligent individuals. So we had to say something that we could connect with and get to these people through pictorial enlightenment, so to speak. In order to do it, expressions were very important."

Although comics usually appear in color, Elder feels black and white artwork is still a very important element to consider.

"Black and white in the picture is everything. Color is an enhancement. It creates a little design by itself. Once you get into a story, the story itself becomes the important thing. Like Shakespeare would say, 'The play's the thing.' And in comics the picture is the thing. Regardless of color or black and white, if you have something to say, the picture will say it."

Regarding the different approaches an artist can take to panel breakdowns on a page, Elder states, "We have to designate who and what the artist represents. Artists are like actors, in a sense. Each one brings his own technique and his own background to express his own ideas. We're all influenced by something in life that comes to the surface when we illustrate. Each artist is his own captain. He knows what feels good for him. If his work is comfortable and he expresses what he intends to express, he will use whatever device he can. Each artist brings to his work his own individuality. I bring my thoughts and ideas, although I might be one of the unusual artists who does that, but I'm sure there's a lot of others who do the same.

"My approach to comics or any artwork is knowing what I am about to do beforehand. My ap-

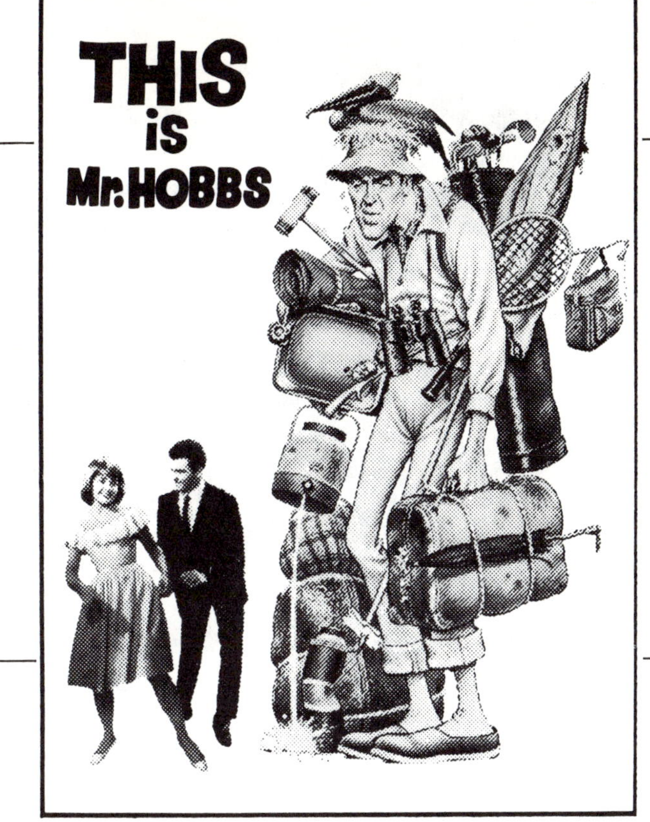

If the story was funny, it didn't matter how you approached it. The story would have to have humor that we all can identify with or recognize, and each one of us has a different sense of humor. The humor and the art and the design are in the eye of the beholder. If it helps to make the story interesting for the reader, then I think it works.

proach to panel designs were insignificant. If the story was funny, it didn't matter how you approached it. The story would have to have humor that we all can identify with or recognize, and each one of us has a different sense of humor. Actually the humor lies in the beholder. I hate to use that cliche, but it works very confidently when I want to express myself. The humor and the art and the design are in the eye of the beholder. If it helps to make the story interesting for the reader, then I think it works. But if it's just a jumble of ideas in order to confuse, then it might not work. It might be superfluous. Then again we have to go back to the original ideas of what makes a story interesting, and it's the pictures. The illustrations. The drawings."

When Elder first started out as an artist, most of his early work was done as an inker rather than a penciller. It wasn't until a few years later that he would come into his own as both a penciller and an inker.

"In the beginning I pencilled very slowly. I was quite young and it was very innovative for me even to get into the field. This goes back about 45 years, and I worked very laboriously, but John Severin worked very rapidly with what he did in pencilling. I inked a lot faster than Severin did and so the two of us seemed to beat deadlines with our combination of him pencilling and me inking. It worked out as a very successful team until **Mad** magazine came along, and that's where I fell into place.

"As far as inking and pencilling are concerned, I would do pencilling later on when I really had the time and the experience and the knowledge to do so. I would take Harvey's layouts, because

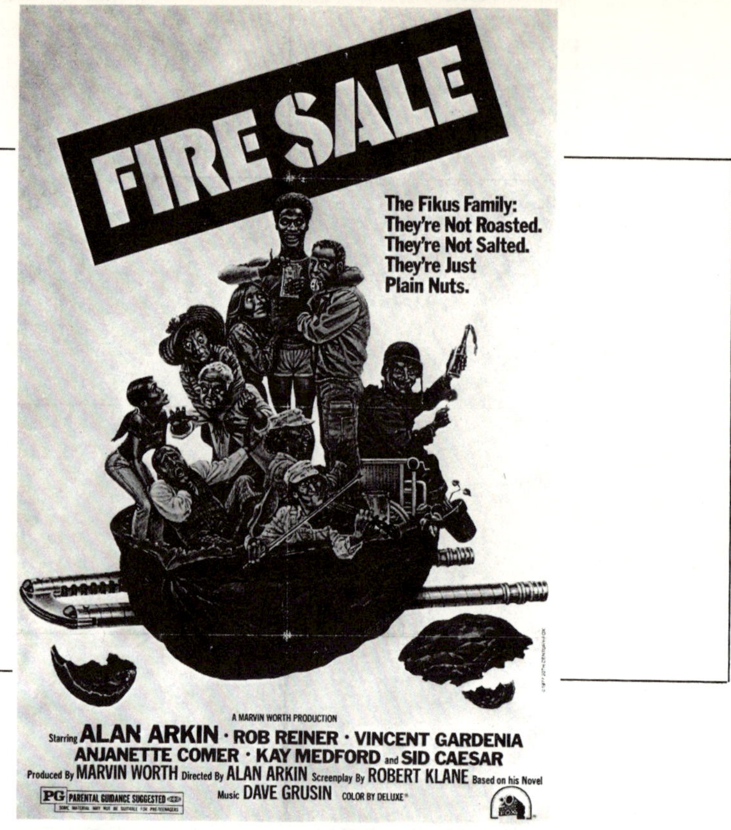

I'd use the watercolor technique to the hilt over the drawing that Harvey had made, so it was kind of a layered system. It was such an involved bit of work that a lot of people don't realize that they were fine watercolor paintings. They were not just line and a flat, two-dimensional tone or four-color print.

you'd know from those exactly what he wanted, and rework them and redraw them so it would fit the finish that I would bring to it. In other words, I'd pencil it my own way after picking up Harvey's layouts and rough pencilling. I'd take it from there, build on it, draw it into a fine pencilling illustration. I would take it from there either in pen and ink, black and white gouache or watercolor. I'd add the final details when I was inking or watercoloring, as in the case of **Little Annie Fanny**. I'd use the watercolor technique to the hilt over the drawing that Harvey had made, so it was kind of a layered system. It was such an involved bit of work that a lot of people don't realize that they were fine watercolor paintings. They were not just line and a flat, two-dimensional tone or four-color print. It wasn't like that at all. We had grays and nuances of color; tones that would go from very dark to very light. You're talking about three-dimensional paintings in effect that had to be built up from a single line drawing."

Elder believes background detail in panel art is important depending, "on the artist. I worked in an area where I had to express my own thoughts and my own ideas. Harvey would write a storyline, which would be accepted by the editor at **Playboy**, or in the case where Harvey was editor at **Mad**, he would have final say. And when the story was completed, he would pass it on to the appropriate artist. When he gave me a story to work on, he would go over it with me, dramatize certain parts, emphasize certain parts, and I would get the picture. I would see it as a film or a layout before me when I got the idea, and he would know instantly that I would take it and change it. But

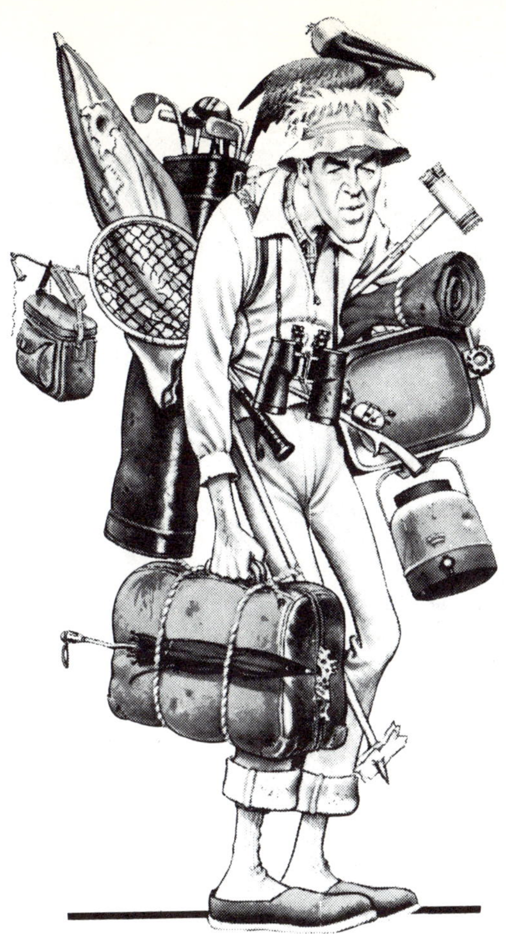

I've had the ability to draw all my life, and being able to make funny pictures was a delight for me. Not only did I enjoy it, but I found that others enjoyed it as well, and it made me feel like I was something special.

what I did change was never detrimental to his story. It was never anything that would obliterate or reduce any of his ideas. It would in many cases enhance it, so Harvey would let me go wild with all of the ideas that I could possibly come up with. But it would have to be something to do with the story. It had to do with the main concept. I would never subtract from the purpose of his story. I would enhance it with little figures running around, but they would be doing something within the storyline. I played with the ideas, and before I knew it, I was creating something entirely different within the story."

Facial expression is very important to Elder's art. He communicates the story through the feelings of the characters as we see them expressed on their faces. But it's not an easy task to master.

"You have to be a frustrated actor," Elder states. " I clowned around in school for years. I was always the class clown. I sublimated my energies as a class clown into being a clowning artist. I had a lot of energy as a kid, and I still do in many areas. But as a kid I would be looking for that vital thing that most comedians look for—love and attention. And finding out that I could get both, I would carry that out to the end. Without breaking my head, or my neck or getting into show business (which I thought would be a very dangerous business), I decided to become an artist.

"I've had the ability to draw all my life, and being able to make funny pictures was a delight for me. Not only did I enjoy it, but I found that others enjoyed it as well, and it made me feel like I was something special. That's a great feeling to have, and it's an

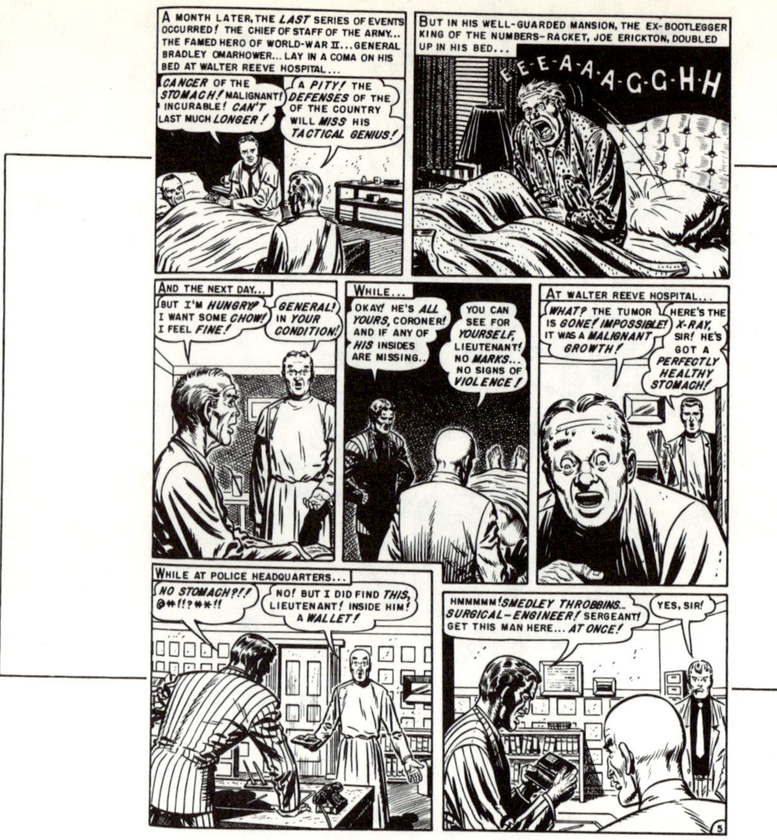

I enjoyed painting and drawing. And through just working constantly at it I improved and my work had more to say.

encouragement. When you feel that way you carry it out to the 'nth degree. You try to improve on everything you do. You try to become a fine artist. A humorous fine artist. Or a humorous cartoonist. Or a humorous illustrator. Both areas, humor and art, work very well for me because the clown was finally coming out in another form."

Elder's artistic talents were refined when they were recognized by his teachers and the young artist was sent to a special school.

"When I was young I went to a junior high school, and from there I was given a scholarship to an art school, the High School of Music and Art in New York City. Al Jaffee, the cartoonist, went to that school. My buddy and my partner, Harvey Kurtzman, went to that school, although we hardly knew each other then. It was a school which culled the better talents throughout the New York City area in both music and art. Kids who showed promise in music and art would be given a scholarship. It was a unique school at the time. That school is still in existence. It's moved since then to a modern building and has gone through many changes.

"At that school we met many friends and it gave us an opportunity to do not only ordinary academics, but three to four hours a day of artwork or music. That gave me a launching pad for getting into the art field. I enjoyed painting and drawing. And through just working constantly at it I improved and my work had more to say. The school would take me to museums where I would look at some of the finest painters of all time; some of the old masters. I envied these masters. I studied their work and they influenced me tre-

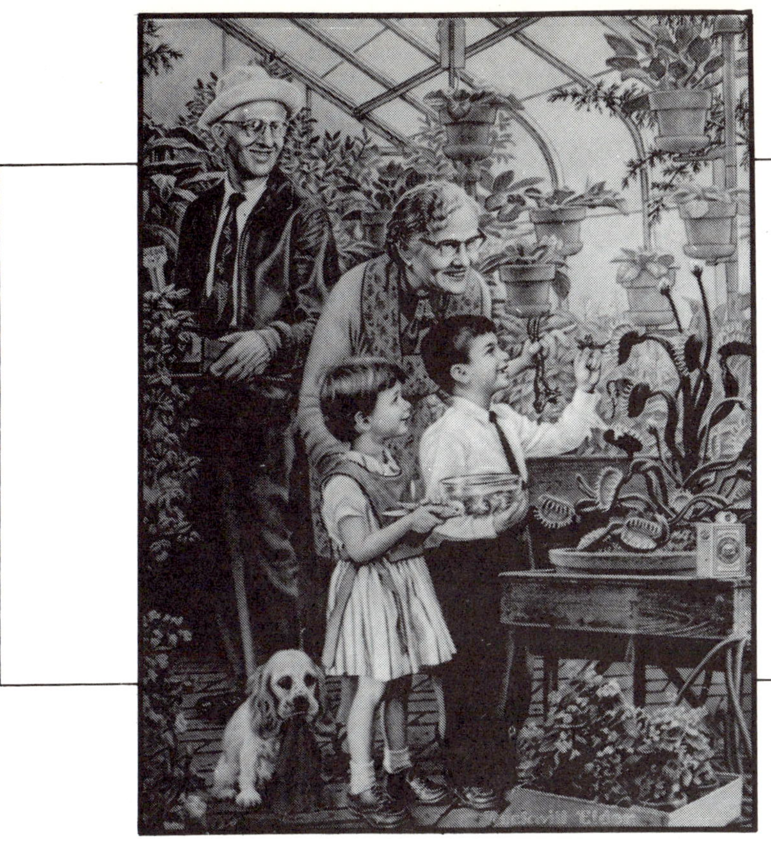

mendously. Early influences play a big part in what you do in later life. It worked for me."

Describing the wide range of art courses at this school, Elder explained how a broad spectrum of art courses contributed to his skills as a cartoonist.

"It was a school that had everything other schools had except there were a lot of gifted kids culled from all over the city of New York. We were a bunch of prodigies walking down the halls. We were exceptional in the areas of music and art. Of course we did have to have passing grades in the regular subjects. Then there were painting courses from a model, and there were sculpture courses from a model. There were graphic arts, and we pretty much covered every phase of art. We were given lectures on art and introduced to old masters to inspire u. It was definitely an influence on my life. I also went to another art school, the Academy of Design, after graduating from high school and just before I was drafted into the U.S. Army.

"Knowledge is forever. To me, as wide as you broaden your interests in art, the more information you gather, the greater the knowledge you pick up from various sources, can only enhance what you do in life. It gives you a broader aspect, another approach. It makes you appreciate what has been done. It just makes you a wiser individual."

there were painting courses from a model, and there were sculpture courses from a model. There were graphic arts, and we pretty much covered every phase of art. We were given lectures on art and introduced to old masters to inspire us. It was definitely an influence on my life.

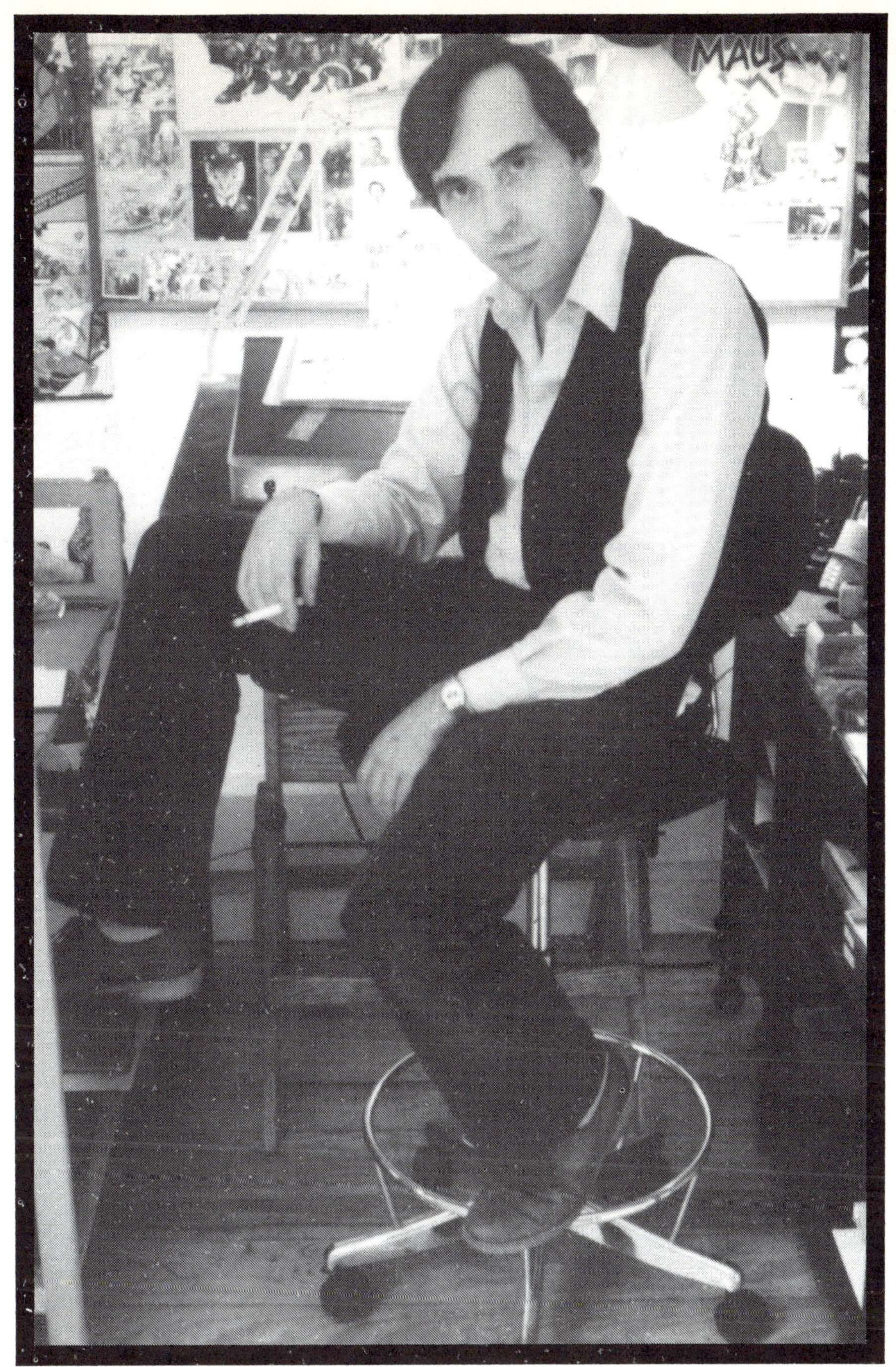

Chapter Seven
ART SPIEGELMAN

*Today Art Spiegelman is known as the co-editor of **Raw**, the modern successor to the underground comics. His long-running strip **Maus** was collected in book form a couple years back and received much critical and sales success. He started out selling gag cartoons to various publications in the Sixties, including the legendary **East Village Other** and the **Gothic Blimp Works**. In the Seventies he co-edited **Arcade: The Comics Revue**, whose contributors included many of the artists who'd come up through the ranks of the underground comics. For seven years, he taught at the School For Visual Arts in New York City. He taught what he calls "Language of the*

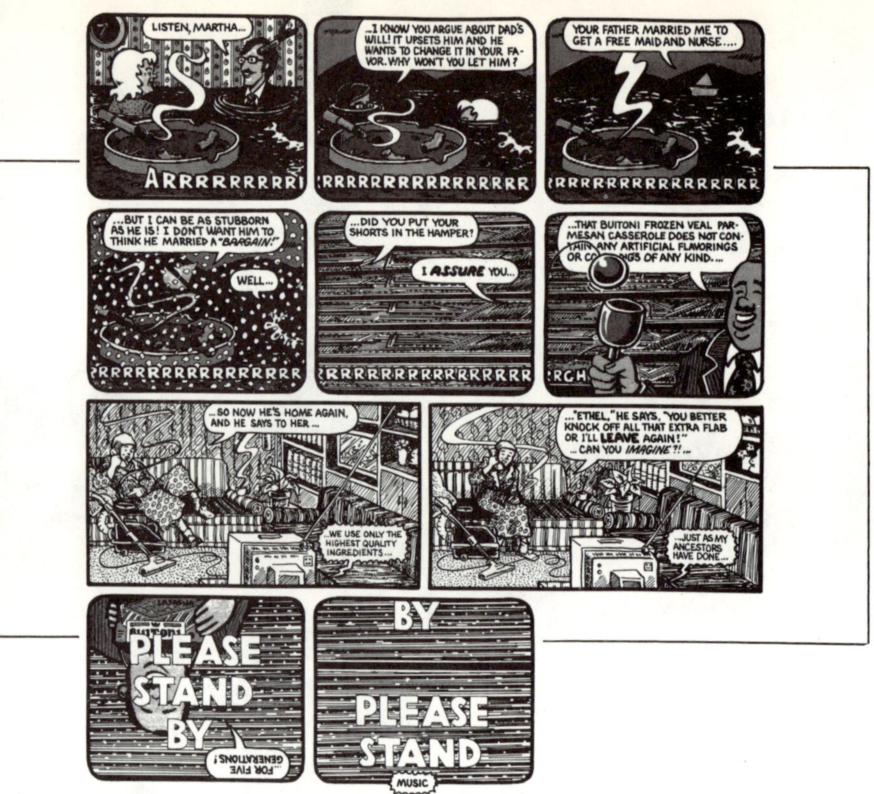

From "A Soap Opera" in Arcade #4

Spiegelman feels that whatever tool will best do the job is the right tool to use. "Each comic strip has its own requirements. For instance, I've done strips using a Winsor-Newton Series 7 #1 or 2 brush. It's been a useful tool. On the other hand, I've done other strips in scratchboard. I've done still other strips with a quill pen. Other strips were done with a Rapidograph and now I'm working with a fountain pen filled with India ink for 'Maus.' That pen had a special point constructed for me that's gold. It's a very flexible pen point in a Pelican fountain pen that'll let me work without paying too much attention to my tool, and still give me a very flexible responsive line and let me feel like I'm writing rather than drawing. This is psychologically important for me on 'Maus.' Each strip has its own mood and different tools seem appropriate at different times. I don't really like to impose one overall surface on all strips because they each have their own demands."

Regarding the custom made pen, Speigelman explains, "This pen is extraordinarily flexible for a fountain pen. It can make a line as broad as a brush line and still make a line as fine as a zero or one Rapidograph. I couldn't find a commercially made pen which could do that, but I discovered an old pen maker who was able to do such a thing. I don't use that as a tool for every drawing I make. It's a tool for 'Maus.'

"I did a strip in the early Seventies called 'Don't Get Around Much Any More.' It was a very still, depressed strip about feeling lifeless and a Rapidograph was the appropriate tool because it gives you a lifeless line. There's something about picking up tools other than the ones you're most used to because it kind of reinvigorates you. I have

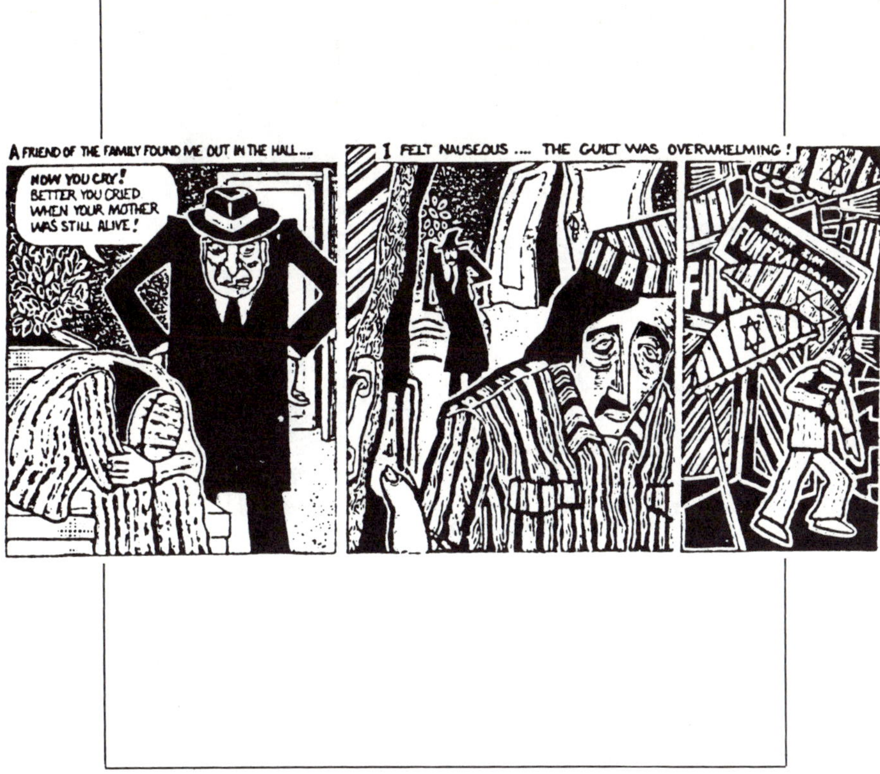

A self-portrait sequence from "Prisoner on the Hell Planet"

no interest in trying to keep my work consistent or developing a signature style. I'm more interested in serving the needs of the strip."

While most artists work in a collaborative venture, Spiegelman has written virtually everything he's drawn. This brings about a very different approach to adapting a story into comic strip form.

"It's more difficult for me to draw a comic strip than to write it, so I wouldn't have the patience to work from somebody else's script when I have scripts of my own I'd rather be working on, although I have written scripts for other artists. I don't write a script in prose form, exactly. I work it out in a rough stage which gets more and more focused as it goes along.

"The first stage is the idea. The second stage is the idea per page, breaking it down into single page thoughts. The next stage is to figure out what can be accomplished in any given panel and how the panels have to be broken down, such as what size and shape. Then comes the writing in the individual balloons. It starts as a note of the content of what has to be said and gets stripped down further and further until there are no extra words. So the comic strip has various stages of focus, and the stage before the last is the stage at which the drawing comes out when I'm sketching straight in ink. The balloons are figured out very carefully. Word for word, the lettering looks very similar, in 'Maus' at least, to the finished lettering because the lettering in 'Maus' is meant to look like my handwriting. So I know exactly how much space and volume the balloon will take up because I composed it as an element in the picture."

Comics," a series of lectures and discussions offering his personal "idiosyncratic aesthetic historical overview." The class consisted to a large degree of choosing about 15 to 20 artists and explaining the historical period in which they worked and what was happening in other comics around them as well as what basic possibilities were open to comics and then analyzing the various artists' work in some detail.

Spiegelman has also created commercial art for Topps Bubble Gum, producing the "Wacky Packs" series as well as contributing to the "Garbage Pail Kids" series and working as a consultant, recommending future projects.

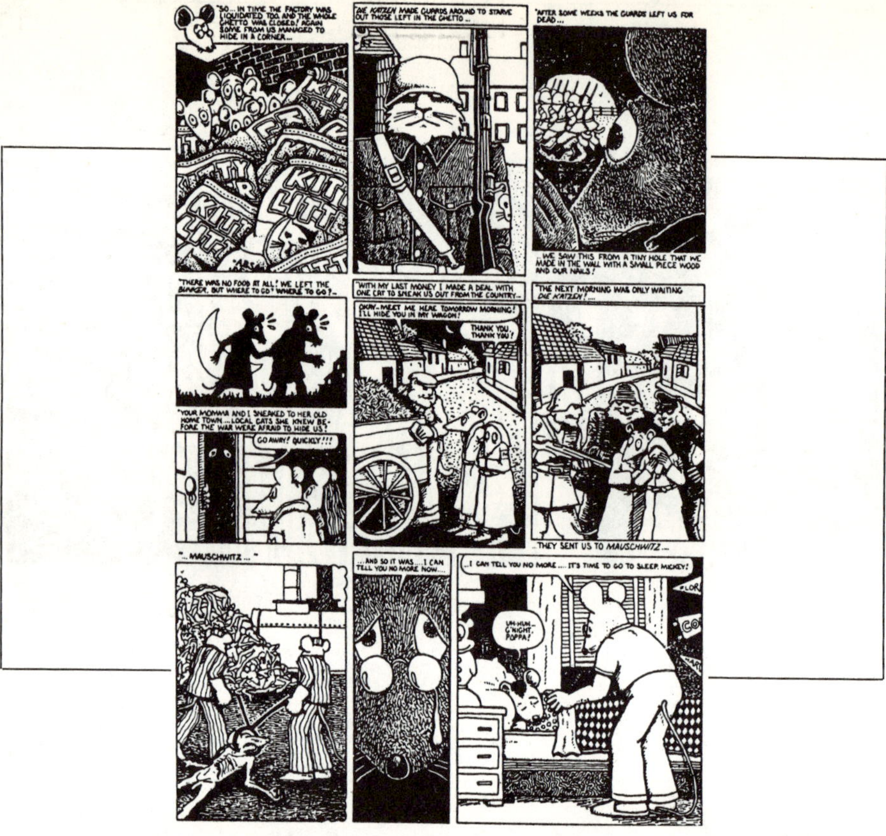

An excerpt from a 1981 three-page incarnation of "Maus" done in a different art style

The pictures illustrate the words, but the words are there because of what they do. The content of a picture in an individual panel is made up of the action the figures are performing, the expressions on the faces and what's being said. It all comes from the idea that has to be expressed in that picture. They're all components.

Since Spiegelman writes and draws his own strip, the artwork is not there just to illustrate the words but rather have a more involved working relationship with the text.

"Because the words and pictures are born simultaneously it makes it very difficult to talk about. The pictures illustrate the words, but the words are there because of what they do. The content of a picture in an individual panel is made up of the action the figures are performing, the expressions on the faces and what's being said. It all comes from the idea that has to be expressed in that picture. They're all components. I have difficulty understanding these things as separate elements, although I understand it can happen since I've written for other people. I don't see my function as either a writer or an illustrator because to me being a comic strip artist means writing and drawing as one process. Getting divorced from one or the other would make me wonder why I was doing this rather than some other thing, like being a writer or an illustrator. I would hate to illustrate a panel if I hadn't conceived of why that panel was there."

The actions of the characters within a panel, particularly body language, are important, particularly in "Maus."

"Body language especially has become more important in 'Maus' than it ever was before to me. I've learned a lot working on 'Maus' since I started in '78, and I'll still be doing it for another couple of years at least. Before that I was working with conventional approaches to both facial expressions and body language. In 'Maus,' because the faces are so minimized, I've had to learn subtler body language. It used to be easy. If I wanted to

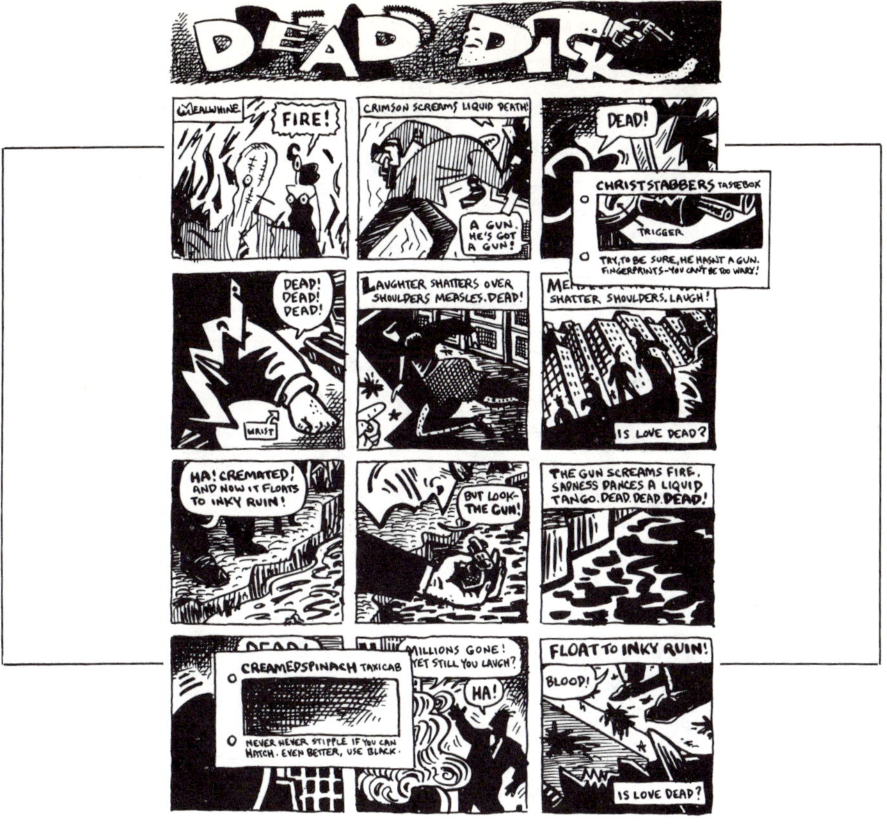

"Dead Dick" from Raw volume two, number one

show somebody looking angry I'd just turn those eyebrows down and get a snarl on the face—Basic Expression #206-A—and that was that. It was part of the vocabulary you learned as a cartoonist. Communicating with only a downturned brow didn't allow for enough nuance because in mouse faces there's no facial muscles, to speak of. They're like little masks. It's been necessary to figure out how to act these things out with the body. There wasn't as firmly developed a received body of syntactical knowledge to work from so I've had to work it out for myself. It's taught me a lot about drawing. I'm sure it's a lesson I'll be able to retain when I go back to drawing human faces. It's become very important in 'Maus' because the faces weren't there to work with, so the next best thing was using the hands and the way people stood."

Comics are a synthesis of words and pictures. Deciding the importance of each to a particular story depends on the intent of an individual strip.

"I've done things that have no words. And I've done parts of 'Maus' where it's just two people talking. You can see two people talking and get some sense of their emotional responses by looking at the pictures, but to find content, the balloons are essential. I don't feel it's a failure if you have to read the balloons. It might be a failure if you could get most everything from the pictures if there were balloons, because then it might be easier just to get rid of those balloons. We're talking about a continuum. The ultimate expression is when the words and pictures interact.

"There's a shibboleth that repeating what's in a picture in the words is bad comics by defini-

You can see two people talking and get some sense of their emotional responses by looking at the pictures, but to find content, the balloons are essential. I don't feel it's a failure if you have to read the balloons. It might be a failure if you could get most everything from the pictures if there were balloons, because then it might be easier just to get rid of those balloons. We're talking about a continuum. The ultimate expression is when the words and pictures interact.

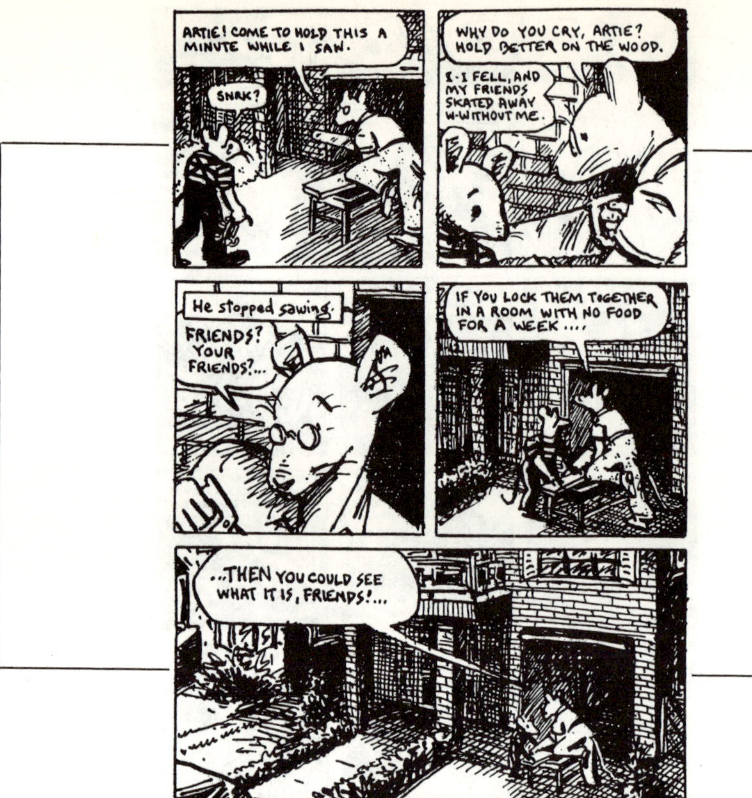

I don't see these things as moving pictures, but accretions of pictures. They're still pictures that never had any other life in my mind. I can see how you can look at a comic and see how it's like a storyboard for a film. But the more it's a storyboard for a film, the less it's a successful comic. Comics are a very specific organization of still images.

The opening sequence from the novel Maus

tion. I used to buy into that, but I buy into it less now. There are instances when it looks like they lettered the instructions to the artist into the caption. There are other times when the repetition creates reinforcement that's very powerful. I don't think by definition this is wrong, although I've seen it used badly more often than not. In 'Maus' often times I need the words to say the same kind of thing the picture is saying. Sometimes when they overlap by ninety percent it can create a strong mood, stronger than when you're given the information only one way or the other."

Unlike many artists, Spiegelman doesn't see his stories in his head as though they're movies which he's capturing on paper. In fact, he says he's never seen it this way.

"I like movies, but I don't think they have much to do with comics except that the language is similar, like wide-angle-shot or overhead-shot or close-up. But I don't see these things as moving pictures, but accretions of pictures. They're still pictures that never had any other life in my mind. I can see how you can look at a comic and see how it's like a storyboard for a film. But the more it's a storyboard for a film, the less it's a successful comic. Comics are a very specific organization of still images. They suggest time and motion, but they exist as still images. A character on the left of the frame in one panel, can, in the next panel, be in the middle and in the third panel be over on the right creating the illusion of a person moving from left to right. But I never saw that as a person walking or tried to figure out how to divide the panels like the frames of a film. I see a kind of patterning, as if you kept the so-called 'camera' still with the figure

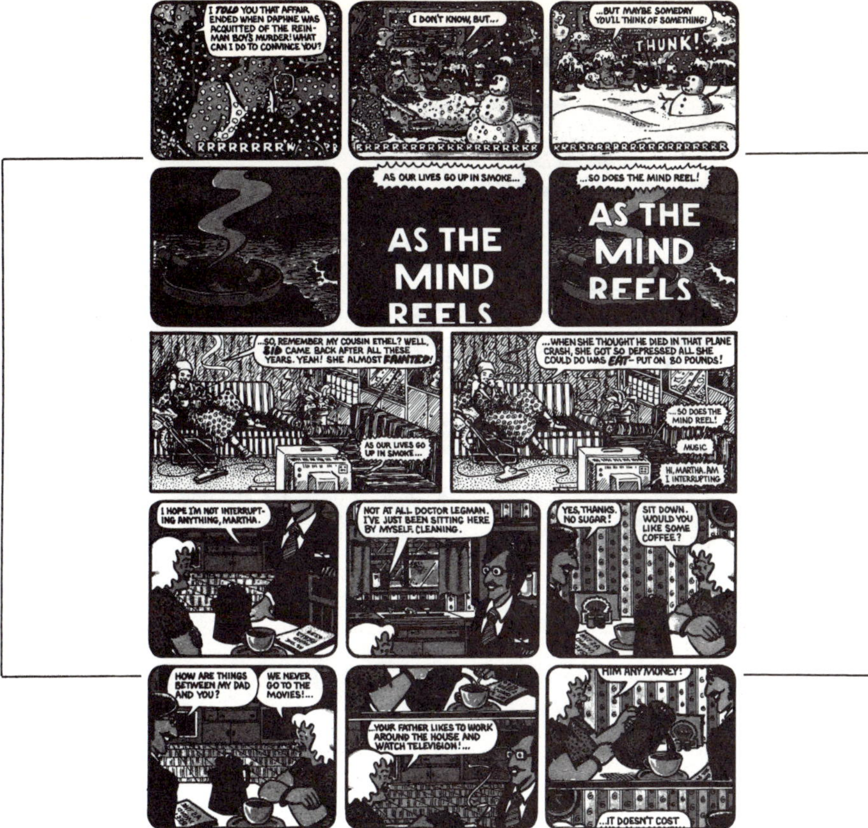

moving across the background. You'd create a pattern that would attract your eye to a certain part of the page and hold it there.

"When I think about comics I always think of full pages and divide them into panels later. And try to find the individual moment that accumulates the full page."

Spiegelman continues, "There's so many other factors operating, such as what size and shape panel to use, which is a problem no film-maker ever deals with because they always have the same ratio of rectangle to work in. And no film-maker has to think of one frame from five minutes ago still being present in the eye because a film is based on retention from a fraction of a second to a fraction of a second. Comics are based on seeing all those things at once because peripherally you're always going to see what happens next and what happened before. It's interesting that Rudolphe Topffer was doing comics that used cross-cutting a good seventy years before the invention of cinema.A lot of cinematic language is actually comics language.

"I find myself influenced by literature and painting. They all play their part. It's what makes comics an exciting medium, to synthesize and be able to use little bits and parts from other disciplines. So I'm not discounting the influence of film, I just think it's overrated. I don't see comics as trying to find interesting angles. Usually it's what will serve the concept and narrative best. Is it something that will jolt you from the rhythm? Or continue a rhythm? Is it something that will focus your attention on one picture or make you ignore the picture and just move through them or see the picture subliminally? I

I find myself influenced by literature and painting. They all play their part. It's what makes comics an exciting medium, to synthesize and be able to use little bits and parts from other disciplines. So I'm not discounting the influence of film, I just think it's overrated.

A page from "A Soap Opera" in Arcade #4

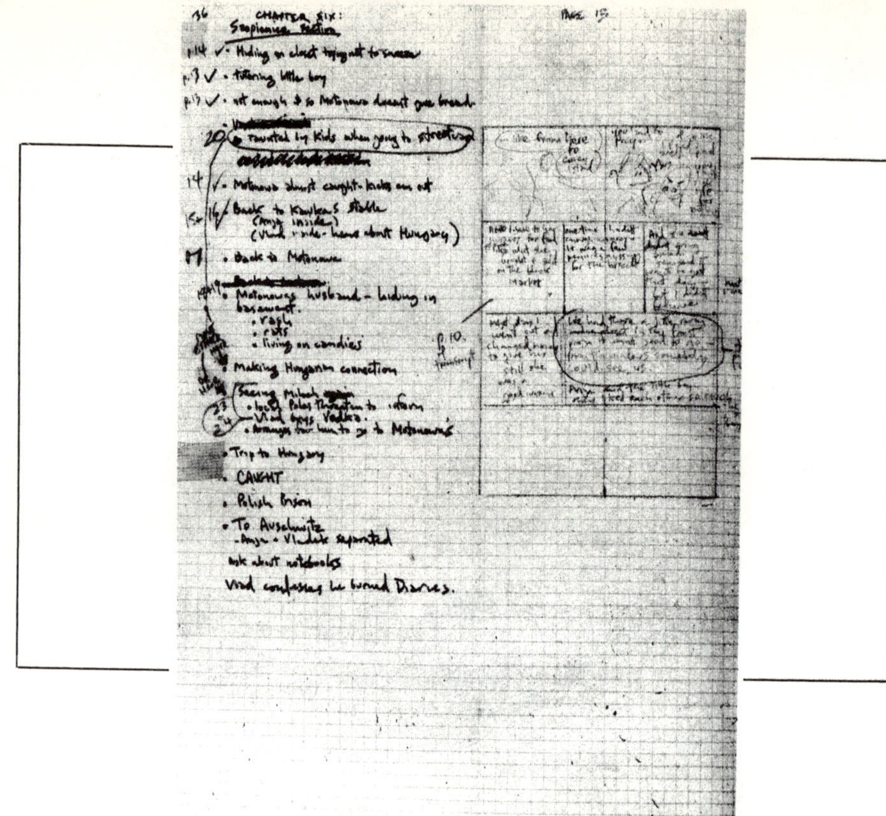

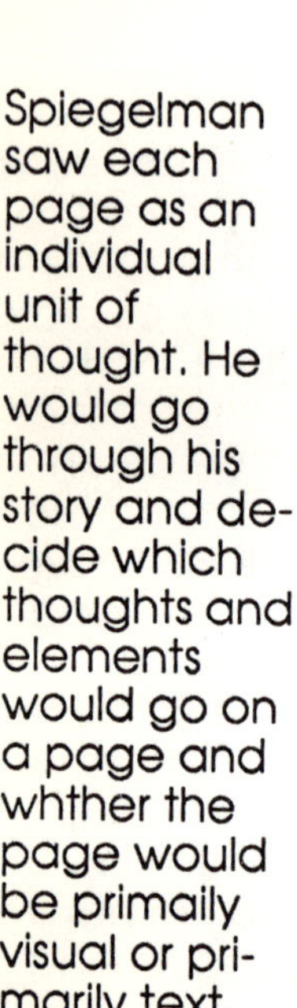

Spiegelman saw each page as an individual unit of thought. He would go through his story and decide which thoughts and elements would go on a page and whther the page would be primaily visual or primarily text.

think of them in clusters and in rows; each row is a concept or subconcept with a basic concept, which is a page. They're clusters rather than storyboarded moments.

"My specific interests might be very different from people involved in the comics industry. The Marvel Comics approach, to me, is an interestingly bizarre one. I can't imagine working like that, where the artist gets to lay out the action and then somebody else goes in and figures out the dialogue. On the other hand, I would hate to receive a script where everything's already been decided. That's why I do the comics I do. It allows the writer and the artist to be in constant communication by being the same person."

Spiegelman works in layers not going through the process of an artist adapting someone else's script into comic book pages.

"For 'Maus,' I work first by blocking out in long hand script form approximately what has to happen in the chapter. Some kind of outline. The events have to be communicated that this action has to happen and this aspect of character has to be revealed. Then I turn that into subsequences, and I'll write down next to it in the outline that this series of events might be tellable in two pages or three pages, and that it will be a page for that and a half a page for this, and so on. Then I go back and try to see if that will actually work or if I need more or less space. Only when I'm at the stage where I know what can be bitten off as a one page chunk would I get down to more specific kinds of breakdowns. At that point I start doing thumbnail breakdowns, like three units of activity or action take place on this page and a three-tiered page is a result. Or I might find that page requires a

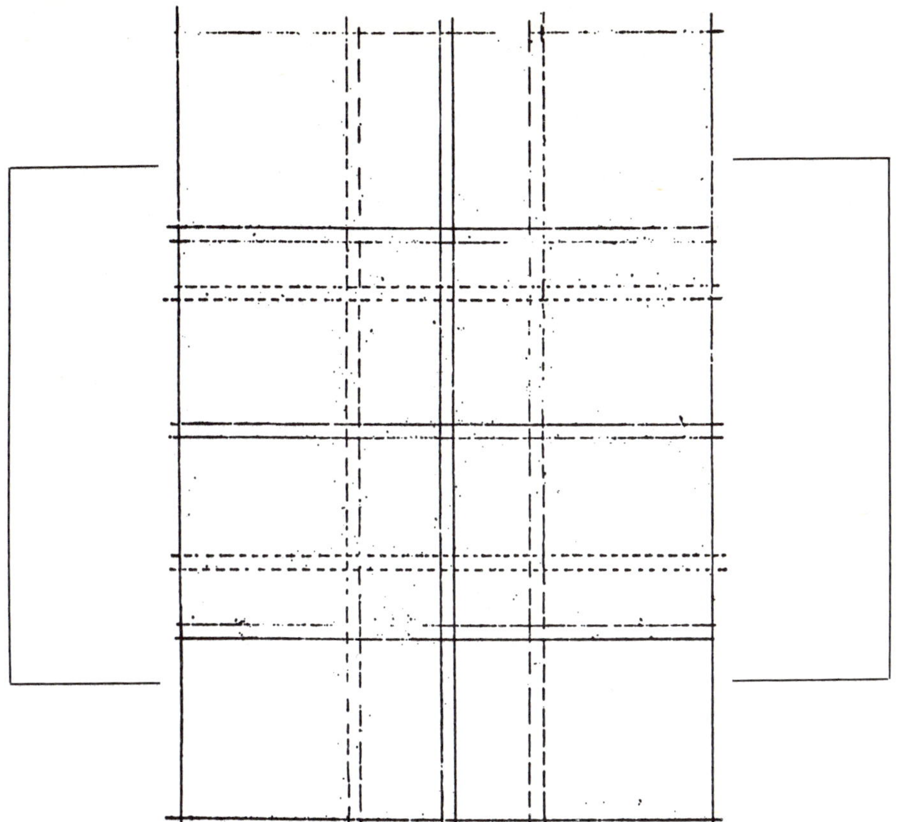

Spiegelman then created a grid, dividing the page in either thirds or quarters vertically and/or horizontally depending on which panels required emphasis.

lot of text and needs bigger pictures, or requires a lot of dialogue and more small panels to have a back and forth effect. So the next thing for me to determine is how many rows and how many boxes will be on a page and what will take place in each of those. Sometimes it'll be configured around: there are three events on the page and I've got to find three subunits on that page to get those events across, not necessarily in horizontal rows but at least in three subunits of one kind or another. Then, still in thumbnail stage, I'll block in what might exist with little arrows going to each of those boxes giving in very encoded fashion what I want to have said.

"The next stage is ruling out on paper the actual finished size, which in the case of 'Maus' is 1:1 ratio with the printed size. So I'll rule out boxes that size. I work on grids for the lettering which is like a piece of graph paper divided into eighths, and I try experimentally writing out the captions or balloons. If it looks like it's hopelessly long, which is often the case, I try to reduce it down to its essence, and if it's still too long I realize I need extra boxes or else I'll have too many words on the page, and I try to find a way to expand my layout to accommodate these extra boxes.

"Finally what I end up with is a piece of 8 1/2 x 11 paper, which is the size I've been working on with the roughs, with the boxes ruled out, the lettering put in quite tightly, and a very rough sketch of the picture. This would consist of what figures will be in the picture, what angle you see them from and so on, but not working out the tonalities necessarily, except in a very coarse way. Then, after that stage is

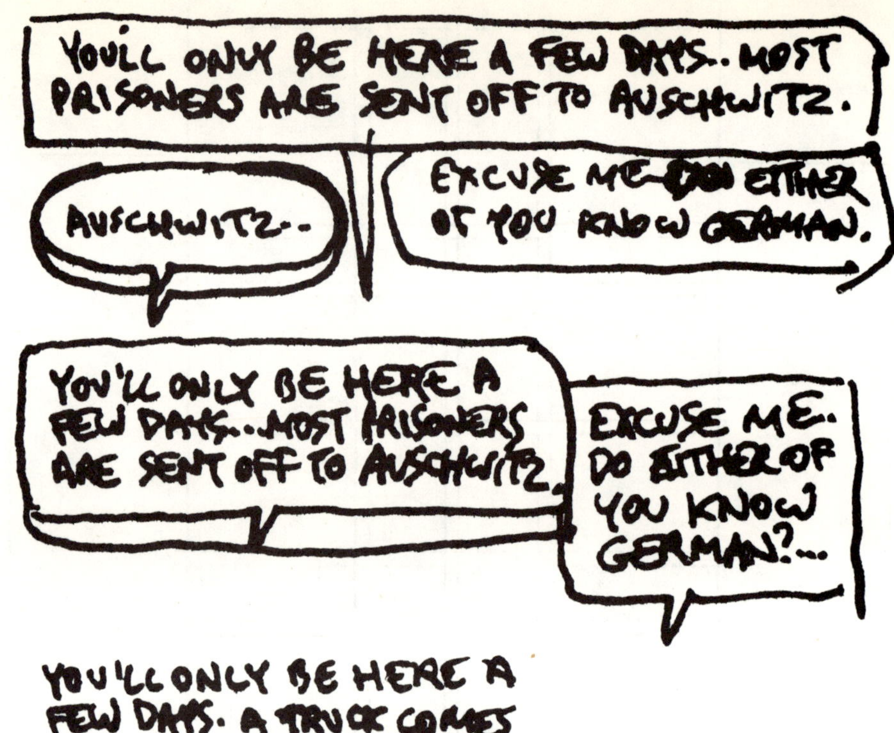

Having decided a page's basic content and grid layout, he then began to select balloon placement and size.

successfully accomplished for an entire section of the book, I start going back and doing individual finished drawings for each box on the page.

"The process then becomes as follows: I work on a light table. On a sheet of transparent acetate is a grid that's been divided up into eighths of an inch for my lettering, and on the top of that grid I've ruled a page of 'Maus' configured in halves, quarters and thirds with dotted lines, which I call a Cartoonograph. So in the Cartoonograph, I have a three-tiered page and a four-tiered page, and I have thirds going the other way so I can get three panels across and I have it divided in half so that I can get two panels across. Now I often deviate from that, but that's the grid from which I deviate. Sometimes I'll have things which are bizarre sizes, bigger than a half or a little bit smaller, but I started from that basic grid and I'm allowed to expand or contract in that space where I'm doing the finished lettering and the rough sketch drawing. I've determined the exact size of each box and approximately what will be drawn in it.

"Then I begin working on the finished piece of paper. I use typing paper rather than bristol board because I want to feel like I'm writing. Like I'm writing longhand. So the finished drawing is done on a higher grade of typing paper, like a hundred percent acid neutral, high rag content typing paper, but nevertheless a kind of typing paper. The finished drawings are very often made of millions of patches, because if I don't get the panel right the first few passes, I'll just do it again.

"I do all my drawing on tracing paper with colored magic markers, starting with a light colored

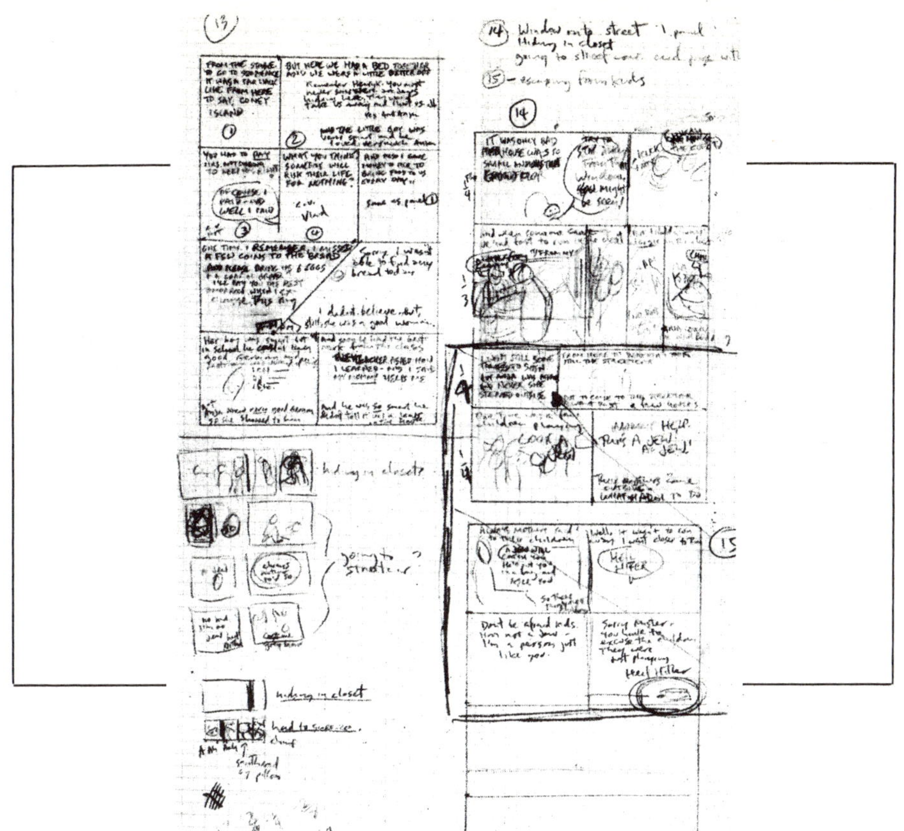

There was a constant process of writing and re-writing to fit words into the spacing available.

magic marker and sketching it in with yellow or orange. Blocking it in the way I did on my rough sketch, or finding something new to do if I wasn't happy with my rough sketch. So I'll sketch something lightly in yellow or orange and then start focusing in on it with darker colors. For instance, I'll put in a figure, and I've now got to figure out how that figure is standing. Is one shoulder higher than the other? Is the figure foreshortened in some fashion? If I started in orange, I'll take my magenta or burgundy color and define that area of the picture more. That works great, but if not then I'll use green and then a dark blue and then a black to keep trying to focus that picture. When any one picture gets too blotted looking and I can't figure out what I'm doing, then I'll trace it over and continue with the same colored marker process. When I've done that for a panel, I then put it on the light table underneath the boxes I've drawn out and draw it with the pen directly, without any further pencilling, but still changing from what I had before. In other words, it's not a line for line tracing of what I had underneath, but I've blocked out all the information and have the perspective ruled. That process invariably involves patching and white out, and sometimes throwing it away and doing it a third time until I have an inked panel.

"Part of that process that I've found useful, and this comes under 'How To' tips, is that when inking, it's sometimes difficult to know when a little bit of crosshatching will be too murky. For that I keep loose scraps of prepared acetate around so I can ink the parts I'm sure of and then try things out by putting acetate over the drawing and seeing whether that section will work

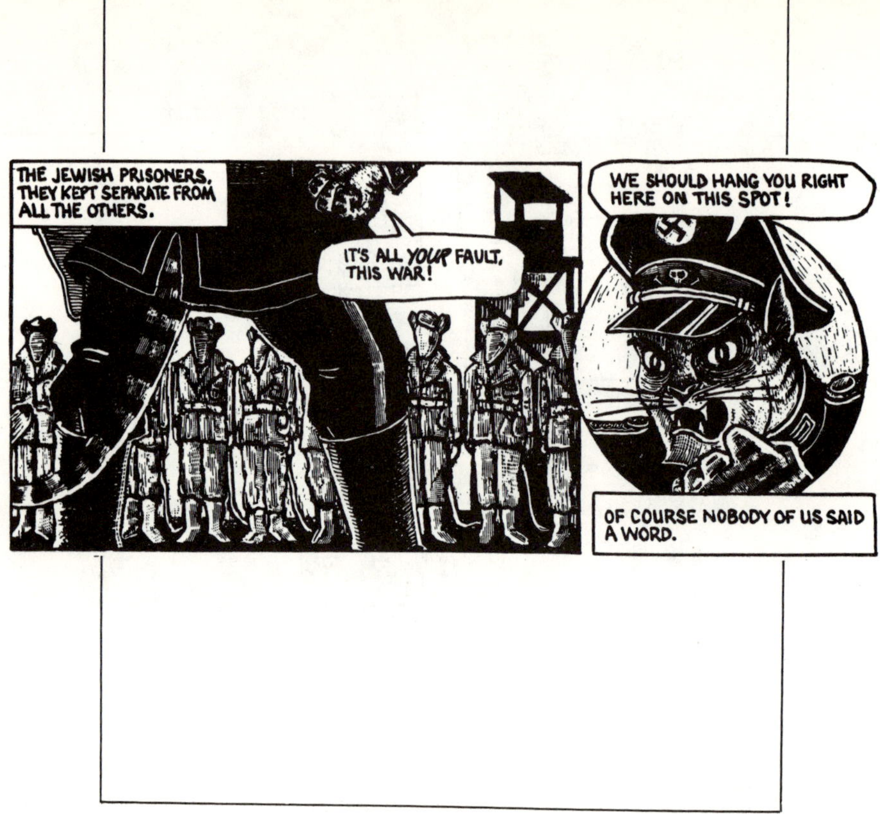

Before selecting the final style of his artwork he experimented with various other methods. Here we see an example created on scratchboard which he found insufficiently fluid.

when it's been crosshatched with blacks put in. That process is repeated through the whole page. After the page is finished, I then go back and change some of the black and whites so that the whole page looks more like what I'd like to see when the whole page is together. I know this sounds incredibly long-winded and arduous, but then it is. That's how I go about it, even though the drawings may not look fancy and sophisticated. Even though 'Maus' is less illustrated, there's still that kind of layered process for me to get to my finished result.

"For comic strips I primarily work in black and white. When I work in color I try to use mechanical color separations. Sometimes, when that's too time consuming, I'll do color but try to keep it flat. Comics are not the same as illustration. I don't believe in giving too much visual information; comics drawing is an extension of writing. A visual kind of writing, rather than things that look too photographically rendered. Drawings like that are too finished, in the sense that when somebody's dead, he's finished. What attracted me to comics is that the drawings are so quirky. You never see anybody who looks like Popeye; it's just drawn with this weird kind of doodle configuration alphabet that Segar invented. That's equally true in a sense of Jack Kirby and Steve Ditko, but less true of the generation of, say, Neal Adams and those comic artists who came after. They seem very enamored of photographic illusionism, and to me that's not necessarily good storytelling. You get lost in irrelevant detail. Irrelevant in terms of the whole concept and narrative."

While many artists have been influenced by the visual splendor

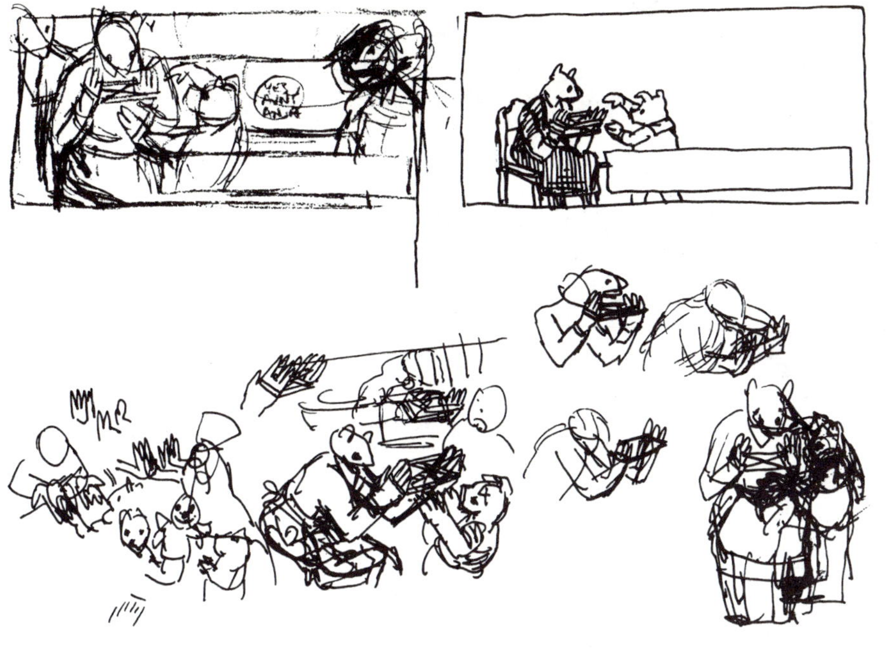

After knowing the exact format and space, but before creating the final drawing, Spiegelman would create as many as fifty sketches. Here we see an example of the sketches he created for the scene in which his mother trains a boy in the German language.

of Hal Foster, Alex Raymond and Burne Hogarth, these artists drew a version of comics largely alien to Spiegelman.

"To me, Foster, Hogarth and Raymond were the bane of comics. That's what killed comics for me. I like comics that are something else. That are specifically working with one kind of information you need for the story. Out of those three people, my favorite is Foster because he at least accepted that he was making a bunch of sequential illustrations. There's a kind of sobriety to those Prince Valiant strips which allows one to rest in them. The others are doing a lot of inking pyrotechnics, such as in somebody like Raymond, who I know is some people's god. On the other hand, I very much admire Winsor McCay. His work borders on a kind of illustration, but he understood and invented a kind of panel to panel understanding that makes all those things work. The detail information is specifically there in support of the ideas of the strip, which have to do with making believable fantasy. They're not illustration technique for the sake of the technique.

"Now all that having been said, there are certain people who do it admirably well and whose work I really admire, like Lorenzo Matotti, an Italian cartoonist. A book of his called **Fires** was published by Catalan and his work is very much inspired by post-impressionist painters. It's very lush, lavish color and makes a kind of comics I'd never seen before, one that I do admire. In it's own way it retains an interest in the kind of abstraction comics are all about, which is also true of the kind of European color in Herge's **Tintin**. It's realistic in one sense but very abstract. There's a kind of

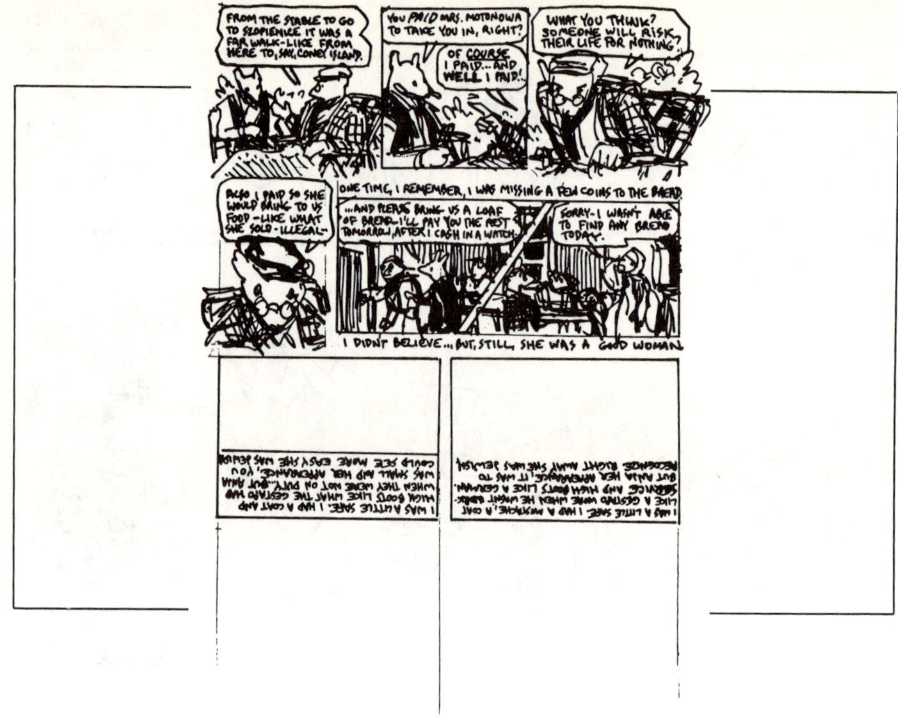

The page format on the grid is never final but open to revision to enhance emphasis. This page started with full panels at the top, with Spiegelman's father telling his story in a contemporary setting.

painted color which has become more and more a part of what's in comics, and it eludes me because it seems to move away from what's central to comics. It's lush, airbrushed color, as one example, that doesn't allow me to enter into the panel to panel continuity, which is where comic book magic takes place. Instead it focuses on the individual image.

"I've done paintings and I've done illustrations, but I've never done illustration-type or painted-type comics. It's not what I want when I look at a comic. I usually can find much better illustrations in the work of people who specialize in being illustrators."

On the other hand, Spiegelman is not against drawing recognizable objects in comic strip terms, such as when an artist has to depend on a swipe file.

"That's absolutely legitimate. I wish I had the discipline to keep more of a file. It's important to understand exactly how something works and looks, even if you're going to abstract from that. It's not necessary to draw every nut and bolt, but it's important to understand how the machine functions. You have to look at it and analyze it. I use photos in my work as often as I can because I draw from life. The end result is not to reproduce that photograph absolutely, but to be able to have all the information there. I can't imagine having to work without that because it would be very limiting. I prefer having as firm ground under me as I can before flying off into my own inept version of something. I've always wished somebody would just publish a swipe file subscription where you could get it all without having to look for it. Whenever I want to try something I have to

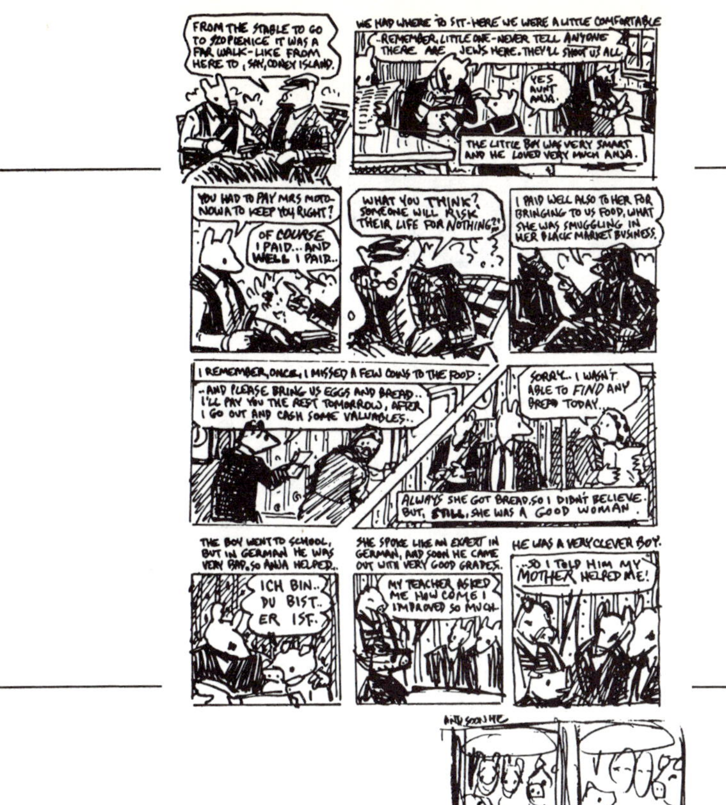

This soon changed to bring the cat's cradle panel to the top of the page, with doodles beginning to shift the emphasis in the last two panels.

remember where I saw a picture of it before, and then go rummaging through endless books. The one advantage of living in New York is a massive file at the Midtown Manhattan Public Library. When I'm starting a project and I know I'm going to need a picture of tanks, horse and buggy, guns or whatever, having access to that central swipe file is quite useful. Also, I'm not above swiping from other artists. I've found occasions where I needed to know how to draw something I'd seen in somebody else's strip. I don't try to trace his picture, but it helps me understand it.Once I've swiped it, I don't think you'd recognize the drawing that it came from. On the other hand, on some level, it's a swipe. I'm not swiping the artist's attitude or the specific configuration of lines, although I am taking advantage of a degree of distillation of something."

Although Spiegelman doesn't depend on rendering facial expressions in his strip 'Maus,' he's used it on other strips. He learned to accomplish this aspect of comic art the way most artists do.

"From books on how to draw cartoons I found as I was growing up, and from copying other people's cartoons, one begins to learn very quickly. There's a basic vocabulary of expression. The Have-A-Nice-Day face. The Have-A-Shitty-Day face. And so on. That's a start. I often work the way animators work, with a mirror handy, method-acting expressions to myself. But again I'm working off a variance of a codified language that has been very successful over the past century or so of comedy."

Although Spiegelman has taught classes in comic art at the School for Visual Arts in New York, he'd never say that attending

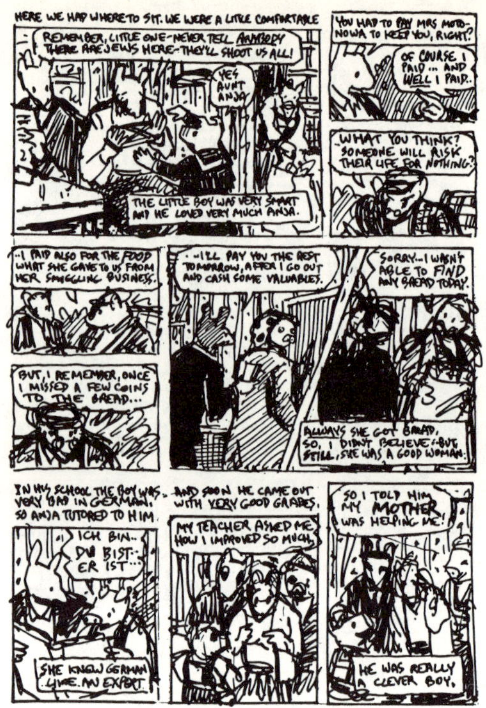

Here the panels are given their final placement with the flashbacks enlarged and contemporary storytelling again using the vertical panel technique. The final two panels are expanded to increase the tension and sense of alarm.

school is the *only* way to become a comics artist.

"A formalized art education is as important as the artist makes it. 99% are self-taught. Ultimately every artist is self-taught, even if he's got twelve years of art school. Part of being self-taught is learning from where you can, and that means learning from artists whose work you're looking at, learning from books on the subject, learning from artists working in other disciplines, learning from whatever art classes you take over the course of your life. Ultimately *you're* the person assimilating it, and to that extent you're always self-taught whether you're in school or not. So I would not say the only way to become a comic artist is to take a class in it. I would say the only way to become a comic artist is to have a passion for comics. Study and read them as much as you can. Copy from them. That's a basic way people learn, and take whatever classes become available. What's more important than classes in comics would be classes in life drawing. Classes in perspective drawing and in lettering, if such a thing exists, and classes in story writing and structure. Those are equally important. It may be important to take classes in psychology, cinema, poetry and theatre. Being a cartoonist may involve knowing as much as you can about everything because I've found myself facing my own inadequacies over and over again from not knowing how a machine might work or where something is on a map. One of the things most useful to know is the history of comics and how to look at and understand what you're looking at. All too often cartoonists are inspired by someone about eight years older than them and that's a very limited resource. The history of comics is

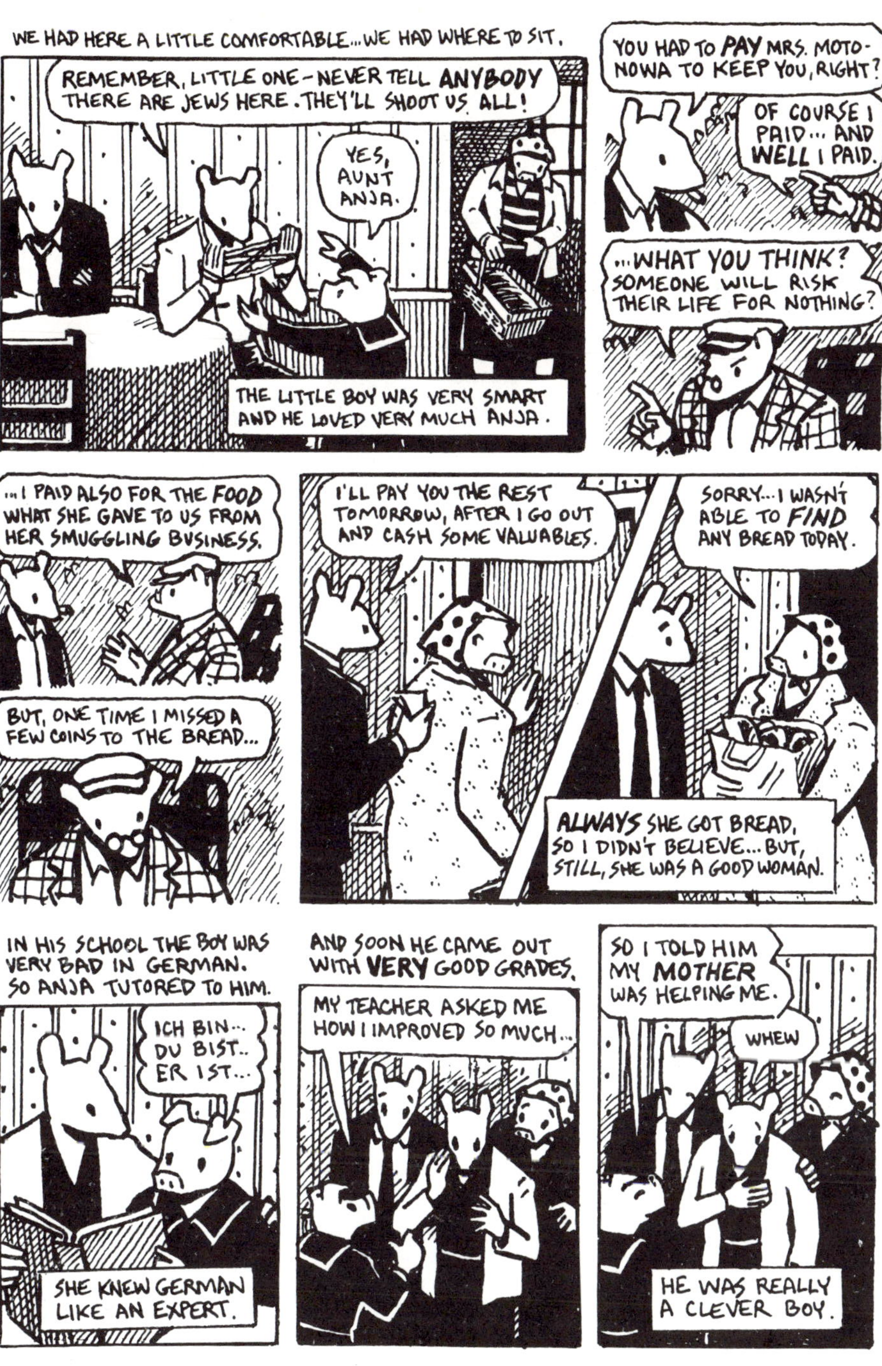

The final page as printed. For the final drawings, Spiegelman replaced his regular pen point with a flexible gold point.

nowhere near as long as the history of painting and it's possible to absorb a good deal of it because so many things are reprinted and available. Also crucial is the history of cinema, theatre, painting. All those things can only feed what you're making."

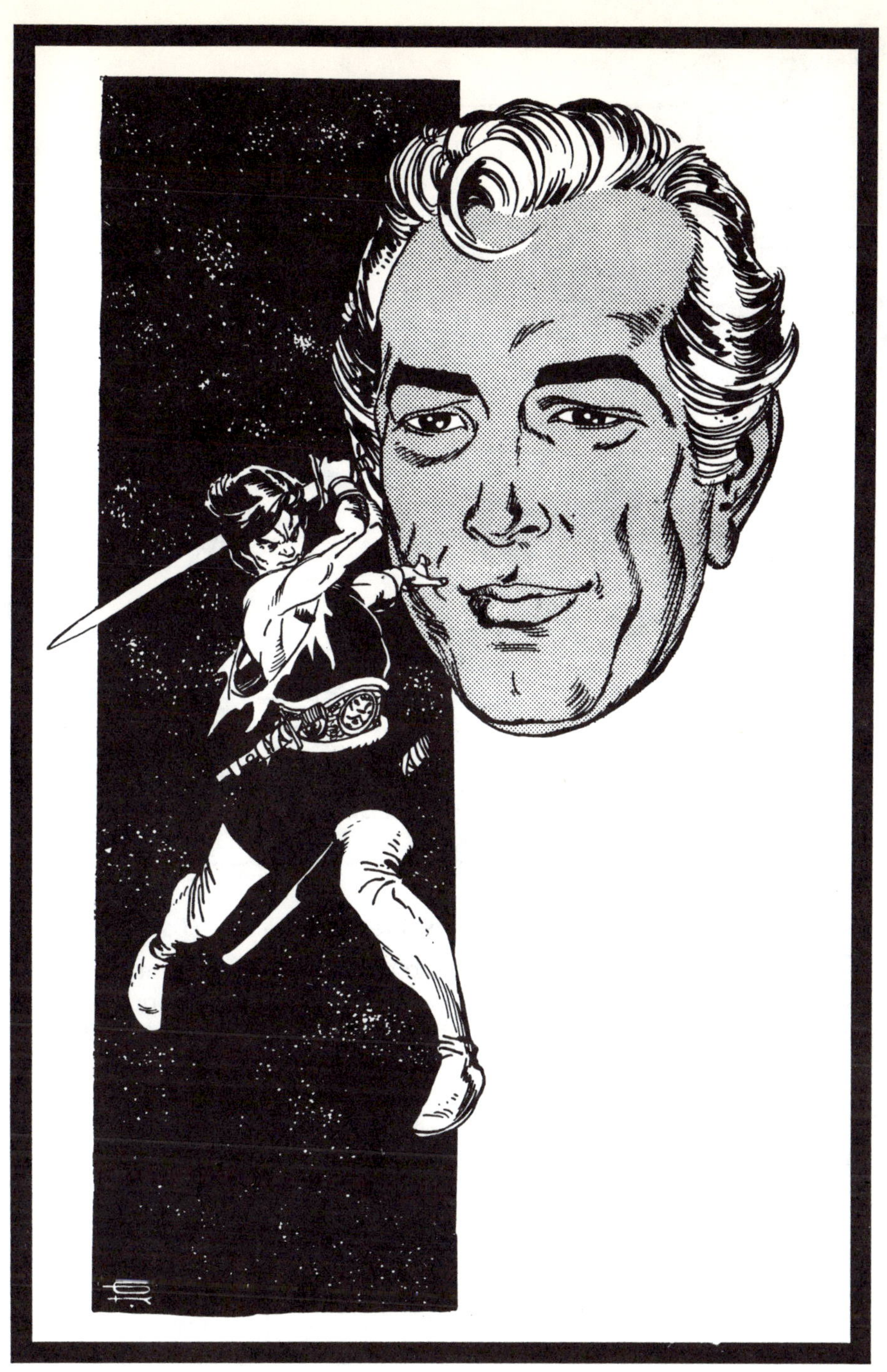

Chapter Eight
GIL KANE

*Gil Kane is reputed to have worked for nearly every comics company which ever existed since he began drawing comics in 1941. His work has been published by Marvel, D.C., Quality, MLJ, Street & Smith, Prize, Holyoke, Aviation Press, Fawcett, Eastern Color, Hillman, Tower, Dell, King, Fox and Avon. In the late Sixties he was the creative force behind the black and white magazine **His Name Is Savage!** which lasted only one issue due to distribution problems, but remains highly praised to this day. In 1971 Kane tried to expand comics into the paperback rack with **Blackmark**, a sword & sorcery strip written in collaboration*

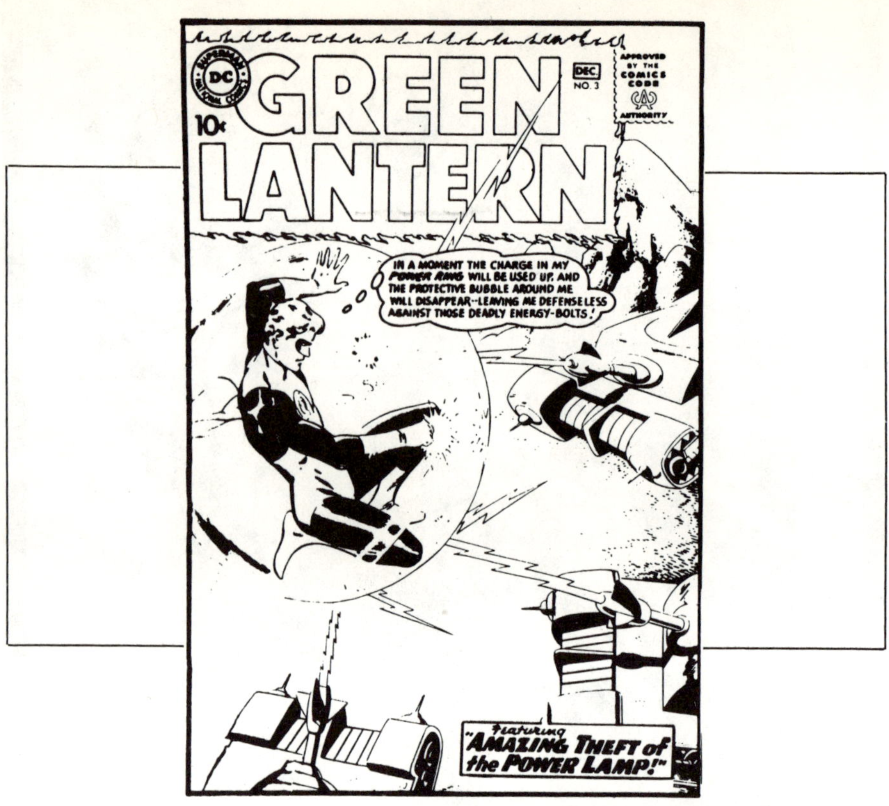

Two series with which Kane wsa most identified in the '60s

Kane dismisses the value of discussing which tools an artist should use as he feels that talent, feeling and intensity are much more important than the search for the perfect pen point.

"Everything depends on personality. We're all victims of our own personality and totally directed by the needs of our personality. When I was a kid I was a terrific athlete, but I was terribly uneducated and came from an uneducated family in an environment which was really sort of narrow. Now at some real distance I understand what happened to me and why, and to some extent how it affects other people in this field.

"Most of the reasons, I feel, that almost anybody comes into comics or pursues fantastic literature of any kind is because it clearly fills a need. I see everybody who reads comics essentially as an incipient creator; somebody who really needed to express themselves and comics presents an accessible form in which they can easily recognize and understand the symbols. They do that without intellectualizing it. Kids are drawn to comics almost immediately, before they're even ten years old."

That different people find common points of interest in comics is evidenced by the influence of one of the greatest adventure strips of the Thirties, Alex Raymond's **Flash Gordon**.

"When I was a kid, Raymond was doing Flash Gordon and there was a point when he was doing 'The Tournaments of Mongo,' and somehow, to me as a kid, that represented the ultimate! First of all it was a direct projection of my own expression, and here it was, articulated beautifully! It was sensual! It filled in information that I didn't have. There were holes in my

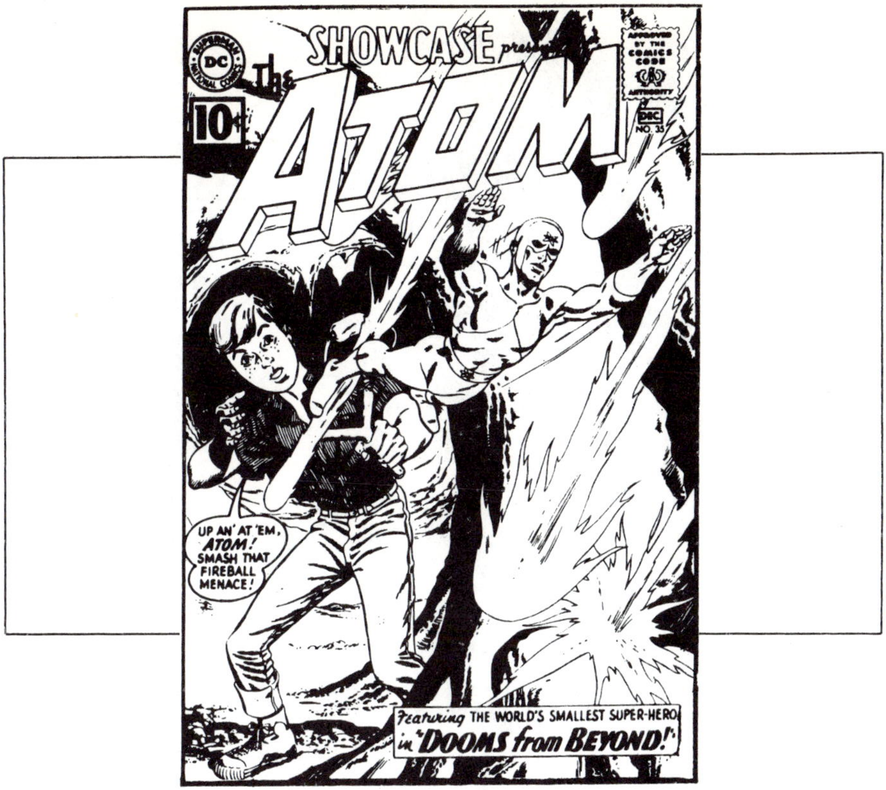

Left: Cover to Green Lantern #3; Right: Showcase #35, featuring Atom

personality that Flash Gordon began to fill. And the thing is that he did it so brilliantly, and so successfully, that I'm just one of millions of people it affected. You must know that (Federico) Fellini was enormously influenced by Raymond and even wrote and drew a Flash Gordon strip for himself during the War. Flash Gordon transcended cultures. It went all over Europe. Clearly there were elements in it that absolutely satisfied deep needs in youthful personalities. That's what makes the determination."

Kane believes there are two reasons people work in comics and feel a need to create.

"One is an allegory of transcendence; some need to push beyond some level of frustration into a state of release. Then there are the guys who purge themselves of anger and for whom working (and they nearly always tend to be the best people in the business) is a way of constantly purging the enormous anger that's in them that drives their talent. Like Jack Kirby and other people I've known that seem to be *endlessly*fertile! They never seem to run out of ideas or have to scratch around looking for possibilities. All they do is dig into this well, this reserve of anger, and just naturally lighten the load for themselves by working.

"The guys at the other end who sort of move into an area of aesthetic ecstasy are guys who have to assimilate something. They don't have to purge something, they have to add something. They're in pursuit of something that they have to add to their personality to be whole while the guys that are angry have to get rid of something in order to be satisfied. Those are the determinations.

with Archie Goodwin. In the Seventies, Kane drew the syndicated ***Star Hawks*** *written by Ron Goulart. Gil Kane's work can be found in some of the most popular comics of the Forties through the Eighties, and he has drawn most of the characters published by Marvel and D.C. including Spider-Man, Conan, Batman, Green Lantern, The Atom, and John Carter of Mars. His striking style loans itslef equally to exotic science fiction or Earthbound superheroes. His vast body of work speaks for itself. But the artist is equally articulate in describing the forces that motivate a creative personality.*

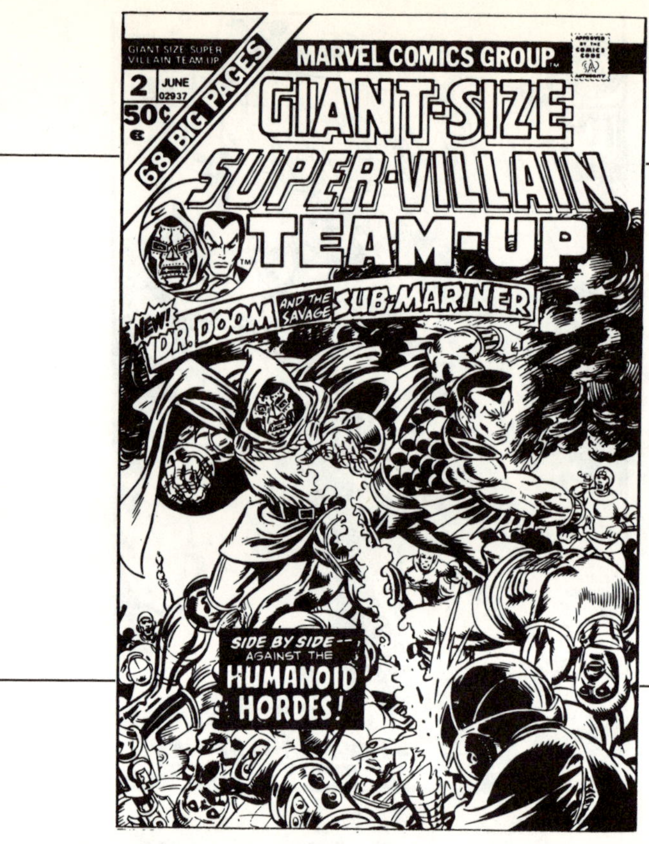

When you're a kid, you tend to be subjective and you're too overwhelmed by experience and too totally involved with experience to even think about examining it. To me, that explains the difference between early and later development.

Typical superhero combat...

"It all depends at what point in your life you start becoming objective. When you're a kid, you tend to be subjective and you're too overwhelmed by experience and too totally involved with experience to even think about examining it. To me, that explains the difference between early and later development. Some people find themselves so emotionally caught up in something that it just overwhelms them, and they never get a chance to catch their breath until ultimately they have to stand and deliver. Then they've found that by not being objective, they haven't been able to develop the perspective necessary to make a coherent whole of all these emotional experiences that they've had and put them into some sort of structure. That's when objectivity comes in—the need to organize and pull together all of these emotional impulses that are beating around in you."

This is why Kane finds questions about the right pencils or pens meaningless.

"Essentially they offer a false suggestion that by getting the right pen you're pulling a sword out of the stone and automatically equipping yourself with what you need. The things that you need to equip yourself with first are an emotional identification with the form, and then ultimately an objective view that allows you to step back and begin to put some sort of perspective structure in place in terms of the material. And then you ultimately need a direction to go in; something that the work has to be about, otherwise you get a kind of uneventful virtuosity. There are people who are really just first rate, except their work lacks the emotional connection a zealot has in pursuing a point of view."

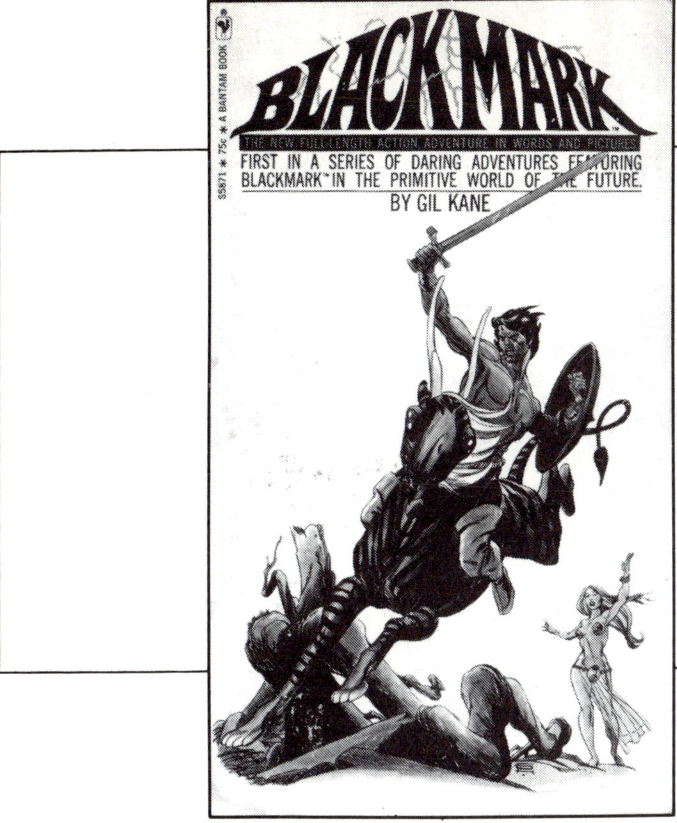

An example Kane gives is the early art of Joe Kubert done back in the 1940s.

"Some guys are lucky. For instance, Joe Kubert is a contemporary of mine. We both started very young. I started at sixteen and he started at fourteen. I always felt that we had a parallel somehow, and that parallel is that Joe was able to be a quick study. He immediately learned how to project. The assimilations that he was making went through a very quick process in his personality or in his mind and started to come out as work on the page when he was fourteen. He was faking, and by faking I mean that since he didn't know anything about structure, he had a mind and an eye that could organize these things into a situation that while it wasn't accurate, it was his*impression* of the material. It took me until I was into maturity before I realized this didn't work for me; that I had to have some underpinning, some sense of structure. I ultimately felt that my emotional connection was such that it was like getting on to a chariot pulled by four black horses with red eyes. Those sons-of-bitches just pulled this thing and I had the devil's own time just keeping them on track. I almost felt like I was at the mercy of my own emotional interpretation. It took me a long time before I recognized how essential a structure was in order to start being able to control the material and direct it and have a point of view that began to place it in a certain context. But Joe didn't need that somehow. He began to fake out stuff that looked sensational right from scratch. By the time he was eighteen he was inking. I had been an assistant to Jack Kirby at sixteen, but Joe was already, at seventeen, inking Jack Kirby as well as Mort Meskin. Some-

He was faking, and by faking I mean that since he didn't know anything about structure, he had a mind and an eye that could organize these things into a situation that while it wasn't accurate, it was his*impression* of the material. It took me until I was into maturity before I realized this didn't work for me; that I had to have some underpinning, some sense of structure.

A sophisticated attempt to bring comics into the paperback format and onto the bookshelf

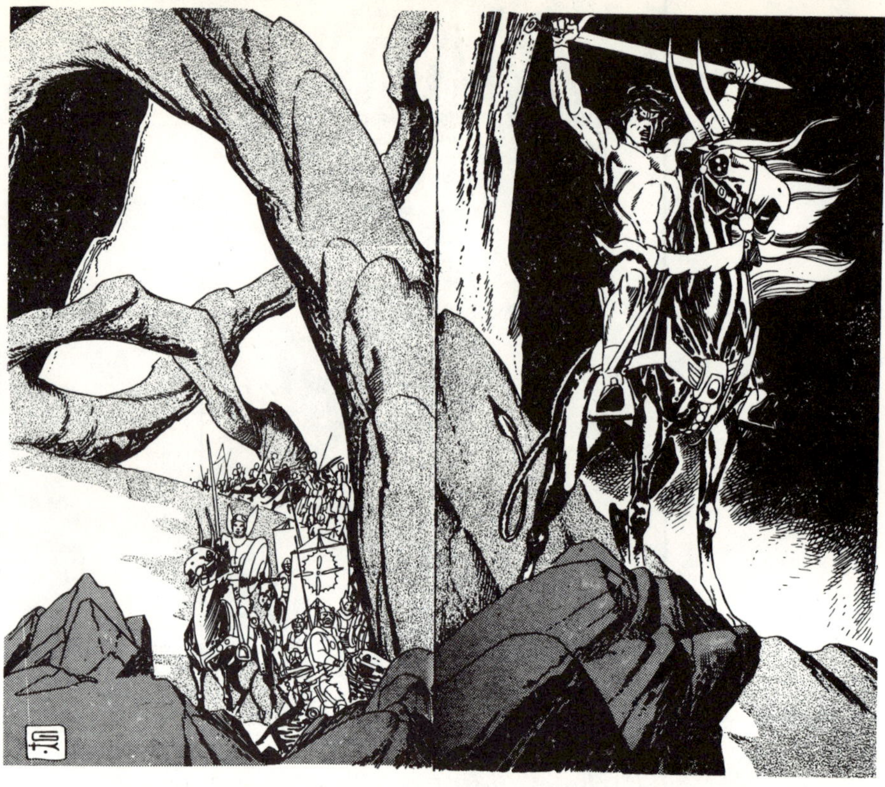

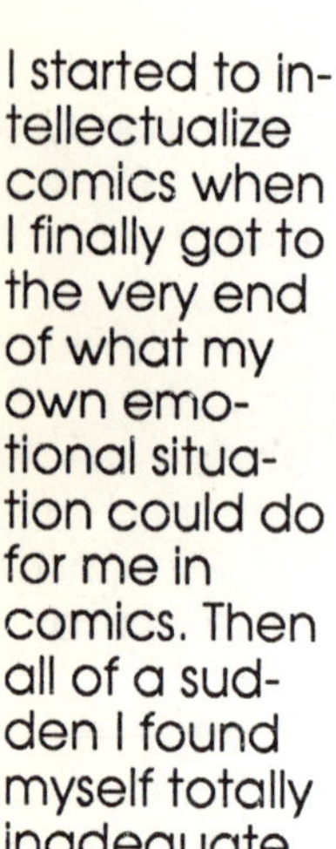

I started to intellectualize comics when I finally got to the very end of what my own emotional situation could do for me in comics. Then all of a sudden I found myself totally inadequate.

where around '44-'45 he wound up pencilling and inking the Hawkman at that character's first go-around. Joe's own personality began to emerge as fairly controlled, beautifully poetic and full of the sort of distortions that only personality can give and put a spin on something. It didn't matter if it wasn't accurate because it so so *emotionally* right! Then little by little, over a period of years, his maturity began to recognize that he needed more of a structure. But his art was always free from structure. He ultimately began to do very sensitive heads and they were terribly expressive as opposed to being just extraordinarily well drawn. He would have a powerful way of drawing fingers even though the hand itself would not seem properly drawn, but he could get by with it. He had a virtuoso inking quality that, when it was poured on pencilling, whether his own or someone else's, was like pouring chocolate—it was so deep and emotional and satisfying."

Kane maintains that an artist's development comes as a result of personality needs.

"I started to intellectualize comics when I finally got to the very end of what my own emotional situation could do for me in comics. Then all of a sudden I found myself totally inadequate, and as a result I had to look at my work. I remember I was twenty-seven years old, and for the first time I began to look at it and realize that I didn't know anything. I began to understand what deep space was. I began to understand what patterns were. I understood about design needs. I began to analyze design. And little by little I had to learn to do all of these things, none of which were natural to me. The only thing that I ever felt natural about was movement. So move-

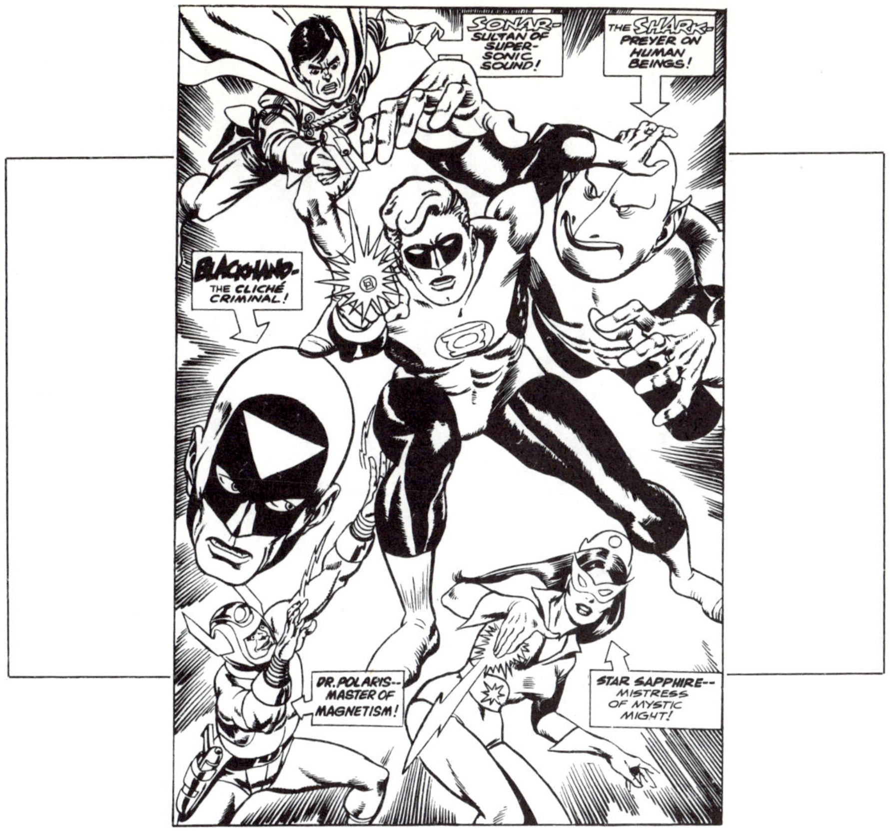

ment was my need. Then I had to build a whole structure; a housing around movement in order to articulate it and give my personality its expression."

What brought Kane to this time of self-realization was that he reached a point when he sat down at his board and couldn't think of what to draw. "I couldn't think of a shot. I couldn't think of anything. The more anxious I got, the less I could draw. I went through every swipe I had, but I couldn't find appropriate stuff. I could feel panic building in me. Then I recognized, by God, I wasn't going to be a slave to this any longer!

"Most comic artists start off swiping different guys until we have the strength to stand on our own. For me it was a longer and slower process, and the only thing I could attribute it to is that I had, what I feel, was a personality that had two mutually opposing sides. I loved things that had a kind of lyrical beauty to it, like the shot of Ken Maynard's horse galloping, his mane flying and his nostrils flaring. Just that extraordinary sense of release. At the same time I had a great feeling for power, for strength, and as a result I had a broad assimilation and I liked everything. I liked things which were mutually opposed.

"Guys like Kubert and Frazetta, for instance, always liked one or two artists who, to some extent, encapsulated their real needs. I know guys who focused on somebody like Milton Caniff and as a result, in no time, developed a professional quality of work simply because the artist they favored gave them the technical answers to a lot of their problems. They were totally satisfied with the kind of naturalism, modernism and the powerful black and white of say, Caniff.

Most comic artists start off swiping different guys until we have the strength to stand on our own. For me it was a longer and slower process, and the only thing I could attribute it to is that I had, what I feel, was a personality that had two mutually opposing sides.

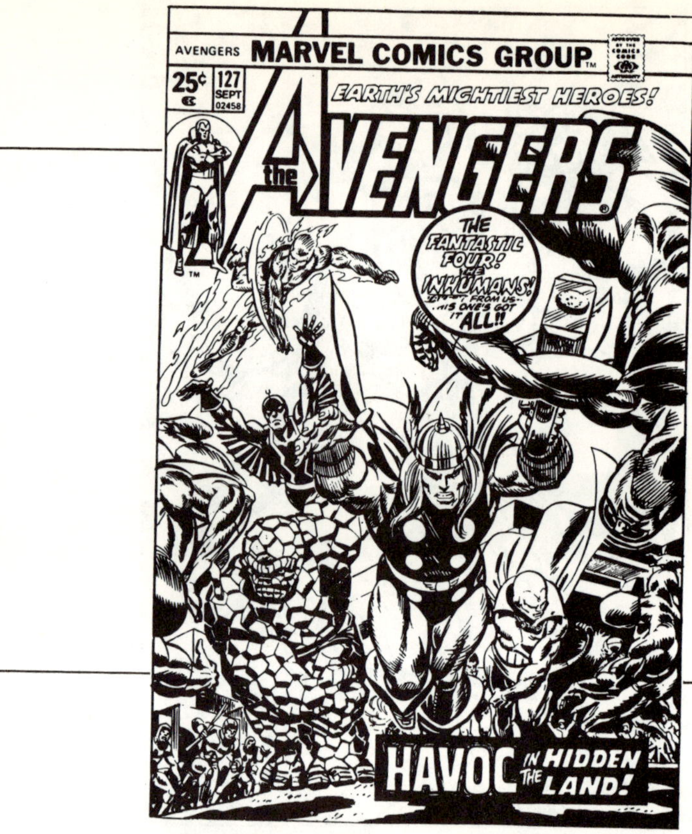

I once told Harvey Kurtzman that I felt like a B-29 with a full load of cargo, revving up the motors, running down the field and just too heavy to take off. That's what the situation was until finally the editorial requirements of having to follow complicated scripts made it impossible for me to swipe cold, and made it essential that I begin to organize pictures on my own.

Or with an artist like Hal Foster for, say, Frazetta, and Foster and Raymond for Al Williamson. It represented a kind of lyrical situation from which they never seemed to stray. I remember when Frazetta did **Thunda**, much of it was lifted right out of Foster's Tarzan. But the point is that it's not so much that Frazetta was dependant on it, but that Foster, at that time, represented what Frazetta himself wanted to articulate.

"Mort Meskin once told me that the artists I liked were my own tastes somewhat down the road, which I always thought was a really bright point of view. The only thing was, I never had an artist that I could settle on. I loved Fred Harmon when I was a kid until I saw Will James, and then I went nuts. I liked Raymond as a boy, and Hogarth before Foster because Hogarth had the kind of dynamism, the artificiality, and the theatrical sense that Foster didn't have. Foster was infinitely more subtle and much more natural without any of those gesticulating postures of Hogarth. But Hogarth brought a kind of unleashed dynamism which was equivalent to what was happening in comic books at the time. I took to him immediately. So I had all of these personality needs and ultimately I was assimilating.

"I once told Harvey Kurtzman that I felt like a B-29 with a full load of cargo, revving up the motors, running down the field and just too heavy to take off. That's what the situation was until finally the editorial requirements of having to follow complicated scripts made it impossible for me to swipe cold, and made it essential that I begin to organize pictures on my own. To do that I had to understand picture-making and that became

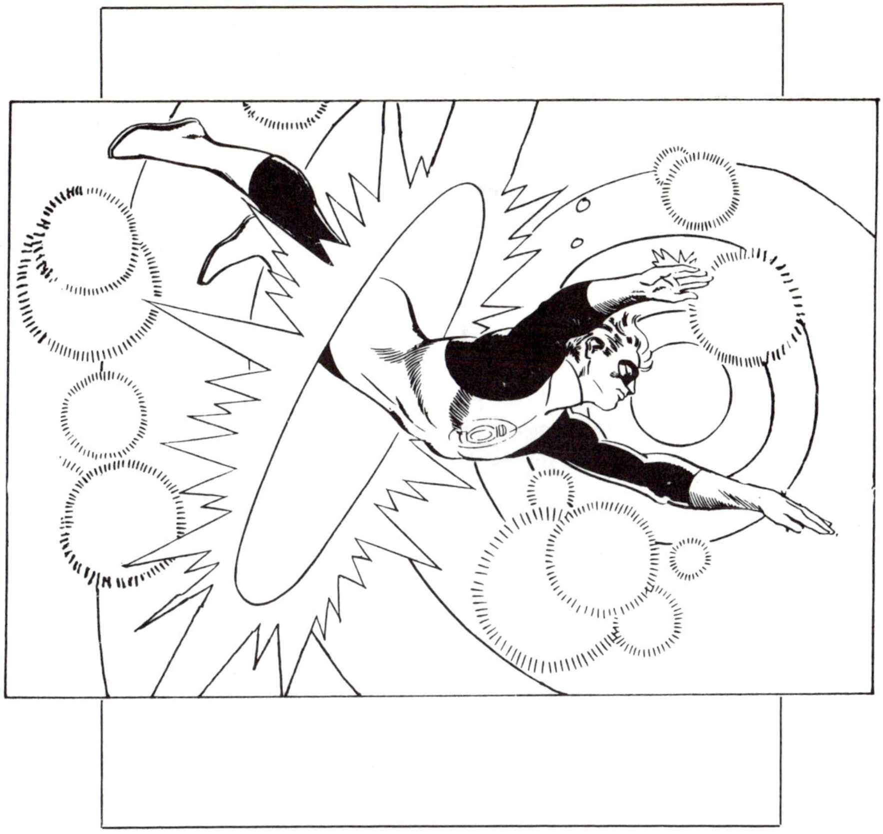

I was just a disembodied lump of feeling without direction, focus and the ability to dip into myself to supply myself with the requirements of the script. People like me, if I hadn't gone into comics, would have gone into something like illustration where there were one picture situations. There you have to learn structure, but comics are really hard. Comics are harder than illustration.

my pursuit over the next couple of years. So I studied the king of picture-making, who in my view at that time was Roy Crane. Roy Crane was absolutely what I needed, and he was much more accessible than, say, Foster who was also the king of picture-making. I had tackled George Bridgeman several times and been turned away each time. I just couldn't get him. He was too hard for me and I couldn't apply him. I would see him brilliantly applied by Raymond and by other artists, like Reed Crandall, but I just could not make him accessible to me. Finally I worked on Bridgeman and he became accessible somewhere between Roy Crane's picture-making and Bridgeman's sense of physical structure."

Kane felt that for the first time he'd lifted himself onto a plateau of professionalism that allowed him to explore other things.

"Essentially that's why I had to do it because I was just a disembodied lump of feeling without direction, focus and the ability to dip into myself to supply myself with the requirements of the script. People like me, if I hadn't gone into comics, would have gone into something like illustration where there were one picture situations. There you have to learn structure, but comics are really hard. Comics are harder than illustration. Having now come out of five years of working in animation and doing presentation boards of enormous scenes for a projected series and then coming back into comics, I realize what a lark that was. Comics is like some sort of commando training. You only learn by blows and humiliation. There's something leisurely about illustration. If you have a feeling for color you can do serviceable pictures and illustration. But comics is just a son of a

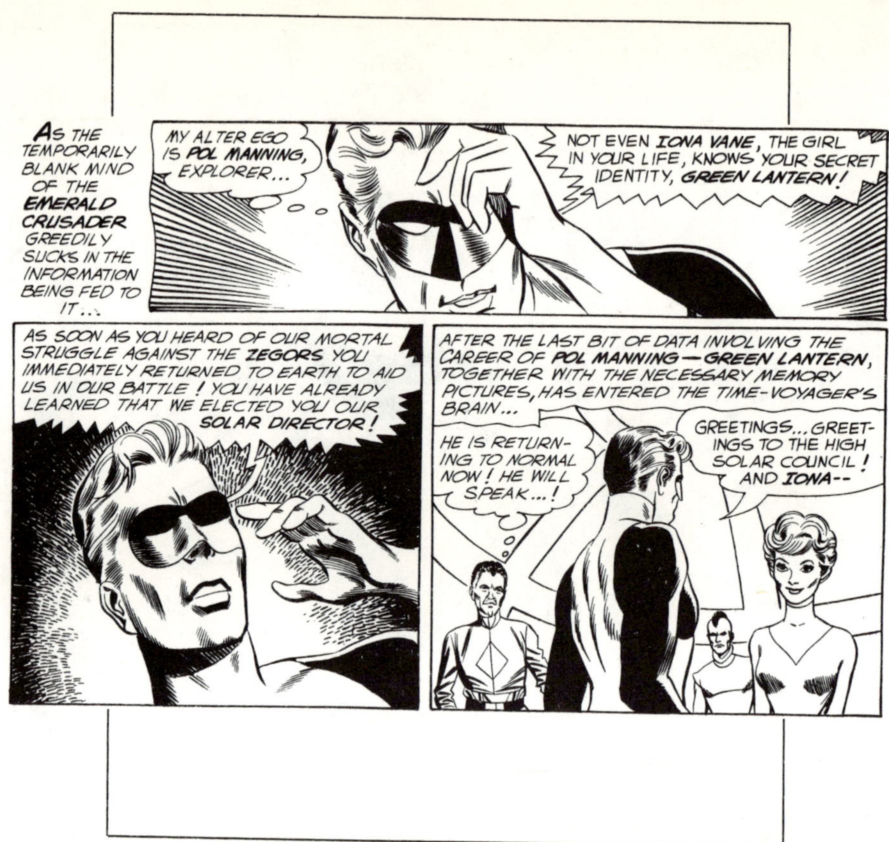

Up until about thirty years ago all scripts described the action and gave the dialogue. You'd have to write that in first before you drew the picture.

bitch where faking is immediately spotted and it just doesn't work."

When it comes to working from a script, Kane prefers to be allowed to participate rather than working from a detailed full script.

"Up until about thirty years ago all scripts described the action and gave the dialogue. You'd have to write that in first before you drew the picture. For instance, I was always at odds with my editor, Julie Schwartz, at D.C. because he was absolutely the strictest guy in the world and just terrified of having the front office come down on him, and so he was a button counter and a line counter. And I'd say, but Julie, this is action! We're doing super-heroes again, now. You need more room for the fight scenes and action scenes, while Julie's scripts continued to be essentially puzzles with a solution. For the action, instead of using six panels, I'd make it eight panels and inject two extra panels of my own which would be action.

"Ultimately the best thing that happened, of course, was Stan (Lee) working with Jack (Kirby) writing a book a night. The only way Lee could do that was to have Kirby or Ditko draw the entire book out after just the most perfunctory discussion, until finally no discussion at all. Lee would get the finished pencil artwork and then put in the copy after the fact."

Kane feels that this recognized for the first time what the artist really contributed to a comic strip.

"The artist didn't contribute an illustration. He contributed *dramatization*! An illustration is an after-the-fact thing. A dramatization is to recognize that when you take material that's articulat-

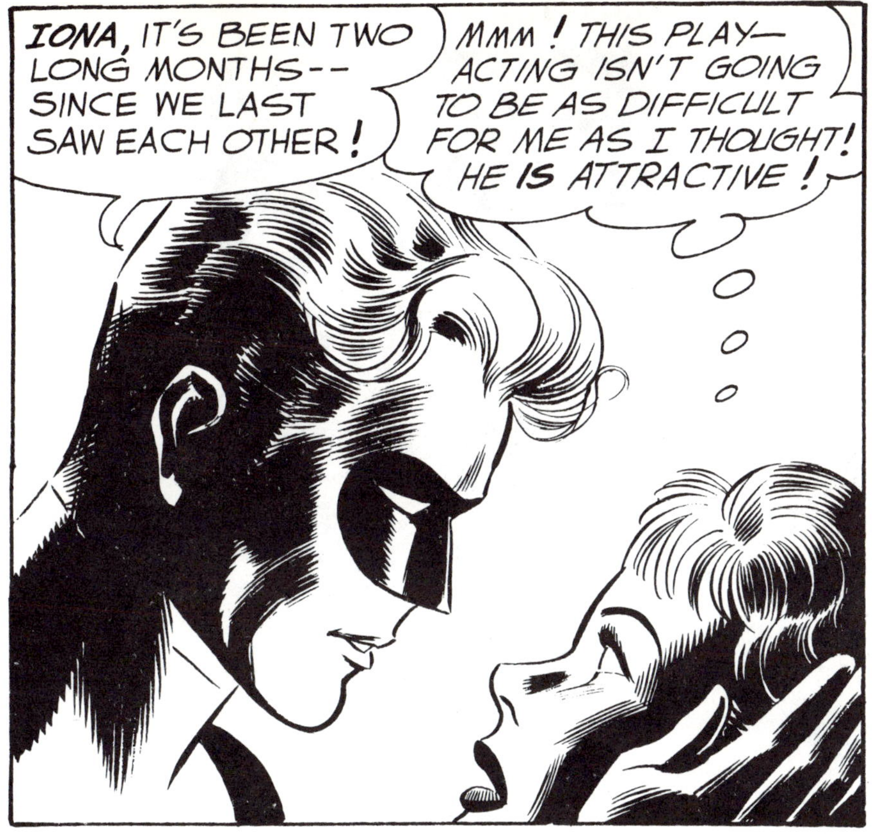

This field only requires writing at a certain level. If it's better, then there's no place for it. The writer doesn't feel like there's any place for his work any more and starts looking around for another place to go. Comics don't attract writers of consequence.

ed but not visualized, it's starting with a blank piece of paper. It's not a visualization of the writer's material, but a dramatization. It's a whole new area of involvement. I think that writing in comics has always been totally overrated. I never thought that comics had many consequential writers, and that the best writers performed what the librettist did for the opera: They performed a structure on which to build, like an armature for a sculpture. But ultimately you did get guys who could write fairly well, like Harvey Kurtzman and Alan Moore, but they really are quite unusual. They're not typical and the thing I think that supports my thesis is that they're both artists. They're both writers who are artists to the bone. So as a result they control the material that they write to such an extent that they have all sorts of sketches and you can see the similarity between Brian Boland's work on **The Killing Joke** and Dave Gibbons on **The Watchmen**. If you look very closely you can see that the point of view on layouts is precise. In fact, sometimes the work seems almost interchangeable. That's because Moore essentially determined the material through drawings and layouts."

So Kane feels comics is unquestionably an artist's medium because if an outside writer comes in and creates a direction and the art to be built on, the institutionalized nature of comics eventually causes the writer to leave the field, if he gets any better.

"This field only requires writing at a certain level. If it's better, then there's no place for it. The writer doesn't feel like there's any place for his work any more and starts looking around for another place to go. Comics don't attract writers of consequence. The only time writing is any good in comics is in newspaper

CHAPTER IV

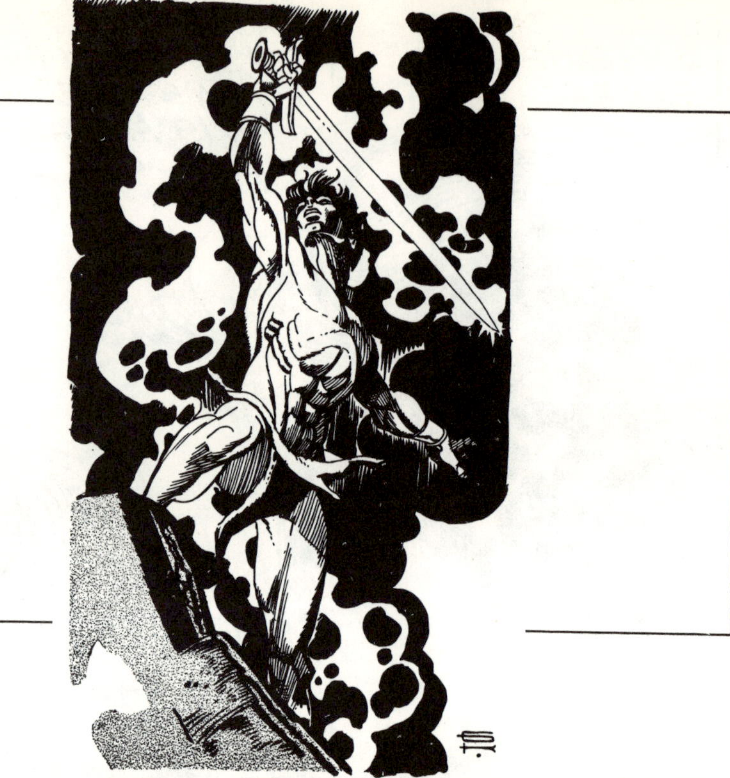

The only way you can transcend the stuff is if you have a desire to do a certain piece of work and you know the kind of audience you want to present it to. That's the only way to override the limitations that are imposed by the institutionalizing of comics.

strips where writing can be wit and perception and sophistication. There you can really do things and get guys like Walt Kelly, Charles Schultz and Bill Watterson. These guys are absolutely brilliant in their compassion, their perception and mostly in their wit and the way they see the world around them. So they seem to be remarkable writers, but they don't come into comic books. Kids pick an audience, which is other kids. When a guy like Watterson picks an audience, he's already starting as an adult looking for an adult audience. It's not that comics can't be better.

"**Love & Rockets** is really a step away from comics, and it's Dickensian, but it also reminds me of a soap opera. They seem to be working for a different audience than the audience that ordinarily reads comics. The only way you can transcend the stuff is if you have a desire to do a certain piece of work and you know the kind of audience you want to present it to. That's the only way to override the limitations that are imposed by the institutionalizing of comics."

Not all artists see freedom in loose scripts. Many actually crave the structure of a full script.

"I know a number of artists like that. I used to criticize different pieces of work because it didn't represent what I thought it should be. But I recognize that any work that has Al Williamson at one end and Jack Kirby at the other end is constantly swinging between those two ends and maybe beyond those two ends. I recognize that they're all part of the same situation. That you couldn't have even a view of an ideal work without all of these different attitudes constantly coming to the fore and creating,

For the space of a heartbeat, the great arena was without motion. No man spoke, no breeze stirred; as though Blackmark's moment of victory were frozen in time forever. Then, in the top of the gallery cheering started, swelling in volume as it filtered down.

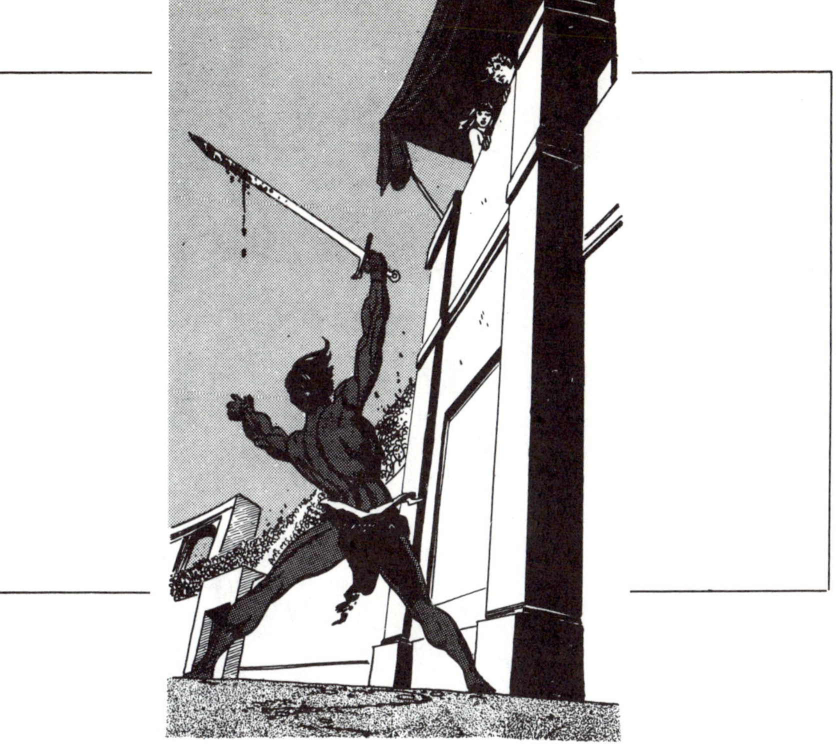

One of the problems with comics is that because it's an accessible medium and you drift right into it from adolescence onward, you don't get a chance to make all those choices you might possibly make. As a result the choices tend to remain the same. You work for the artist whom you most admire. An education is an invaluable thing in comics but for the most part we're all self-taught.

unconsciously, a range of choices that people are constantly making. The extremes of work are sensitive to elements in the culture, and by representing those extremes they simply actuate the choices that we can make. For instance, Williamson and Frazetta developed together and had similar qualities, the difference being that Frazetta had a sensual, lyrical and a power need while there is something in Williamson's work that doesn't require power. So his work has essentially become almost aesthetic. The characters are very delicate and there's a kind of aristocracy to their quality which is because they're generally inexpressive facially. There's a Victorian quality in Williamson's work that suits it at its best. When I was a kid and I loved **Flash Gordon**, I particularly loved 'The Tournaments of Mongo' segment. I talked to Williamson years ago and he liked the part when Flash is in with the Power Men and so on, in the early Forties. But to me that was the end of Raymond and I saw no value in that material at all. I never saw anything of Raymond's that transcended the 'Tournaments' or the 'Witch Queen.' The personality extracts those elements from the same material. So artists like Williamson and Frazetta represent two absolutely diverse points of view.

"One of the problems with comics is that because it's an accessible medium and you drift right into it from adolescence onward, you don't get a chance to make all those choices you might possibly make. As a result the choices tend to remain the same. You work for the artist whom you most admire. An education is an invaluable thing in comics but for the most part we're all self-taught so we're at an enormous

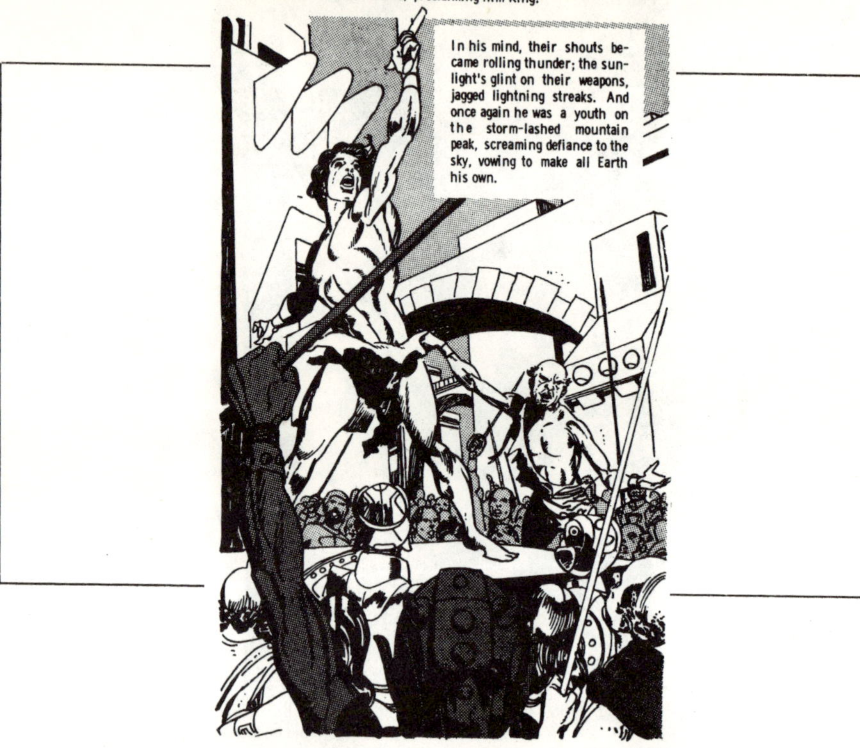

disadvantage. We're self-taught in every sense and we're just like blind people who are feeling an elephant to try to determine what it's like. We don't know enough. The things we anticipate are not large enough, broad enough, expansive enough and not deep enough. All of our choices are shallow ones. The only things that aren't shallow in terms of the work we do are the needs of our own personality, which are profound. I haven't always seen it this way, but I've more or less seen it this way for awhile and I've thought about it a lot and I really believe it."

We're self-taught in every sense and we're just like blind people who are feeling an elephant to try to determine what it's like. We don't know enough. The things we anticipate are not large enough, broad enough, expansive enough and not deep enough. All of our choices are shallow ones.

Not all artists agree on how closely words and pictures should work together in a comic strip. Some, like Kurtzman, believe it essential while others feel it depends on the story. Another view holds that artwork is the star of the comic. Gil Kane has his own very views.

"My own biases favor certain things, but I recognize immediately that anything that's effective is right. It's very hard to do a strip dependent entirely on dialogue and pictures. When I was doing romance material the editors wanted expressions on the characters that would have put Spencer Tracy to an enormous test. In a continuity it was almost impossible to achieve the subtlety they required, and in romance you didn't have to because they were very heavy in captions. As a result you never were in doubt as to the turmoil that was going through the heroine's mind and heart because you were constantly informed about it. That stuff was too heavy. There was an imbalance between pictures and text. The page was overwhelmed, and so were the pictures. That happened at E.C., too. But there's no question that the E.C. stuff really had impact.

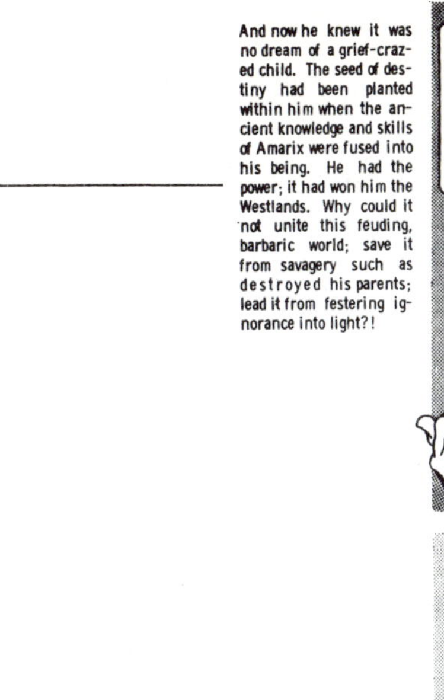

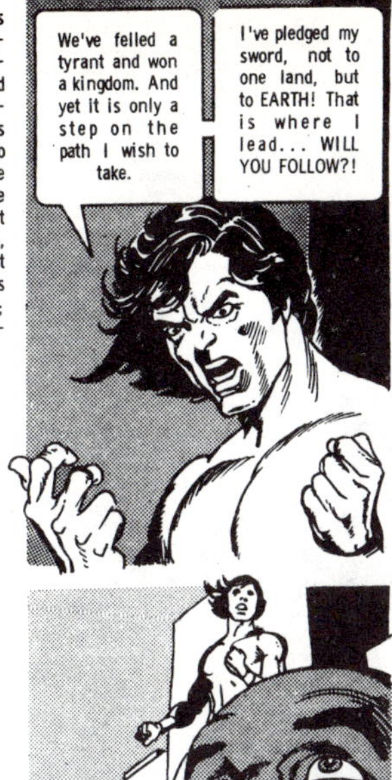

If it's over-written, and by that I mean too much copy for the picture, the copy doesn't have to be censored, there just has to be more pictures so that it's not so cramped and over-whelming.

"Pictures without captions is not necessarily a prescription for material that is not highly evolved. But I tend to think, by and large, that if I had my choice I would involve caption writing without having it interfere with the pictures, but definitely to support them, although not in every instance. Certainly there are times when silence — nothing at all— is an eloquent expression. There's a difference in action. What most artists who draw action do is state the action, but I always felt that it wasn't enough to state the action. You must make them *feel*the pain. By that I mean you have some intense sense of the result or the reaction to the action. That's why I went in heavily for captions because I needed to intensify what was happening and to communicate that intensity to the reader.

"If it's over-written, and by that I mean too much copy for the picture, the copy doesn't have to be censored, there just has to be more pictures so that it's not so cramped and overwhelming. I definitely feel that the more information you communicate, the better. But if in trying to express information you eliminate the picture, one of the sources of information, that's bad, too. So it's a balance and definitely it's a matter of choice and a matter of personality, but I wouldn't think of trying to go into a character's head without using captions."

Like many comics artists, Kane sees the story in his mind like a film, but that's largely because comics are action oriented.

"In fact, most of us are best when the story is really rolling and is action. We're at our worst when there's no action, when the action is essentially internalized and people are standing and talk-

Blackmark opened the case, lifting the sword from the base of wine red velvet it rested upon. Though long of blade and oversized of hilt, there was perfection in its balance. In the hands of the proper warrior, such a sword could weave arabesques of razor-edged death through any foe's defense. The temper of its silver blade would never yield before battle axe or spiked-head mace.

But it was the ornate, oversized hilt that drew Blackmark's tawny eyes. Inscribed upon it, amid delicate drawings and finely wrought decorative swirls, was a name.

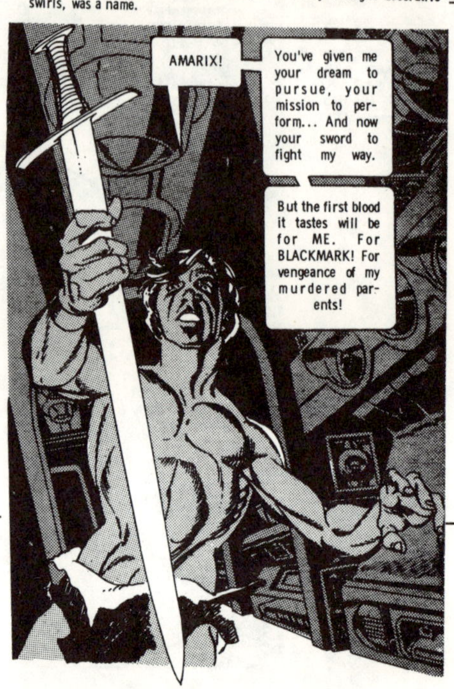

So much of the story now has to do with the internal lives of the characters that they deal less with cosmic villains. So crime lords are back in business and you're not dealing so much with cosmic villains.

ing to one another for an extended piece. But in spite of the fact that we're still doing superheroes, there's been a step away from Jack Kirby's monstrous scale and the whole scale of superhero material. It's been scaled downward. Figures are smaller. They're not quite built like Jack's any more. So much of the story now has to do with the internal lives of the characters that they deal less with cosmic villains. So crime lords are back in business and you're not dealing so much with cosmic villains."

Although comics are usually done with color in mind, black and white drawings by themselves have their own individual impact which should be considered when drawing the art.

"Because color's always been so cheap, the best thing to do is make the black and white as formidable as possible so that you're hurt as little as possible by the color. Joe Kubert always did that. But now you have to accommodate color and more and more it will be a kind of full color process that you use primarily over black and white. My own choice is to do black with a full color overlay. but more and more you'll have to let go of the heavy blacks and let color take care of that the way they do in Europe. Their drawings are practically all outline and the color takes care of both the darks and the lights, like an animation cel."

Returning to drawing comic books after having spent several years working in the animation field in Hollywood, Kane has found the field changed in substantive ways.

"Comics are a really difficult medium, and the only way I can rationalize my involvement is that when I was in animation it wasn't anywhere near as satisfying. Except for one particular

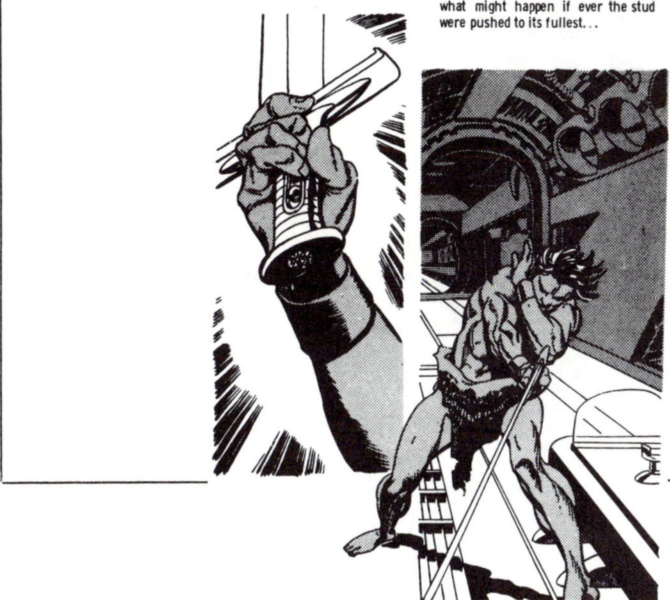

point, and that is that I made much more money in animation. But I always wanted to get back to comics. Now that I'm back, I've found the entire situation changed in that volume doesn't do it any more. You have to turn out very carefully crafted pieces in order to build an audience who will follow you from one piece of work to another. In other words, it's not unusual now for an artist to spend close to a year on a single book. We used to do a book a month. Sometimes two books a month. Jose Garcia Lopez, whom I admire enormously, takes six months to pencil a book. He's got three books that he's going to finish penciling in a year and a half. Now he happens to be excellent so he brings a variety and degree of skills to bear that are very impressive, and given that much time to develop the work, he develops it to a point where he creates a standard for other people to try to equal. Little by little the work is moving away from the kind of stuff that would've been acceptable five or ten years ago where you could pencil three pages a day.

"When it comes to action, as I say, I usually don't have any problems. But when it comes to people in repose I find that you just can't fake the figure. It becomes another problem entirely. You really have to be very thoughtful about what you're doing and recognize that falling into a pose is very, very bad. You have to be less an actor now than a director. You have to not react to material, but in effect know the intent of figures and what the entire point of the design in a picture is and what you're attempting to evoke to the reader. As a director, you say to yourself, 'What's the point here? What are you trying to say? How are you going to say it? What's

I've found the entire situation changed in that volume doesn't do it any more. You have to turn out very carefully crafted pieces in order to build an audience who will follow you from one piece of work to another. In other words, it's not unusual now for an artist to spend close to a year on a single book.

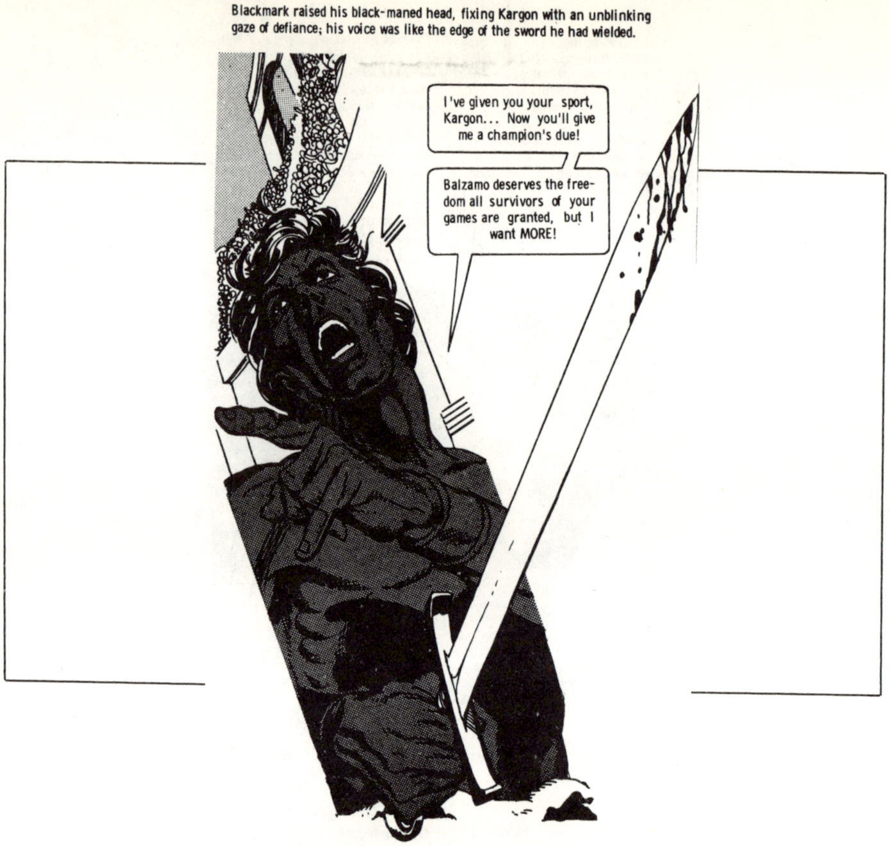

Blackmark raised his black-maned head, fixing Kargon with an unblinking gaze of defiance; his voice was like the edge of the sword he had wielded.

I've given you your sport, Kargon... Now you'll give me a champion's due!

Balzamo deserves the freedom all survivors of your games are granted, but I want MORE!

There's a need to scale my work down so that I can do figures that are natural and more understated in terms of the heads. There's a certain verisimilitude that's essential now to aspects of the work.

the point of view?' You understand that all these things come into it and all of a sudden it becomes a puzzle, both emotional and intellectual, looking for a structure through which you can express your emotional feeling for the material. If you're totally out of touch with the material that you're handling, that's an enormous disadvantage. You can't fall back on professionalism any longer to any great extent. Not if you want to distinguish yourself in the field or at least distinguish yourself with your audience. You now have to give it a focus. The field has moved forward in a challenging way, not in terms of content, but in terms of the way we interpret the adolescent content we've had to deal with up until this point. It's simply treating super-heroes more thoughtfully as opposed to the point where we used to treat them without being thoughtful—just emotional. The content of the material isn't any stronger, it's just presented in a stronger fashion."

Kane has also found that new demands are being made on his work, demands different from those expected from the comics artist a decade ago.

"There's a need to scale my work down so that I can do figures that are natural and more understated in terms of the heads. There's a certain verisimilitude that's essential now to aspects of the work. Each artist applies that in the way he sees fit. Some are still applying it in terms of advertising art standards, so externally there's a sophistication. Internally there's no change. I've had some control over the work that I've done in the past, and when I did, the thing that I was preoccupied with was form as opposed to content. Now I'm preoccupied with content, but working within

Blackmark paused a moment before shouting his demand; paused before calling down the Warlord he'd dreamed of facing for fifteen years; paused to relish the time of vengeance at hand. And in that moment, the woman whose favors he'd scorned leaned forward to Kargon.

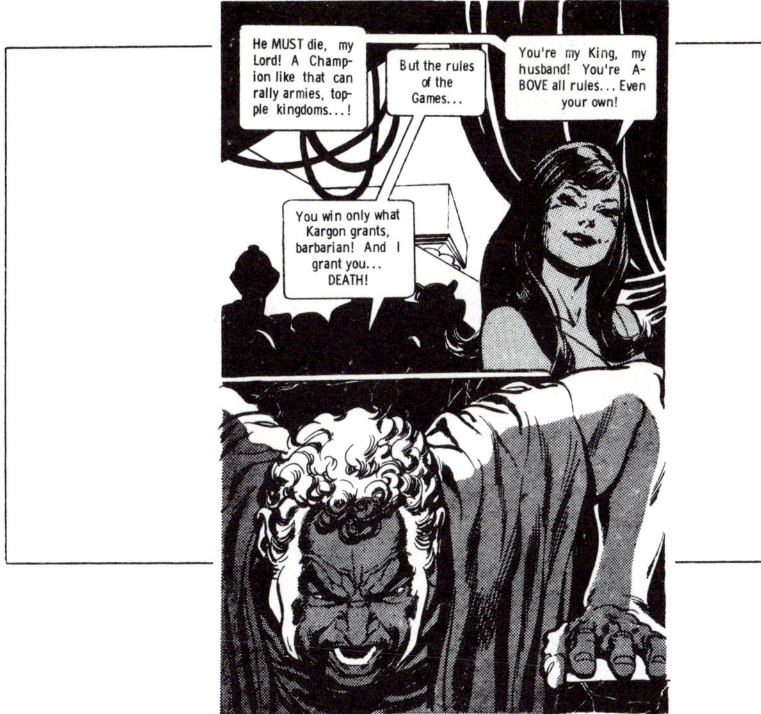

Distinction is what the audience is buying now and they have a different yardstick for it than they used to have. The publisher just puts his money where the distinction is.

the institutionalized content of the comic book field. I'm still preoccupied with the abstract elements of doing the work rather than with the need to make content more substantial. The only way I could think of making content more substantial for the audience is to make the work more intense and I think that's part of what's happening. Comics is reflecting what's happening in movies. Movies aren't any better, but they're certainly more intense. And the violence in the films, now. I'm not making any moral comment about the violence but only that it's been escalated to a point and has creatively evolved so that it's simply incredible. The kind of wild choreography, like in James Bond's **License To Kill**, and the Indiana Jones' movie and **Lethal Weapon** is so brilliantly conceived and carried through that they just need enough story to keep it spinning, but not enough to get in the way. So the action has a life of its own. It dominates the field and is part of the intensity that I see now in comics.

"When I was a kid, I used to get assignments from doing samples that would take me all week to do. But when I finished them, they were good enough, always, even at sixteen years of age, to get me jobs. Well that's what's happening now with guys who spend an entire week doing one or two pages. They're simply pouring every bit of their resources into the material, and the effort is such that it transcends their normal level of work had they just spontaneously generated two or three pages a day.

"Distinction is what the audience is buying now and they have a different yardstick for it than they used to have. The publisher just puts his money where the distinction is. He tries to get those artists and writers who

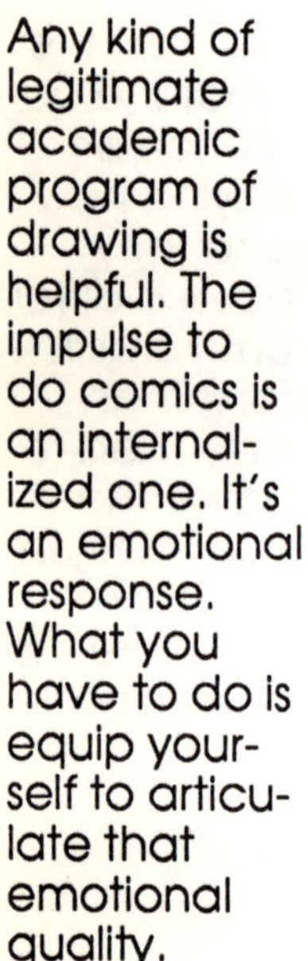
Any kind of legitimate academic program of drawing is helpful. The impulse to do comics is an internalized one. It's an emotional response. What you have to do is equip yourself to articulate that emotional quality.

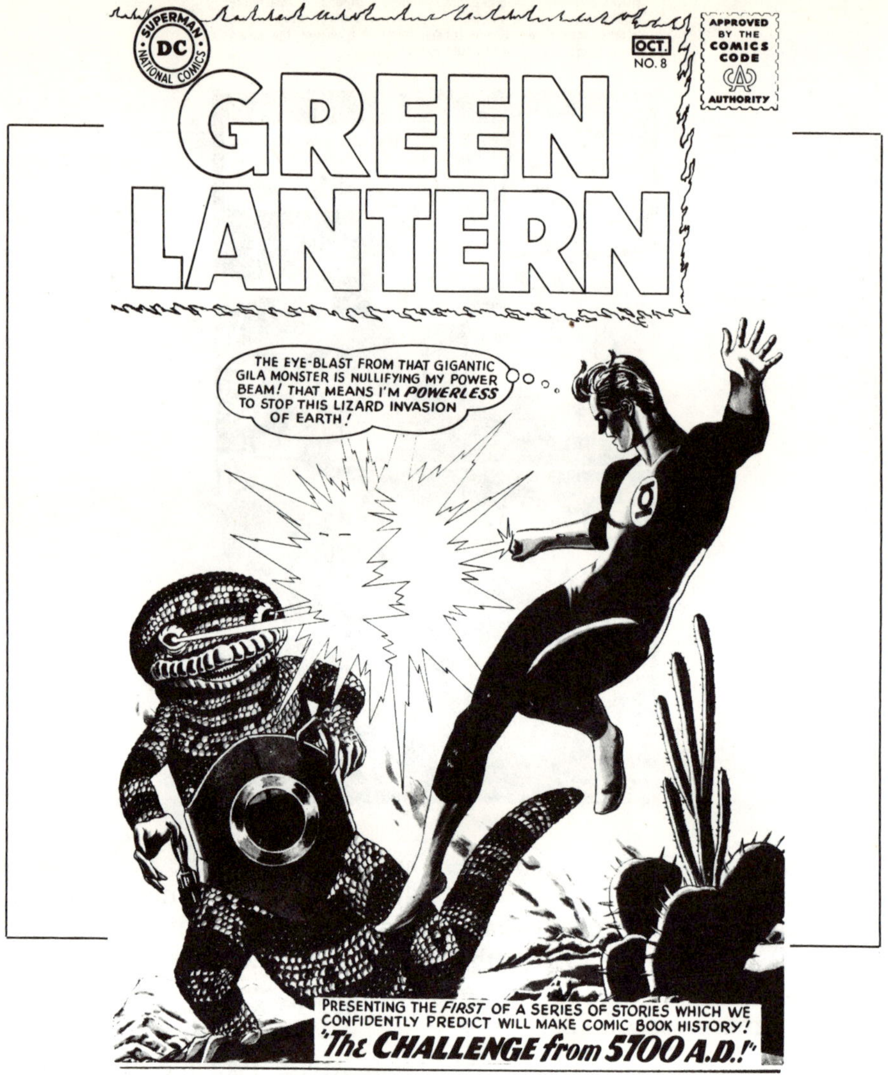

seem to be able to generate an audience, and they are the ones who do best in this field."

Kane agrees with others that formalized art training is important for an artist who wants to draw comics.

"Any kind of legitimate academic program of drawing is helpful. The impulse to do comics is an internalized one. It's an emotional response. What you have to do is equip yourself to articulate that emotional quality, and so the best academic programs are the best things you can have. We didn't think so years ago because we didn't know anything and weren't educated enough to know anything about how valuable an academic structure was to launch any kind of personal point of view. The academic structure isn't an end in itself, it's simply a springboard to help you evaluate and make judgments. It informs you and information is essential. As long as it's legitimate drawing it has a direct application. There's nothing better than life drawing and understanding of design, painting classes, and working from models. Those are exactly the qualities you need to succeed in comics."

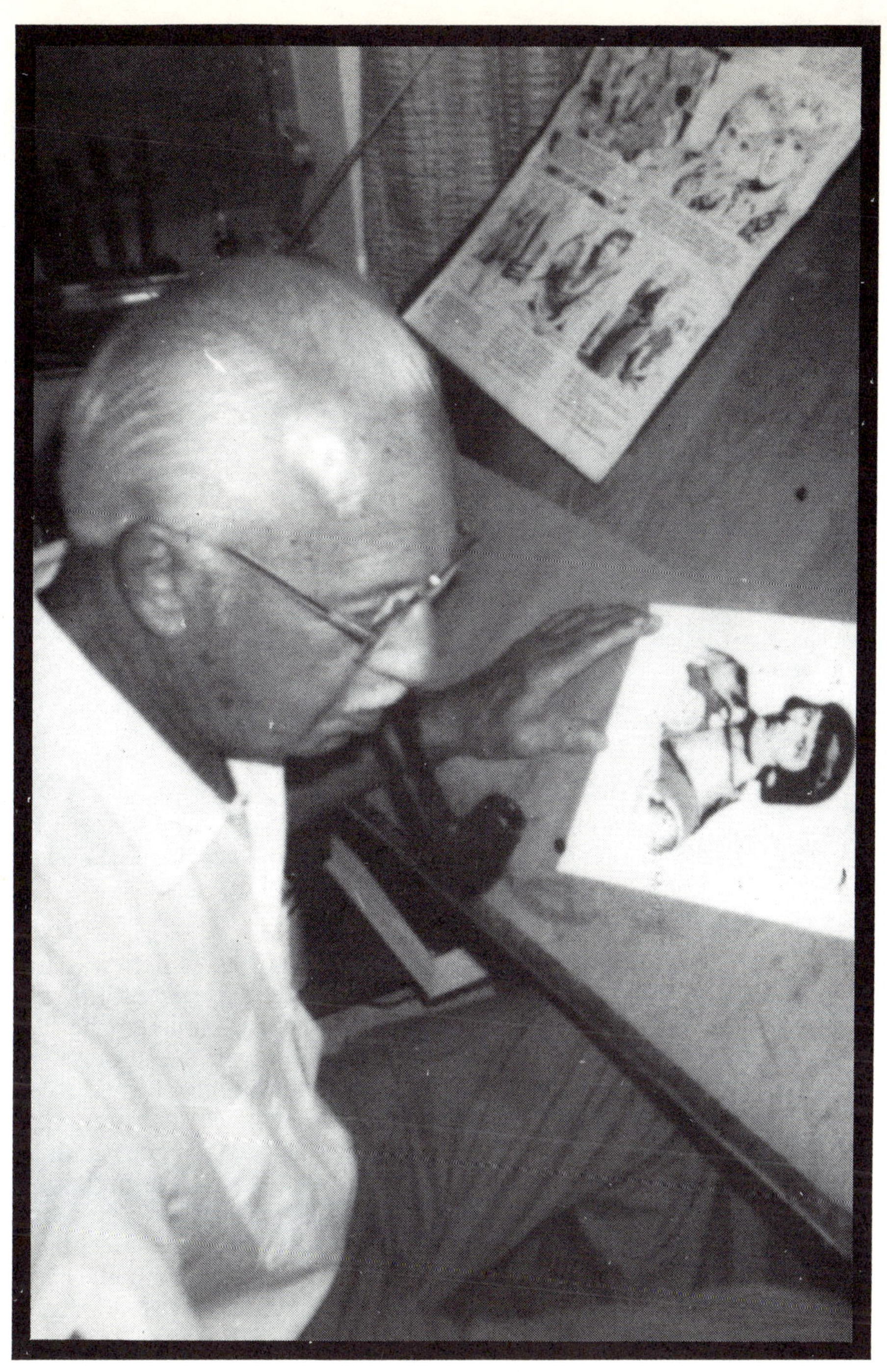

Chapter Nine HAL FOSTER

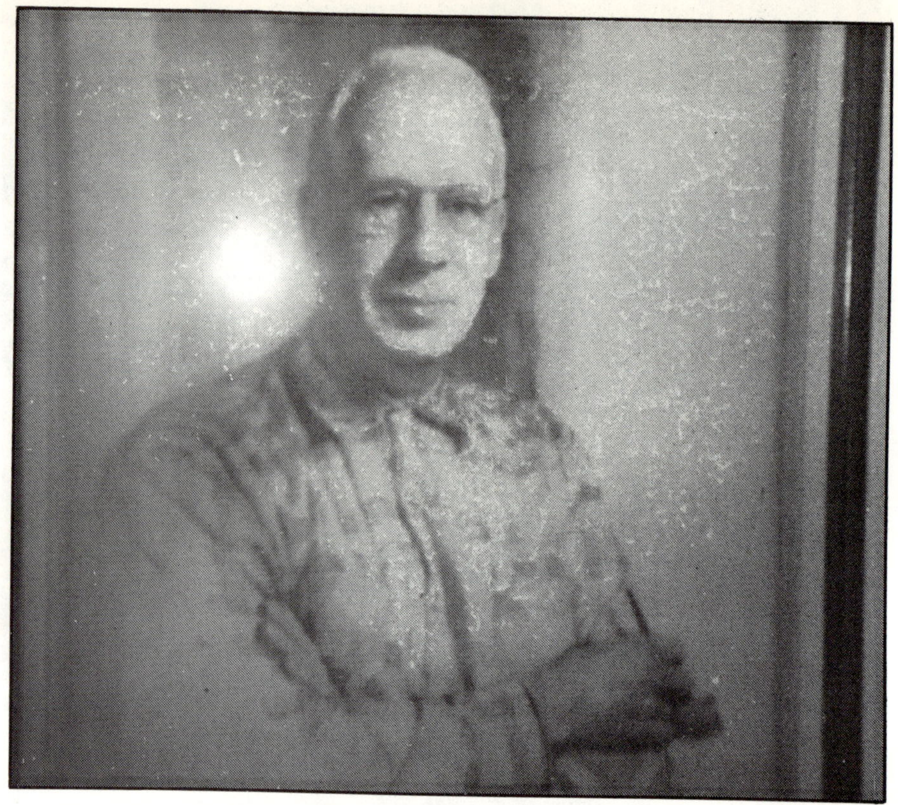

A selportrait of Hal Foster

The era of the illustration strip began on January 7, 1929, for this is when Hal Foster's work first appeared on the newspaper comic strip page. That initial ten week trial run was Foster's adaptation of Edgar Rice Burroughs' **Tarzan of the Apes**, and it launched Foster on a career he had neither planned nor looked forward to.

Harold Rudolph Foster was an advertising illustrator back then, with an eye towards being a gallery artist, and had even been encouraged by having some shows of his work in the late Twenties. He took the job of adapting Tarzan as just another assignment. Familiar with the format of newspaper strips, Foster disliked the concept of word balloons on sight and so his panels featured artwork with text above or below the drawing like passages lifted from a book. It made for an interesting and very different approach, and one which was ultimately deemed successful. But when Foster completed the Tarzan assignment, he thought no more about it and returned to advertising work. A **Tarzan** Sunday feature was begun and became an instant hit, and when artist Rex Maxon couldn't handle both the daily and Sunday chores associated with the strip, the Sunday strip was offered to Foster in 1931.

"At first I didn't want to do it," Foster told **Cartoonist Profiles**. "I thought I was prostituting my art doing Tarzan and being a funny page artist. Then I realized it was the Depression, I had a family and I was hungry." Foster admits not putting a lot of effort into those early strips, but when he began receiving fan mail he became more self-conscious of the art and applied himself with renewed interest. But while Foster wasn't bored by his work on

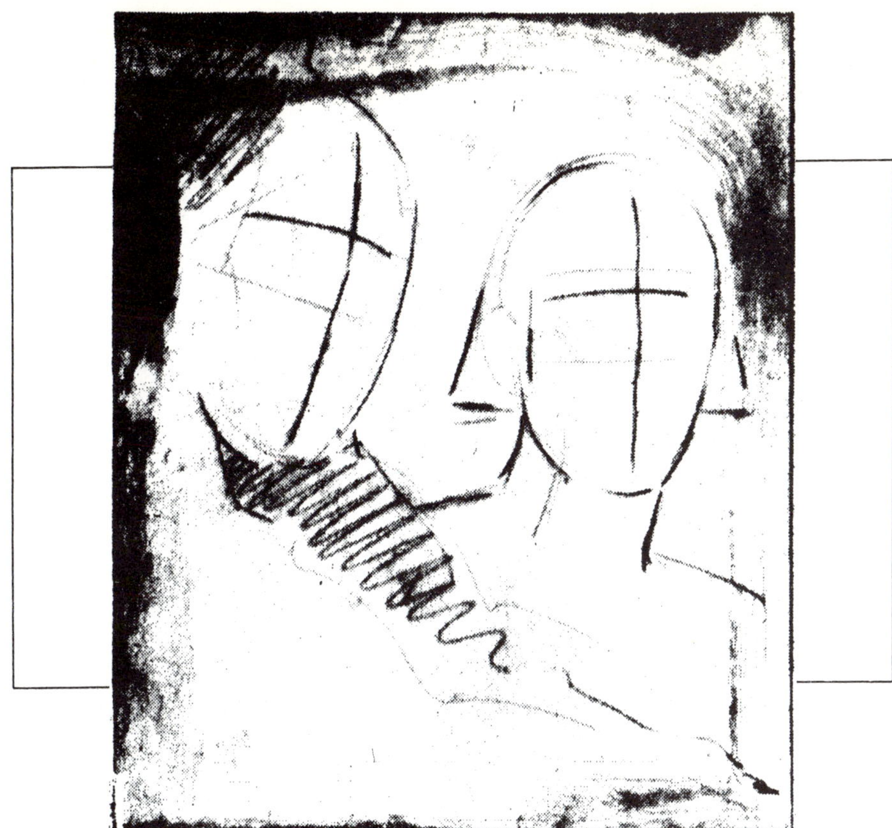

This and following pages: a finished panel goes through a progression of steps

Tarzan, neither was he entirely satisfied with the feature. "The art was always a challenge, but I thought some of the stories were silly and some of the writing sloppy." Foster found himself wishing he had more control over the material, but since the character was not his own he realized that would be impossible. Still the writer in him was yearning to be expressed. A reader himself, Foster was very much influenced by such writers as James Branch Cabell, Lord Dunsany and others of similar vein, and his appreciation of a good tale well told waited to be expressed with his own artwork as well.

Foster got the chance to write as well as draw when King Features approached him in 1936.

"King Features first approached me because William Randolph Hearst liked my **Tarzan** artwork so much," Foster recalled. "They wanted me to do a strip and offered to create one for me. I refused at first because I wanted to create my own. **Prince Valiant** was the result and I own the strip." It was rare in those days for an artist to own his strip, but this is a mark of how highly respected Foster had become in just a few years. It's also an indication of how important comic strips were to newspapers in the first half of the Twentieth Century, something difficult to imagine today. Foster's **Tarzan**, and then his **Prince Valiant**, were almost always published in the full page size in the newspaper comics sections in those days, something no one practices today.

Foster had learned a great deal about drawing successful comics during his years on **Tarzan**, and he continued to experiment and expand on his technique when he began **Prince Valiant**. The first appearance of **Prince Valiant**

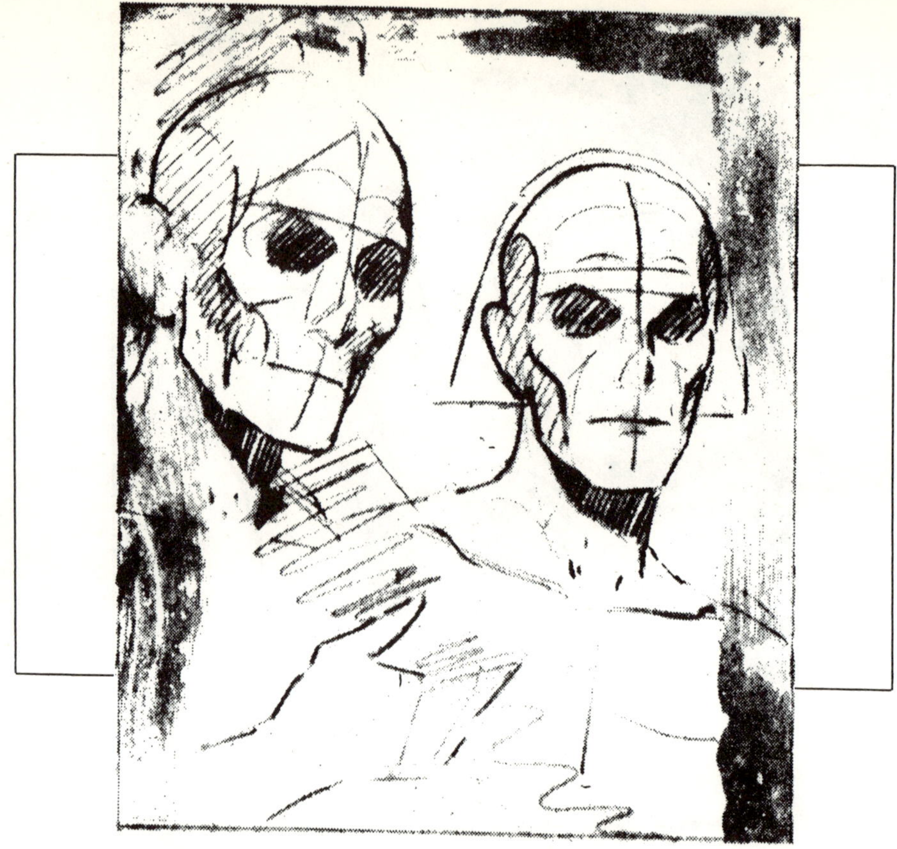

was on February 13th of 1937, and the first dozen or so strips stuck close to the kind of straightforward composition he'd employed on **Tarzan**, with generally a dozen identically sized panels to a page with the long accepted use of text above or below the art instead of word balloons. But then he began to expand the art, using fewer panels to tell the story and creating great mood and atmosphere with the art and the size of the panels he used. He popularized the concept of the "big panel" in which occasionally nearly half the page would be dominated by one dramatic scene. Foster continued writing the strip, even after he retired from drawing it in May of 1971, at the age of 78. Foster wrote it for several more years, and also drew layouts for his hand-picked successor, John Cullen Murphy. Finally he had to retire, even from this aspect, several years later so that the last page scripted and layed out by Foster appeared on February 10th of 1980, almost 43 years to the day after his first **Prince Valiant** page was published.

Hal Foster died July 25, 1982, but he lived to see his work influence many artists and to a degree shape the industry due to the lush, illustrative technique he'd brought to the adventure strip. Artist Arn Saba has described Foster's work as "a legacy of uncommon beauty," and it is certainly that, and more.

Although interviews largely dealt with historical questions about his career and vast body of work, they did occasionally touch on his artistic philosophy, training, technique and views on how writing and drawing interrelate. The following is taken from various interviews. Together, for the first time, they provide some insights into Hal Foster's personal approach to drawing.

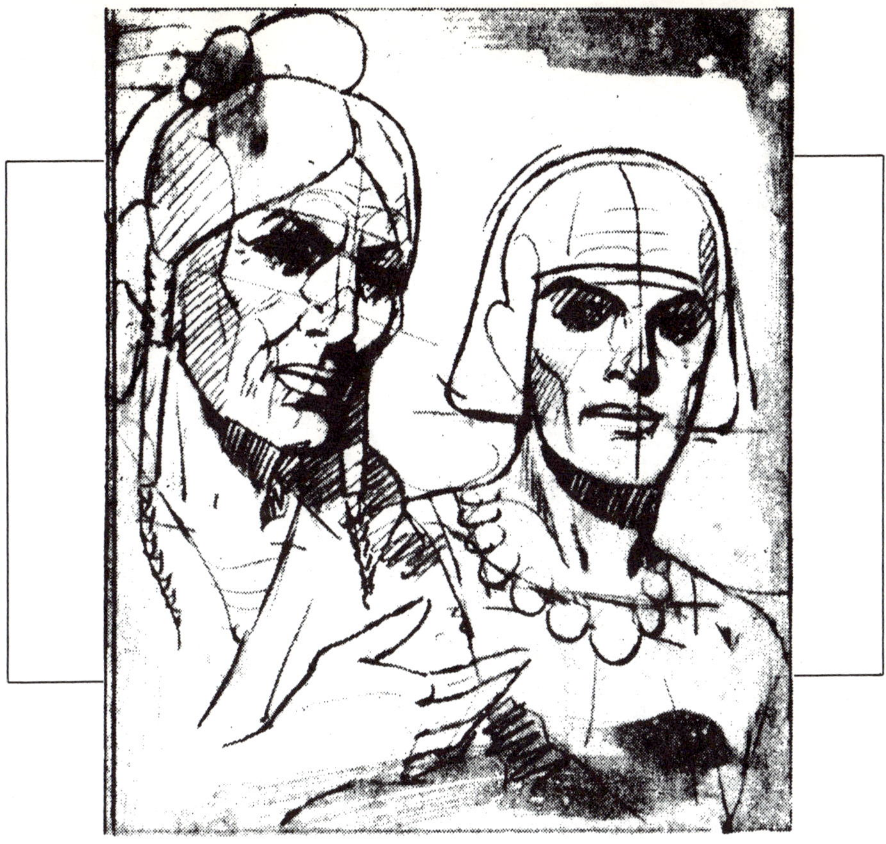

Regarding his early years learning to be an artist, Foster stated, "I was very fond of drawing. I put my easel up in the attic and, since I couldn't afford any models, I'd strip off and start to draw. When it gets down to twenty or thirty below zero in Winnipeg, you have to sketch pretty quick—so I learned to sketch quick. I had a cracked mirror set up and I'd set up my easel beside it and I'd sketch myself and learn anatomy. I'd really sketch fast. As soon as I turned blue I'd quit what I was drawing."

Years later, Foster still occasionally used himself as a model.

"I hate to admit this. I used myself in an idealized version as the model for Prince Valiant. I deleted what I disliked and he's sort of my body with muscles. He's all the things I would have loved to have been. The haircut was simply designed in a traditional cut. It was padding for the helmet. However, it's been the single most famous thing from the strip. I made him have black hair because it would show up more prominently when reproduced. After all, his mother was a Roman woman that had married King Aguar. Prince Valiant has sort of a Roman nose. Besides, you always think of a blond in terms of a beautiful woman."

On the subject of drawing for reproduction, a fact he had to be constantly aware of, Foster had this to say.

"A good painter can put so much feeling, so much atmosphere into his work that an illustrator can't. An illustrator must draw and color for reproduction, and right there, there's a line drawn. You have to use colors that the printer can imitate. They used to be able to, the platemakers; they used to be artists. I have some proofs that are really

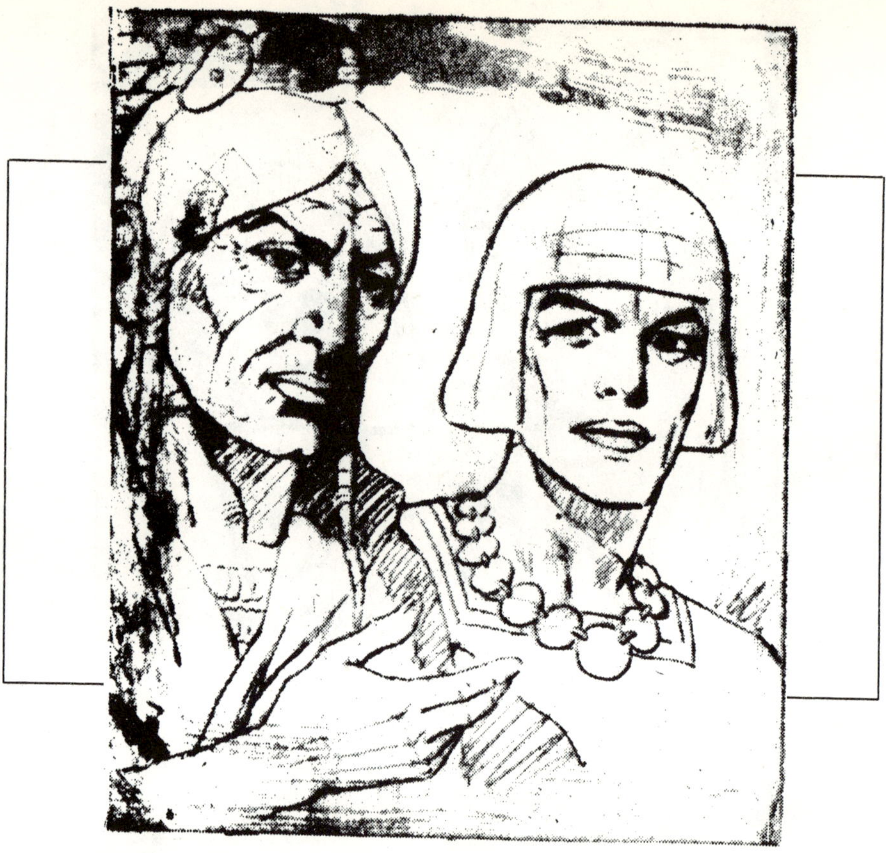

masterpieces of their work, but they did every color and every tone and everything, and those are all gone out of business. They're too expensive. Now they have a reproduction system. I've been through a printing place where they print, or make the plates for cartoonists, and a bunch of girls were there, with plates in front of them, and one woman, the superintendent, she goes around and marks certain colors and certain half-colors and certain quarter-colors. Pretty good, but nothing like the old engraver. Everything has to be done cheaper."

In the June, 1974 issue of **Cartoonist Profiles**, Foster gave a rare description of what his work technique on **Prince Valiant** had been during the decades when he both wrote and drew it, including the types of tools he employed for his rendering.

"I'd go to my studio about 9 a.m. and work through until 5:30 with a break for lunch. My schedule was seven days a week including most holidays.

"In drawing the human figure, I started with the outline of the body for proportion and then dressed the figure. The result of all my years of studying art in Chicago is that I can visualize the human body and don't need a model to work from. Back then I studied the body from the skeleton out. I thought I was going to medical school.

"I never did roughs on separate pieces of paper. I'd just sketch it out using a Venus HB pencil. Before the comics shrunk I used to work on a 27 x 34 piece of 3-ply Strathmore with a kid finish. Now the originals are down to 16 1/2 x 24 inches. It was a pleasure to work in that larger size. Now that it's smaller I'm sort of glad I'm not drawing it.

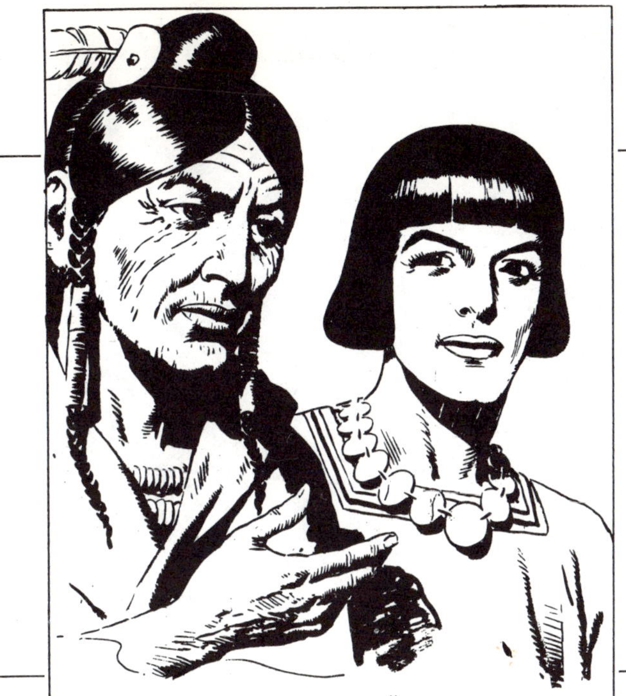

"I used the background to show time and place. The trees, architecture and landscape differ all over Europe. It would take about three panels to do any sort of panorama effect. The shrinkage of the size **Prince Valiant** is printed has all but removed the panorama from reality as a tool available to use.

"I use Higgins ink and for the delicate work a Windsor Newton #2 brush. Then for fine detail I like a #170 Gillot pen. For coloring, Windsor Newton watercolors are my favorite. I used the color to either bring figures out or place them in the distance.

"It's true I've brought traditional art and illustration technique to the funnies, but it wasn't done consciously. This has always been my style. Some people dissect their art in formal terms, but I've never done that with my work."

Foster explained which artists influenced him when he was first learning and how what he observed eventually became absorbed into his technique.

"I copy the work of anybody who solves a problem that has bothered me. I was in commercial art when I first started out—catalogue work—then in advertising, and finally book illustration. In those days I admired Leyendecker, Abbey, Howard Pyle, Arthur Rackham—all the great ones. I started out without any formal training, so I had to learn from others, to see what they did. It was like getting cloth samples, then, when I finally did get some art education, I could bring it all together. Formal education was like stitching cloth samples on to a blanket."

When Foster said "copy," he didn't mean it as exactly swiping somebody else's work.

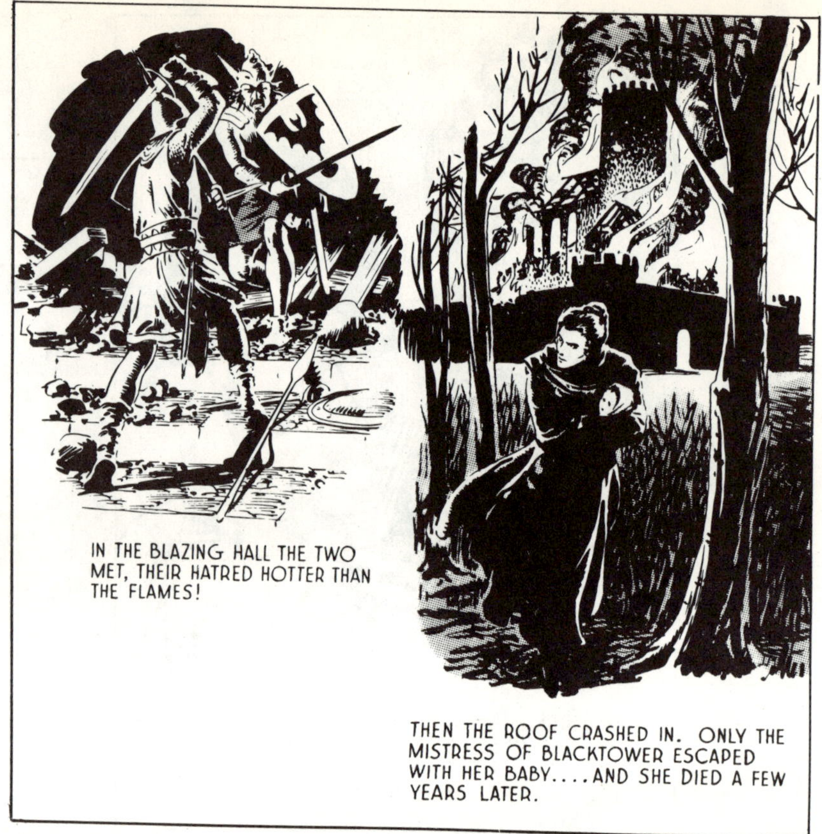

"No, I never copy anything. For instance, I'll look through some of those books I have on Vikings if I'm making ships or a crowd of Vikings. I'll take a look through there and I'll get some attitudes, expressions, the shape of the ships to reassure myself. But to copy direct you lose all originality. Once you copy something, well, now you've got to copy everything, so there's no use in it. I make my sketch first, what I want, the position, whether it's a man on a horse or a horse galloping or something like that. I'll put that into my drawing, but I won't copy it directly."

Part of the reference Foster did for **Prince Valiant** was in capturing the character in a landscape when he traveled in Europe.

"Every country has a different character. Every tree has a different character. When you go to Rome you see the flat-top pines, the long, thin cedars, the rocky hills—you just *know* this has to be Rome. The terrains, the type of mountains, of trees, things like that tell you what kind of country it is.

"So I've always made a point of studying, not only the architecture and costumes, but the trees. You can tell a picture, you can tell it's Italian or Roman by the square buildings, and the columns, and the trees. These pine trees run up straight and have an umbrella top on them. I've always been interested in the whole country, not just the people or the architecture and things like that, but everything has to do with it."

Foster's interest in writing infused every panel of **Prince Valiant** because he felt the story as important as the art and that the two must work together to achieve maximum effect.

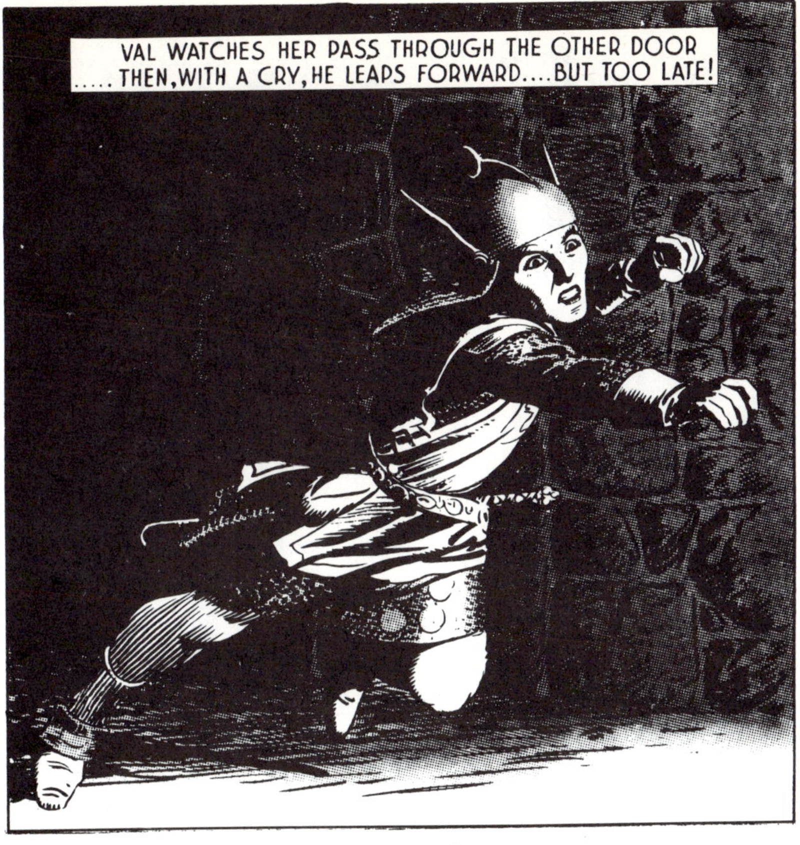

"People think if they can draw, they can be a cartoonist. That's wrong. A real cartoonist needs writing ability and a formal education in drawing.

"I can't 'cartoon'; I am an illustrator. But where the cartoonist ends and the illustrator begins is pretty hard to say. It all hinges on the writing, on the story. In my estimation the story is the most important thing. The illustrations are just meant to give another dimension to a story, which has to be cut down into little captions; the illustrations are necessary to carry the story on from the captions. But of course, it doesn't make any difference how well you illustrate the story—you can get away with a good story poorly illustrated, but not vice versa. If the illustrations are good, why, it's one thing, and if the story's good, you don't need such good illustrations. No matter how pretty the picture is, if there is no story or meaning in it, there will be no interest. Milton Caniff, he wrote well. He knew how to be dramatic and he had great artistic ability."

The way the story meshes with the art has to do with how the art expresses what's in the story. Part of this is in the body language of the characters, which is one of the reasons Hal Foster chose John Cullen Murphy as his successor on the strip.

"He's a very good illustrator and he can make hands talk. Now, if you'll notice any other illustrator that you see, they'll paint the face, and probably feet, and they'll paint the hands, but the hands are useless. They're not doing anything. They're turned over too much, or they droop too much. Every expression on the face has to be confirmed by the hands."

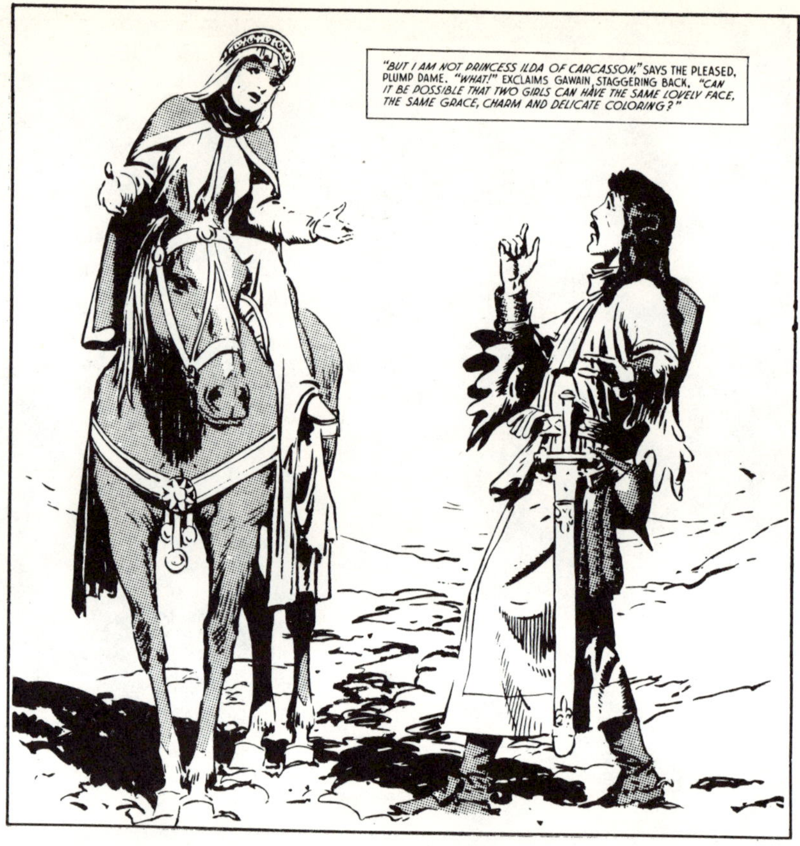

What kept Foster interested in drawing one feature, week after week, for over three decades, is that he wasn't really working for King Features so much as he was working for himself. **Prince Valiant** belonged to Foster and because of this he was never in the position that he was on **Tarzan** where he might be made to feel like an assembly line artist. Because he created, wrote and drew **Prince Valiant**, the strip was like a part of himself that he was bringing to life each week and sharing with the world. So it was never just a job to him.

At one point Foster said, "I work 53 hours— even 65 hours a week, when I first started out. But then I am doing work that I created myself; my own creations, so it's really not *work*. It's really what I *want* to do. I don't consider myself as good as people tell me I am. I appreciate the flattery and the affection that I get. For instance, when I go to New York and meet a bunch of cartoonists, they treat me much better than my golfing and hunting companions do.

"I sit out here all day, and look out the window, and everything is so normal and natural. I suppose that if I mixed with the boys—with the cartoonists—more, I would feel probably that I have done pretty good!

"What I've done is what I had to do, what I enjoyed most. And if I've lost the use of one leg, and I can't remember anything, at least I can give up quietly and feel repaid."

Foster also kept his work in perspective, being very self-effacing even though many of his contemporaries idolized what he could do.

"When I'm gone, I won't know about it. And I'm not doing the kind of work that will last for fu-

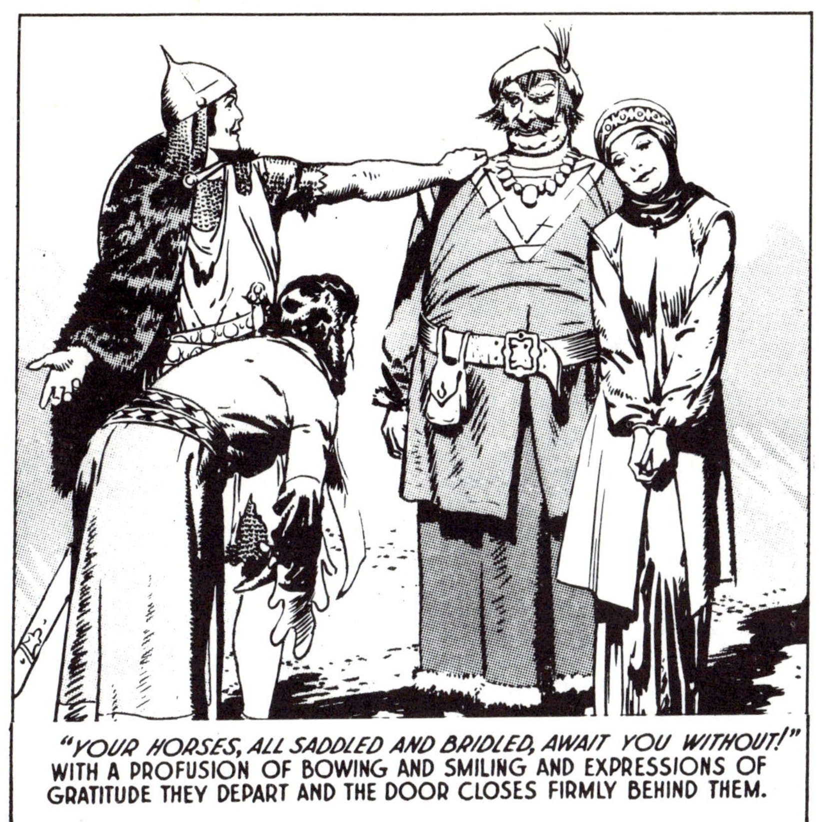

ture generations. Mine is a comic, during this century. What people like in this century might not be popular in the next one. Besides, paper doesn't wear well."

Even after all he had accomplished, the vast body of work he had created, Foster never felt completely satisfied because he felt that when an artist is satisfied he stops growing. In a 1971 interview he said that he remained very critical of his work, and when asked what he would wish for, he replied, "I don't know; a touch of genius I guess. No, you're never satisfied with your work. Anyone who's pleased with their work will stop right there, because if you're pleased you're satisfied and you don't have to improve. You've satisfied yourself. But, no, I'm not satisfied. I can pick out my own faults. When the story gets boring there's nothing you can do about it. You've written it and you hate to tear it up. It's not right and you just hope the customers will forgive you."

Foster had reprints of Alex Raymond's **Flash Gordon** in his studio, and when asked about them he remarked, "Yes, I take them out and look at them every now and then, and get sick. He has the most beautiful lines. I can't imitate his lines. I'd like to copy some of his stuff, but he was just too darn good."

He remained fascinated by the work of other artists, and not just adventure illustrators. Foster also admired the cartoons of Charles Schultz.

"I don't know why it is that some fellows can draw a little kid like Charlie Brown, with just a round head, round nose, and no particular body, and yet give the thing a personality. I still can't understand that and see where

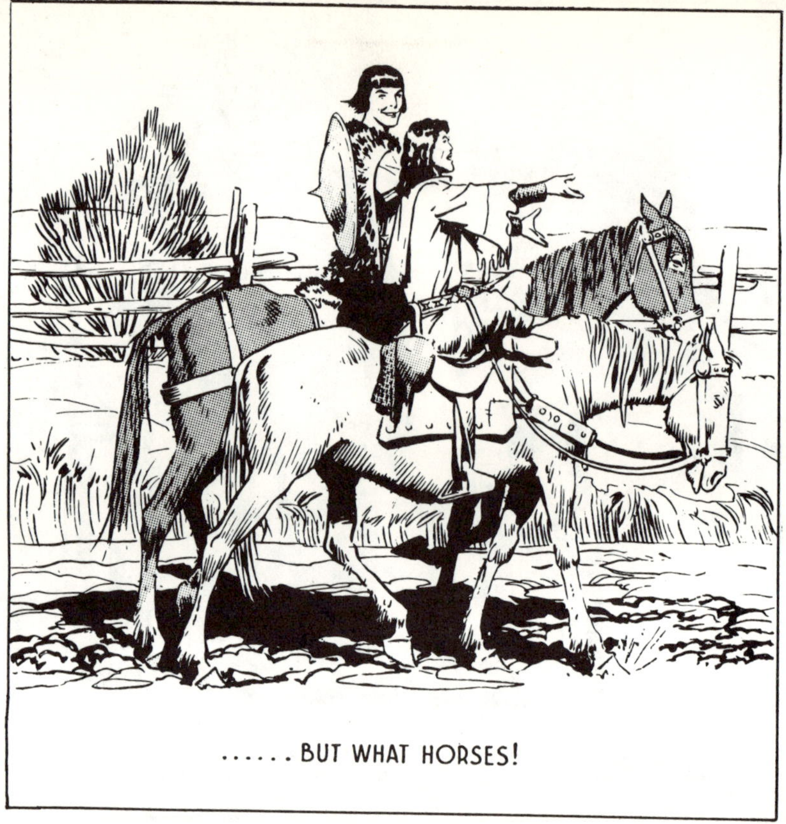

...... BUT WHAT HORSES!

the little things he says and the funny little illustrations seem more real than some of the best-drawn adventure strips."

Some days creating artwork can be a living hell and an artist longs for any other type of work. What kept Hal Foster drawing comic strips for more than fifty years?

"You cannot do good work unless you enjoy it and like it, and I would correct it, and improve every now and then on something. That's what keeps you going. You look at your work and say, 'Oh, I couldn't have done that 10 years ago.' "

BIBLIOGRAPHY

CARTOONIST PROFILES #22 (June 1974) Hal Foster interview by Bill Crouch, Jr.

NEMO: The Classic Comics Library #9 (Oct. 1984) "The Hal Foster Interview" by Fred Schreiber (Interview conducted in 1969)

THE COMICS JOURNAL #102 (Sept. 1985) "Drawing Upon History" by Arn Saba (Interview conducted in 1979)

KING COMIC HEROES by James Van Hise (Pioneer Books, 1988) "Foster" by Van Hise, A. Warner, L. Bigman, C. Springer and M. McKenney (Interview conducted in 1971)

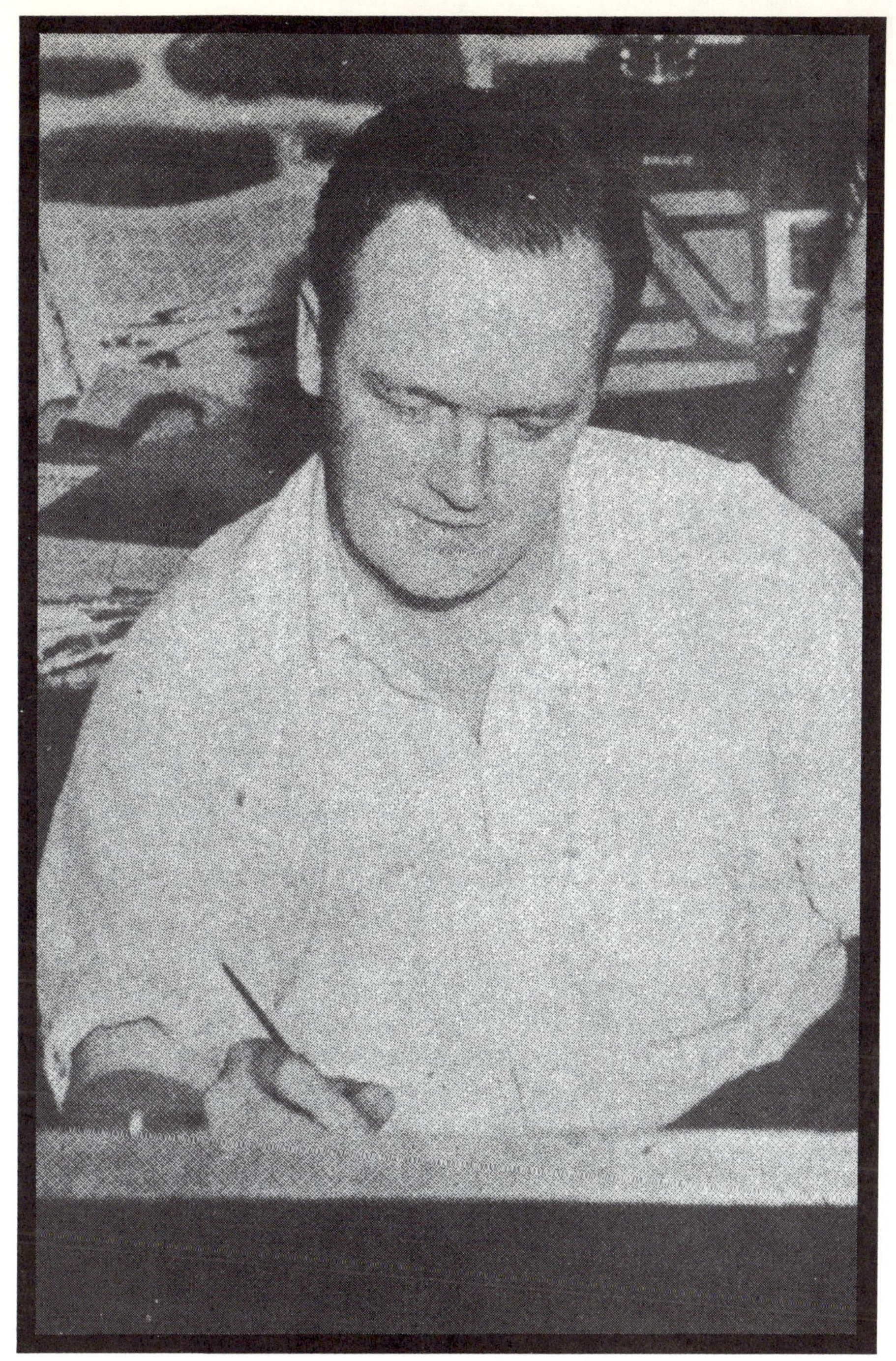

Chapter Ten
ALEX RAYMOND

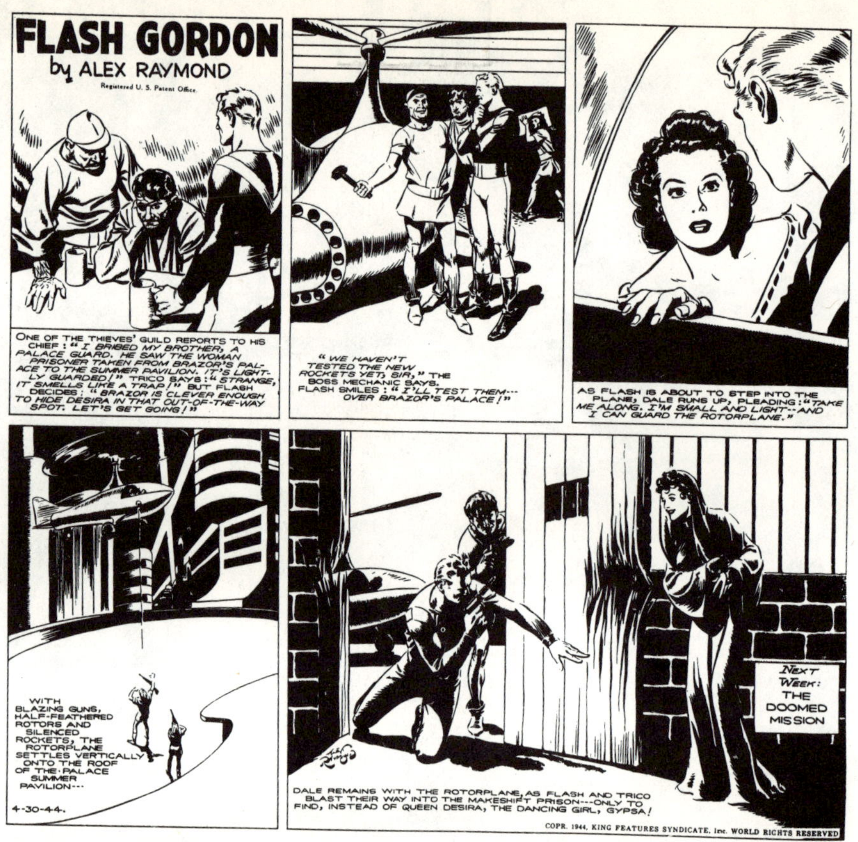

"Alex was a great influence! He was such a wonderful delineator of character; I admired his work very much. It had a great truth to it, and his lines were so accurate and delicate.

Any time I look at his work to refresh my memory of certain things that he achieved, well, I just get an inferiority complex."

—-Hal Foster

Alex Raymond drew several newspaper strips during his career, but the one he remains most famous for is the one he created, **Flash Gordon**. Alexander Gillespie Raymond was born October 2, 1909 in New Rochelle, New York. The eldest of seven children, he displayed a flair for art at an early age and was encouraged by his father. But when Alex was twelve, his father died suddenly, and without his greatest fan to cheer him on, Alex put his interest in art aside. He attended Iona Prep in New Rochelle on an athletic scholarship and turned down a football scholarship to go to work on Wall Street. The crash of 1929 ended his career as an order clerk.

Returning to his first love, art, he enrolled in the Grand Central School of Art. He also resumed his acquaintance with Russ Westover, the creator of **Tillie the Toiler**, and secured work as Westover's assistant on the strip. Raymond also worked on Blondie with Chic Young and with Lyman Young on **Tim Tyler's Luck**, and ghosted the latter for most of 1933.

While working at King Features, he sold them on the idea of **Flash Gordon**. His initial idea for the strip, which would have been about a group of scientists taking a rocketship from Earth to

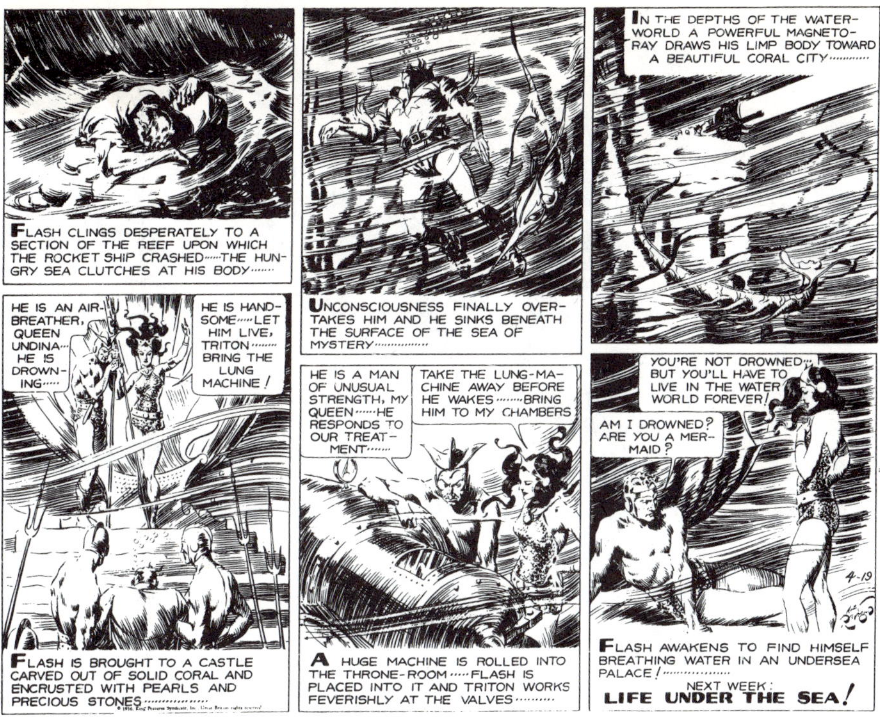

another world, was rejected by the syndicate. Raymond then revamped it completely, reducing the number of scientists to one and adding an adventurer, Flash Gordon, and a pretty girl, Dale Arden. **Flash Gordon** started out as a full page and later **Jungle Jim**, also by Raymond, was added as a single tier top piece across the strip. Raymond was also drawing the **Secret Agent X-9** daily strip when he began **Flash Gordon**, but after a year and a half he dropped it to devote his attention to Flash.

When Raymond began **Flash Gordon** in 1934, his style was stiff and flat, but later in 1935 it began to loosen up as his technique became more illustrative and stylized. Raymond derived inspiration from the work of Charles Dana Gibson, Matt Clark, Franklin Booth and John Lagatta. In fact Matt Clark had been King Features' first choice to draw **Secret Agent X-9**, but the popular magazine illustrator didn't care for the medium of comics and Raymond soon proved that he could deliver what the syndicate wanted. His dry brush technique brought a new look to the comics page, a style more familiar in the magazine illustrations of the day, something which Raymond also drew during his tenure on **Flash Gordon**. He drew illustrations for **Colliers Weekly**, **Blue Book**, **Esquire**, **Look** and several other leading publications. He also painted covers, book jackets, movie ads, advertising art and illustrated a book titled **Scuttle Watch**. Raymond draw **Flash Gordon** until the strip published on 4-30-44, which marked his departure to join the Army. Following his service, he found that King Features had another artist under contract to draw the strip, and not wanting to wait around for the contract to

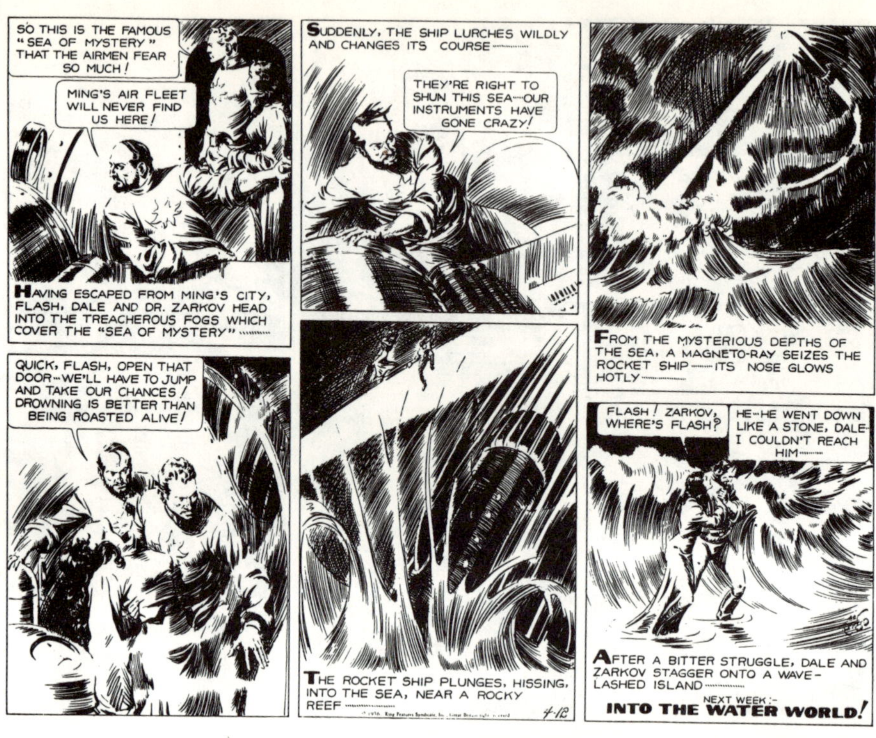

expire, he instead created another strip, **Rip Kirby**, which he drew until his death in an automobile accident.

Alex Raymond was the first artist to bring an illustrative technique, rich in brushstrokes, to the comic strip page. He was soon imitated by so many artists that by the late Thirties his approach no longer appeared unique, but by that time Raymond's technique had moved on; what he'd been doing in 1936 was very different from what he was drawing in 1940.

In a rare interview, Raymond's philosophy of art was expressed when he said: "I decided honestly that comic art is an art form in itself. It reflects life and times more accurately and is more artistic than magazine illustration since it is entirely creative. An illustrator works with cameras and models; a comic artist begins with a white sheet of paper and dreams up the whole business—he is a playwright, director, editor and artist all at once."

Even on **Flash Gordon**, set on a world unknown to us, Raymond captured the realism in the fantasy realm by grounding his figures firmly in reality. His people came to look more and more real, and therefore became characters more easily identified with. Part of the reason for this was Raymond's use of models. The accompanying photos show Raymond posing a model for a sequence which appeared in 1941. Although the use of live models for commercial illustration had been common for many years, this was primarily done for paintings by such notables as Leyendecker, Norman Rockwell and others. Raymond was one of the first comic strip illustrators to go to the trouble of posing models to achieve greater realism in his character poses. Ray-

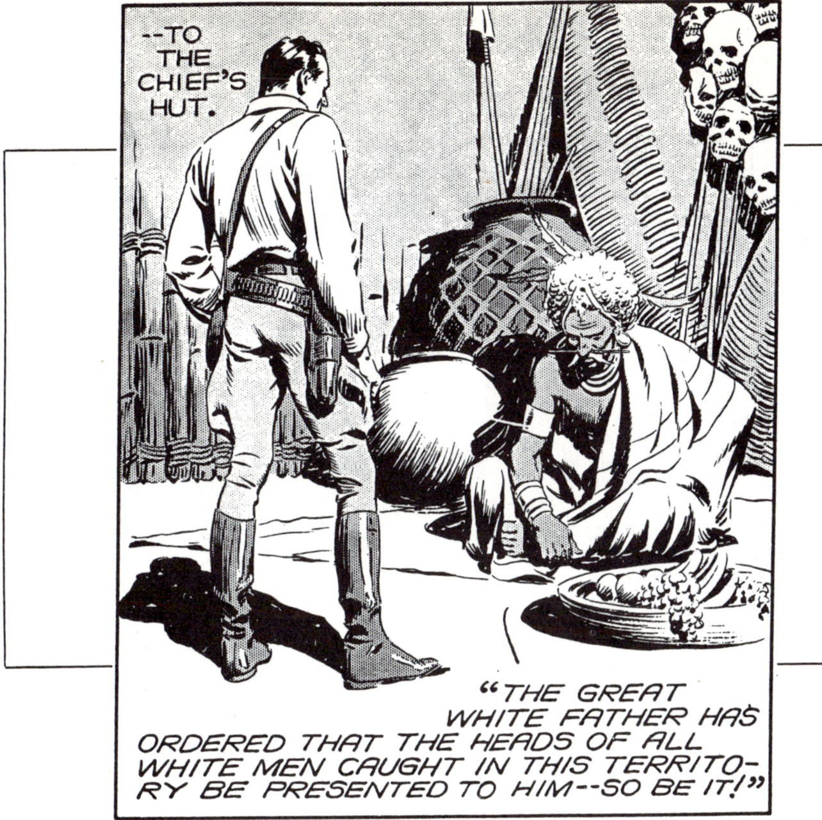

mond also established many of the formulas now taken for granted by artists in rendering figures and clothing realistically. Even Raymond's inking style established a form in comics which has been followed ever since. And yet Raymond's style never stagnated. Rather he kept evolving his linework throughout his years on **Flash Gordon** (1934 through 1944). One can look back over the strips in each year and actually see the art progressing. Raymond grew away from his thin-lined, cartooney looking art of 1934 so that by 1936 a more fluid approach was much in evidence. There was a flurry of brushwork evident as Raymond practiced and expanded on his technique. But by April of '36, and the beginning of the story called "The Water World of Mongo," he had refined his art still further into delicate yet luxurious lines which give the images sweep and density.

This was the time in the history of newspaper strips when the most popular, as **Flash Gordon** certainly was in the Thirties, appeared printed as a full page, not reduced to the third or quarter of a page we're used to seeing strips printed at today. So while now artists have to be certain their drawings aren't too complicated to come across when reduced to the size of a postage stamp, Raymond drew to have his artwork experienced in the large, full page richness that Sunday comics were blessed with in the Golden Age of the newspaper strips. Raymond evolved his art to the point where each panel could stand alone as an illustration, so that even after reading the story, one could go back over the art again and again, luxuriating in the linework. The water world Raymond presented to his readers was his most other worldly vista, both eerie and menacing, and swept

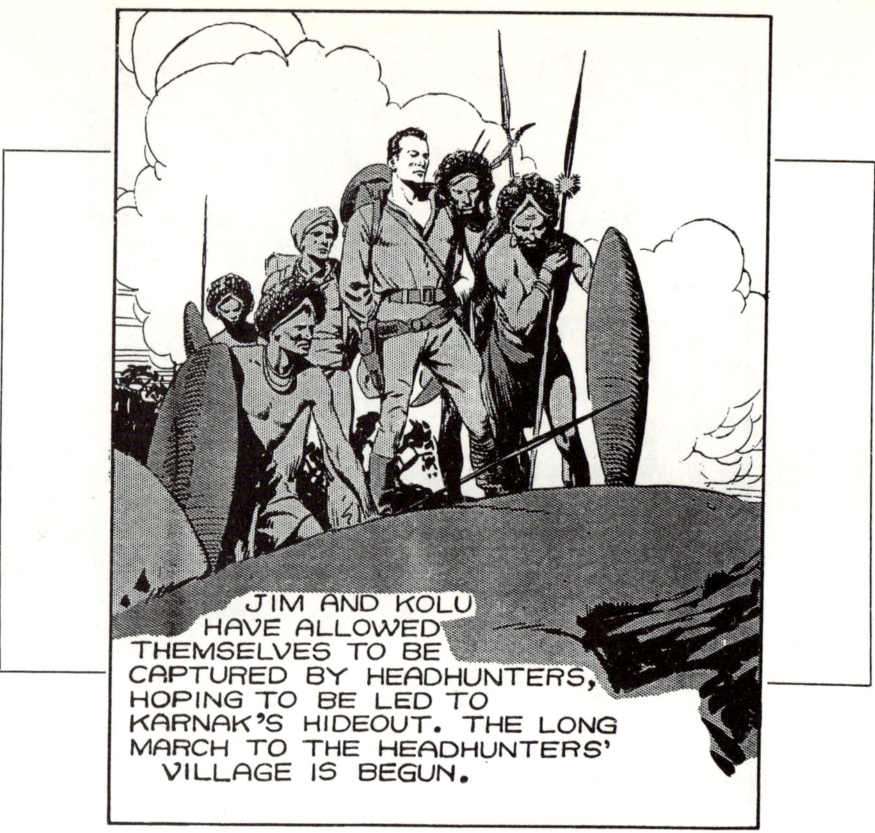

by torrents of brushwork so that the tides in that aquatic realm seemed to be sweeping through the drawing. But only those who saw it as a full page experienced the full majesty of the art, for Raymond still had to contend with the alternate, half-tab size which the syndicate would create by rearranging the panels from a vertical format into a horizontal one, and cropping the artwork in the process.

In black and white Raymond's pen work is both vivid and remarkable, for even though he knew he was drawing for color, he never neglected the depth and texture his art would have when seen in black and white. Raymond did not depend on color to add the finishing touches, at least not during this period. That would come much later. The use of color was often interesting in the strip, for even though the water world series was dominated by purples and greens to achieve the sense of the murky depths, the colors were done with graduated tones.

Raymond didn't stay with that technique but continued to refine his work. Gradually throughout 1937 he seemed to be striving to achieve a balance in his composition where the linework did not predominate. In 1938 he began achieving this cleaner style while retaining the rich detail. Rather than furious lines delineating the action and the scenery, his work became tighter and yet kept texture and expressiveness.

In his introduction to the 1967 edition of the Nostalgia Press reprint of three years of **Flash Gordon** (1938 through 1941), Al Williamson writes, "Raymond's style is never stagnant; it is always flowing and changing. He was constantly experimenting with new ideas and techniques, seeking always to im-

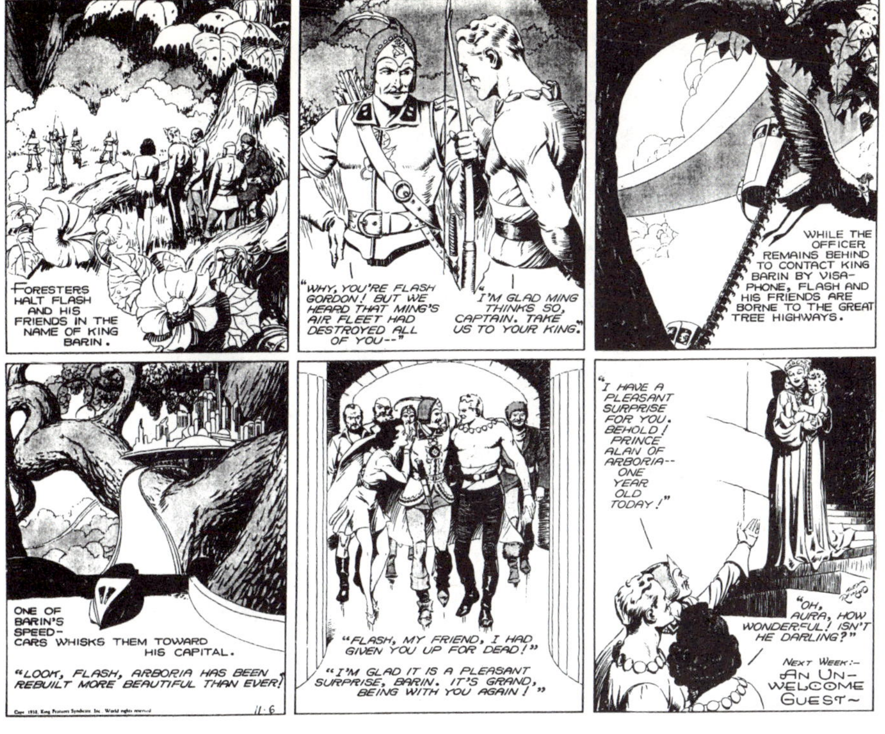

A tribute to Foster by Raymond

prove his presentation. Every story looks different, but there is no doubt that the work is his. It is never confusing or ostentatious; it is precise, easy to read at first glance—alive. There is a wealth of knowledge behind every line, and not many cartoonists have been able to achieve his simplicity in drawing realistic adventures. Raymond's work is the inspiration behind many artists in the field today, and is evidenced in many current strips, both foreign and domestic."

By this time everything was in black and white linework and color added another dimension without necessarily improving on it. In 1941 Raymond's refinement of his technique took a different turn. In black and white the art became simpler in intent because Raymond began looking letting color add depth something he had not done until then. Thus black and white reprints of Raymond's **Flash Gordon** from 1941 through 1944 present a more Spartan approach to art which belies the effort Raymond put into the strip. It is comparable to seeing black and white art from Frank Miller's **The Dark Knight Returns** and being startled upon realizing how much the printed art depends on rich, finished color for texture, life and intensity.

The control Raymond began bringing to his art in 1938 can no doubt be traced to his great admiration for Hal Foster, an artist whose work was the epitome of control. In Foster's work every line was in place and not a trace of flourishing design could be found. Looking at a page of **Prince Valiant**, one gains the impression that Foster was rendering a scene precisely as he saw it. Raymond was much impressed by this evidence of detail and control, what some have re-

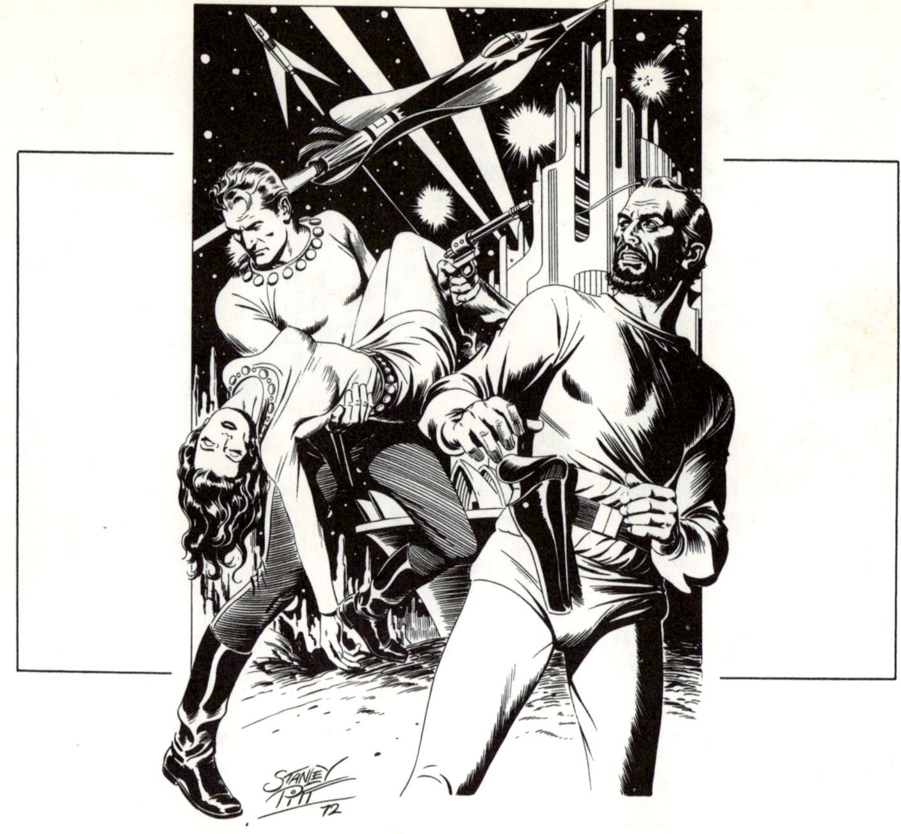

Stanley Pitt was much influenced by Raymond

garded as Foster's painstaking craftsmanship and puritanical industriousness. On the other hand, Foster greatly admired Raymond's often florid linework, and never hesitated to admit his envy of Alex Raymond's technique.

While Foster admired Raymond without altering his routine to absorb his techniques into his own style, many other artists couldn't wait to imitate Raymond. The work of Phil Davis on **Mandrake the Magician** in the late Thirties looked very much like the work of Raymond while other strips introduced science fiction heroes who looked a lot like Flash Gordon. In comic books of the time, artists often swiped Raymond with casual earnestness, one of the most blatant being Sheldon Moldoff (who signed his work "Shelly") on the Hawkman strips he drew for **Flash Comics**.

In Australia, a young artist named Stan Pitt saw Raymond's work and at the age of fifteen became a lifelong devotee. "I saw a page and was really knocked out," the artist said in a 1976 interview in **Comic Crusader**. "I just could not believe it; it was so magnificent. So far above everything I'd ever seen. So I devoted the next five or six years to studying the style." And study Stanley did. In 1946, at the age of twenty, he sold a newspaper strip to the Sydney Sunday Sun called **Silver Starr**, whose artwork, technique, sensibility, composition, everything captured the style of Alex Raymond's art circa 1940. That Raymond wasn't drawing like that any more by 1946 didn't bother the young artist. He knew what he loved. Although the wholesale lifting of an artist's entire artistic repertoire tends to be frowned on these days, one cannot argue that Stan Pitt absorbed

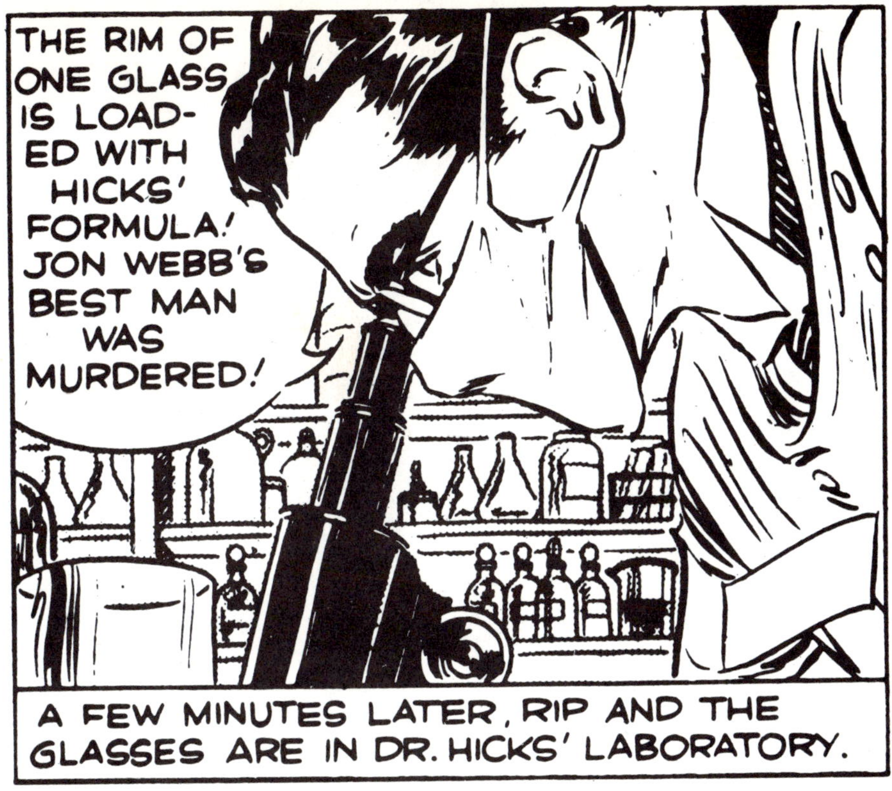

the style and made it his own. Decades later his linework was unmistakable, and even though he had refined it, the work still looked like it was drawn by the ghost of the 1940 Alex Raymond. Pitt internalized the style so completely he didn't even have to swipe from Raymond's art to do draw in Raymond's style. By the Sixties, while there were other artists around certainly influenced by Raymond, such as Wally Wood, Al Williamson and Russ Manning, they also showed many other influences and had established their own styles. But Pitt remained the standard bearer of Raymond's romantic tradition in comic strip illustration, and certainly the only one who had immersed himself in it to such an incredible degree. Since no one had drawn quite like Alex Raymond for decades (unless they were doing a deliberate *homage*), Stan Pitt's artwork actually came across as fresh, exciting and energetic.

What Raymond would have thought of this tribute to his craftsmanship is unknown. Although Foster lived for decades producing a wonderful body of work, Raymond's artistic output was cut short after only two decades, yet his influence is in many respects just as powerful. Raymond is still studied and marveled over fifty years after he began his work. His work remains rich in feeling and intensity. Raymond loved what he was doing and his artwork continues as living testament of his infatuation.

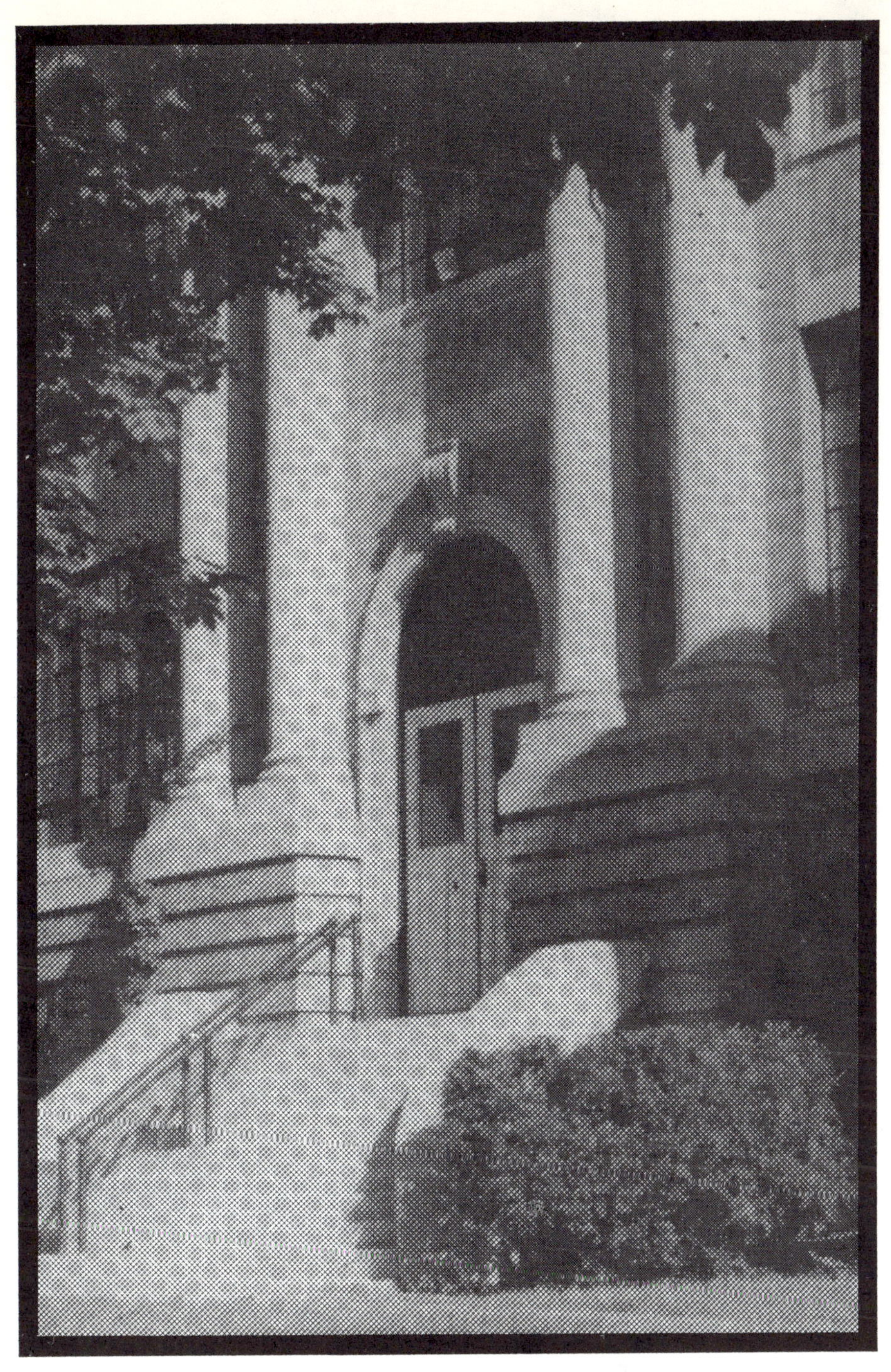

Appendix One
THE JOE KUBERT ART SCHOOL

In 1976, Joe Kubert and his wife, Muriel, founded the Joe Kubert School of Cartoon and Graphic Art, Inc. Muriel Kubert is a graduate of Rider College with a B.S. in Business Administration and is the school's Administrator.

Kubert founded the school because he perceived a need for it due to the lack of any formal schools educating in this specific area, and knowing that there were many fledgling cartoonists wanting to break into the profession of Cartoon Graphics and Illustration.

Having started as a two-year school, the courses of study were extended to three years in September, 1978 as the school's attempt to indoctrinate professional acumen within a two year span was soon recognized as being too demanding. Even with the three year schedule, full time students are required to be at a drawing board from eight to ten hours a day.

As a result of the school's continued growth, additional physical space was needed. In 1983, the former Dover High School building (containing almost 100,000 square feet) was purchased. Besides a full gymnasium and a two-tiered auditorium, the number of added classrooms allows for further expansion. The original building (called "The Mansion") where classes were taught, is a twenty-three room facility located on several acres of picturesque landscaping and now acts as a students' residence.

Michael Chen, an administrator and teacher at the school was interviewed regarding the history of the Joe Kubert School and its day to day operation. Chen teaches "Narrative Art" to the first year students, and "Business of Cartoon Illustration" to the second year Cartoon Graphics students. Chen himself has worked for both DC and Marvel Comics. The Kubert School is primarily keyed to teaching comic artists, but it also has a parallel program which teaches animation, although the number of students in that program is much smaller.

In explaining the procedures for admission to the school, Chen states, "The prospective student must submit a portfolio to Mr. Kubert, who does the initial screening. He interviews all the applicants himself. An applicant can either be interviewed over the phone if he lives too far away, like in Germany or Australia. Or he can come in person. In either case, Mr. Kubert must have a portfolio in his hands when he talks with the student. In the case of the portfolio, it is strongly recommended, but not mandatory, that the applicant must have fifteen or so pieces of work in there. I have known applicants to come in with close to a hundred pieces, which is really unnecessary. When Mr. Kubert interviews the applicant, the primary quality that he's looking for is a sense of commitment on the part of that applicant. That they really, truly want to be a cartoonist. If the portfolio shows an extraordinary amount of skill, there is always the possibility that the student can just bypass the first year and go directly into the second year, but that is not the crucial reason for having them come to the school. Mr. Kubert and the rest of this faculty realize that the only way you can teach a student anything is if they are receptive to being taught. If the applicant is extremely talented, there is a good chance that he is not looking for any information, but simply wants the applause of either the students or the faculty, and so he's not going to learn anything from us. Then the best thing is just to have that applicant, or that student, go off on his own and get a job if he's that good."

Being a three year institution of learning, the Kubert School is very much like a college except that all it teaches is art whereas a university would also teach math, science, foreign languages and other subjects unrelated to drawing.

"Since we do not require any academics, such as mathematics and the usual, we do not issue a Bachelor's Degree. Consequently we can offer the courses in three years instead of four years as you'd have in a college."

The staff at the Kubert School is drawn from longtime working artists in the industry, such as Tex Blaisdell, Jose Delbo, Hy Eisman, Irwin Hasen as well as Joe Kubert himself.

"At any given time on any day, I would say there are about a dozen instructors. The faculty this year is our largest. We have about thirty instructors on the faculty. Al Williamson taught here for a semester a few years ago, and so did Bill Sienkiewicz. In terms of guest speakers we've had Curt Swan, Will Eisner several times, Sergio Aragones, Jim Steranko, Murphy Anderson, Ray Harryhausen, Jeff Jones, Mike Kaluta and several others over the thirteen years we've been in business. A lot of that comes from Joe's involvement with the National Cartoonists Society, which he's been a member of for years. But also a lot of the instructors ask their friends to come out and talk to the students. Rowena (Morril) came out here at one point, and Boris (Vallejo) came by when we had our reunion of alumni back in 1988. We had 200 alumni get together and Boris dropped by to talk to the students.

The way the Kubert School operates is by a school year, like any other school. It runs from September through May and it is broken into two semesters. This time around (1989-90) they have 170 to 180 students just in the day program. The evening classes, the workshops and the like, tag on an extra hundred students. If they fulfill the curriculum to the school's expectations, then the student continues throughout the year

"Roughly about fifty percent of those students who enroll in their first year graduate," Chen states. "That would be in two different sections: The Cartoon Graphics and the Animation section. The Cartoon Graphics is the larger of the two. These are two different sections of the school.

"Animation is self-explanatory—these students are learning the principles of cel animation, stop-motion animation, computer animation, and Claymation (which is all the rage nowadays). They also learn how to do storyboards. How to prepare for the business end of it. The mechanics of working the video equipment and the film equipment. They would have to prepare for their portfolio, in order to graduate, roughly a minute or two of videotaped animation work so that they can show people that they have the ability to do the animation.

"With the Cartoon Graphics, they would also cover storyboards, but their viewpoint, the way they approach art, would be to handle comic books, comic strips, political cartoons, gag cartoons, advertising illustrations and anything that doesn't involve the illusion of life. Although an Animation student can do some of what the Cartoon Graphics people do, they can't do everything as well, and vice-versa.

"Right now in the third year we have six students in the Animation program. In the Cartoon Graphics third year we have twenty-two students. In second year Animation we have sixteen, and in Cartoon Graphics we have roughly forty-five students.

Although the Kubert School was initially founded to teach an artist to be a cartoonist, they make sure that the artist's skills are sharpened as much as possible so that the broadest applications of their talent will be opened to them, including how to paint, something which a lot of cartoonists are not ordinarily trained in.

"We do teach illustrative painting as well as other techniques used in illustration. The students learn acrylic, oil, marker techniques, pastels, guache, water color, air brush and dyes. They would all have to learn that to take Cartoon Graphics."

Having this broad range of knowledge and ability to draw from doesn't automatically guarantee people are waiting to give graduates of the school a job, it just means that they're in a better position to prove themselves than other artists may be.

"I wish it were a guarantee, but it doesn't work that easily," Chen admits. "Within the comic book industry, the Kubert School's reputation has grown over the years, but it's not yet at that point where editors are going to drop everything just to talk to our people, although more and more of our people are getting into the comic book industry. Marvel comics, at least at this point, has at least six full time production people from the Kubert School, not to mention all the freelancers working for them. DC does not have anybody working full time, but hires more of the freelance people than Marvel. There's Jan Duursema, Ron Randall, Tom Mandrake, Rich Veitch, Steve Bissette, Tom Yeates, Tim Truman, Karl Kesel and Kim Demulder all working or having worked for DC in the recent past, and because of the nature of freelancing, they may well be working for them again in the next few weeks. (Pioneer Comics, a newer publisher, currently employs six Kubert Art School graduates on a freelance basis.) But the way we do things here at the school, we stress flexibility in our students. We don't want them to just be a comic book artist. We want them to be as versatile as possible, which is why we make it mandatory to take the illustrative courses as well to know how to do paste-ups and mechanicals. To be able to do a marker-comp for an advertising firm, or to do storyboards.

"A number of our people are working for Hasbro Toys designing characters for the G.I. Joe and COPS line. Mark McNab, David Hasle, Dave Dorman, Mark Pennington, and Bart Sears are all working or have worked for Hasbro fairly recently.

"Also we have people working for Hallmark Cards. Both Hasbro and Hallmark regularly send people out to scout talent here at the school, to check out the portfolios for the third year students.

"We have several people working at Archie Comics as well, either full time or on a freelance basis. Many of our graduates are working for advertising companies. A few of them are even Art Directors. They're pretty much all over the place, and it's kind of a kick that every time you turn around, there's another Kubert alumnus in the business, whether it's advertising, toy design, greeting cards, animation or what have you."

The Kubert School also has partial scholarships available, such as one which was established in the memory of one of Joe Kubert's oldest friends.

"For the last two years we've had a Norman Maurer Commemorative Scholarship. Norm was a very old and dear friend of Joe's back in the Golden Age of comics. They broke into comics at the same time.

They pioneered the use of 3-D techniques in comics. Norm also worked as the manager, producer and writer of The Three Stooges back in the 1960s, as well as for Hanna-Barbera on the Scooby-Doo series. When he died a few years ago, his family and friends got together and established a scholarship in his memory of a thousand dollars to be given to a second year student going into their third year."

Recently another scholarship was added which is for the benefit of a student who would just be entering the school for the first time.

"This year the Newspaper Features Council instituted a scholarship which is full tuition to a first year student, but only minorities are allowed to participate. This is our first year and our winner was Terry Wilson.

"Also, the Comic Book Retailers International Organization of comic book retail shop owners throughout the United States have established a scholarship starting this year where people from outside could apply for the scholarship by competing with a portfolio. Judges will be appointed by the CBRI from a list provided by the Kubert School of teachers and alumni. That should be getting under way in 1990. Right now we're setting up a preliminary competition throughout the New Jersey-New York area."

Although many of the students entering the Kubert School do so right out of high school, there is also a sizeable majority of older students as well.

"I would say that roughly fifty percent are straight out of high school. The other fifty percent are broken up into a large number in their early twenties, then we occasionally have students who are in their late twenties to early thirties. In the past we had one student who graduated who was in his fifties when he attended the school. I remember that four or five years ago we had one fellow who was in his sixties come to the school. He was a retired plumber, but he only lasted one year because he said he didn't have the physical stamina to keep up with the other students and keep doing the assignments that we demanded of them."

The Kubert School also has special courses available to both beginning and advanced students including Saturday Cartoon Sketch classes, evening classes in Basic and Advanced Paste-Ups and Mechanicals, as well as a Life Drawing class offered one night a week.

Additional information on the Joe Kubert School of Cartoon & Graphic Art can be obtained by writing: 37 Myrtle Avenue, Dover, N.J. 07801

Appendix Two

GLOSSARY

BACKGROUND: Those elements in a panel which create the setting and the ambience and indicates if the scene is in a city, a forest, in the sky, etc.

BALLOON: Used by most artists to contain the dialogue spoken by the characters in a strip.

BODY LANGUAGE: The stance of a character, their gestures and the way they are posed in a panel.

BREAKDOWNS: How the elements of a script are transferred into comic strip form. The stage in which panels are roughed out before they are fully rendered on the art board.

CAPTION: The words in a panel, set off in a block, which describe action or an unseen element of the story.

COMIC ART: Panel art whether done in the form of a comic book or a comic strip.

COMIC BOOK: Felt by some to be a misnomer as it applies to both humorous as well as dramatic stories. The "comic" actually does not indicate humor but refers to the arrangement of consecutive drawings in panels. Refers to stories which fill most of the pages of the periodical.

COMIC STRIP: An arrangement of drawings within panels in strip form in one tier or over just a few pages.

CARTOONIST: One who renders subjects and objects as line drawings, usually in comic strip form. Adding detail achieves more realism in the drawing while simplified linework creates a more impressionistic cartoon, such as when one is attempting to achieve a humorous effect.

COMPOSITION: The arrangement of elements in a panel wherein certain attention is placed on figures or action depending on their importance in the story. The composition of one panel might emphasize a character who is speaking while another panel might emphasize someone sneaking up on the speaker. This is shaped by the focal points of the story.

DRAFTSMANSHIP: The structure of the elements within a panel and how they relate to each other.

FULL SCRIPT: A comic strip script in which the story is broken down into pages and all of the dialogue the characters speak is included so that the artist will know how many balloons to allow for in each panel.

INKING: Going over the pencil art with ink to finish the drawing and enable it to be most easily shot for reproduction. On rare occasions artwork can be shot from pencils, but this is difficult to accomplish with any success.

GAG STRIP: A single-tiered humor strip, such as "Calvin and Hobbs" and "Crankshaft."

MARVEL STYLE: This is a type of comic book script in which the plot for an entire story is described in some detail, but it is generally not broken down into pages and little or no dialogue is included. The artist is then expected to break the plot down into pages and panels. This requires a great deal more creativity on the part of the artist than other comic strip scripts demand.

PANEL: One of the elements in a comic strip which serves to contain and control the action.

PENCILLING: The stage of drawing after the script has been roughed out and layed out and the detailed art is rendered in each panel prior to being inked.

PROGRESSION: The manner in which a story flows from panel to panel.

SCRIPT: The story an artist uses to base his drawings on. This can either be written by the artist himself, in which case is it sometimes just roughed out and very simplified, or by another writer. When written by someone other than the artist, the script tends to be more detailed and is broken down into pages, sometimes even describing the number of panels and the contents of each.

STORY STRIP: A single tiered dramatic strip, such as "Spider-Man."

STORY-TELLING: The manner in which the artwork in a comic strip communicates the story to the reader. Does the action flow from panel to panel or does each panel seem disconnected from the other panels around it?

STRIP: An arrangement of panels, whether vertical or horizontal.

THUMBNAIL SKETCH: A tiny breakdown showing the arrangement of panels and action on a page to experiment with the structure before it is actually pencilled.

SPECIAL SECTION..

Over the next few pages you will find a special section for ambitious artists. On each page you will find one stage of a Hal Foster drawing of Prince Valiant. Each stage is progressive from the one before it resulting in a completed printable work. The first stage, for example, is unfinished pencils, while a later stage is finished pencils that have not been inked. This will provide a unique opportunity to create finished pencils over a Foster layout or to provide the inks for a completed Foster pencil drawing. The last page reproduces the completed Foster work which can be used for comparison.

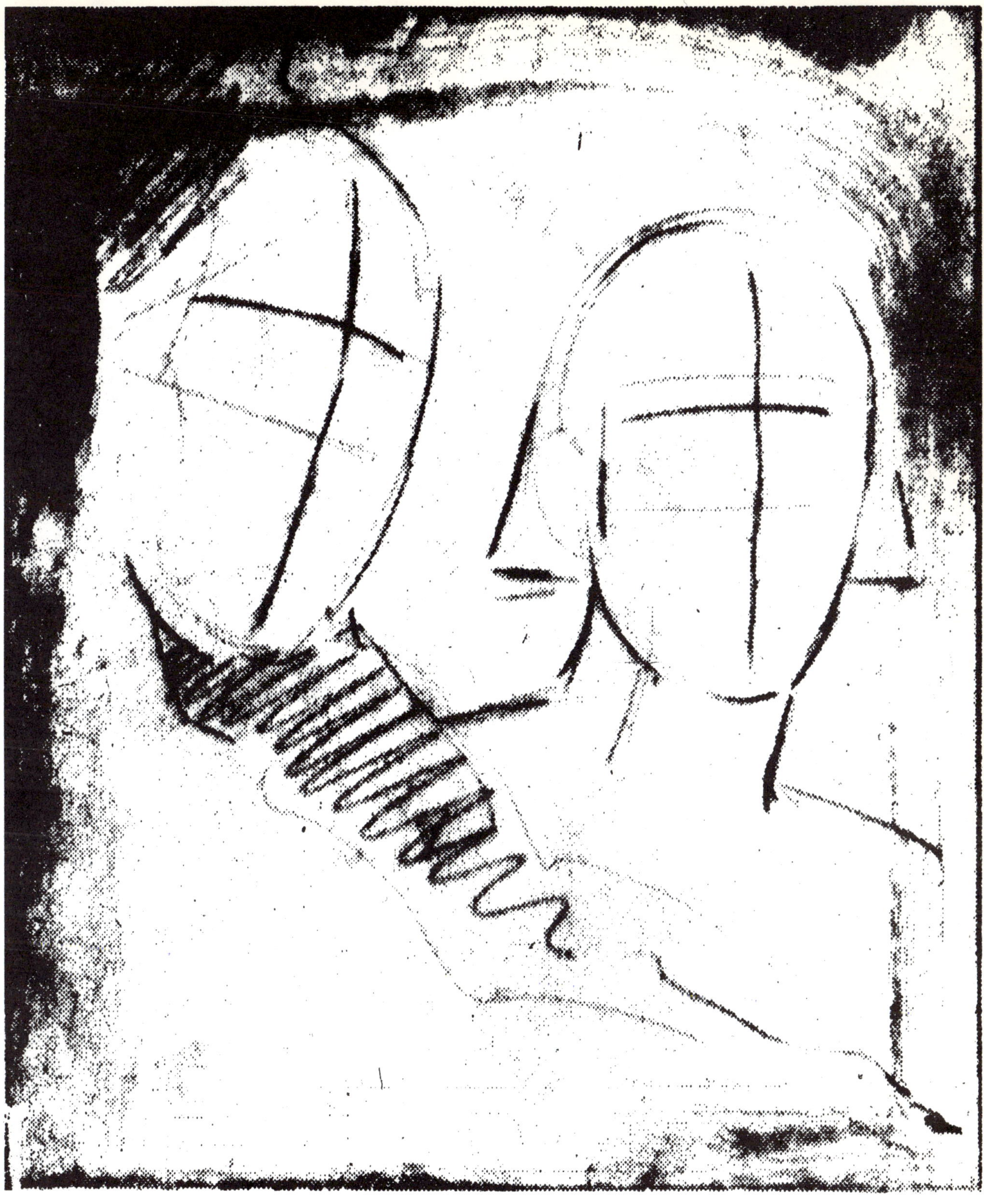

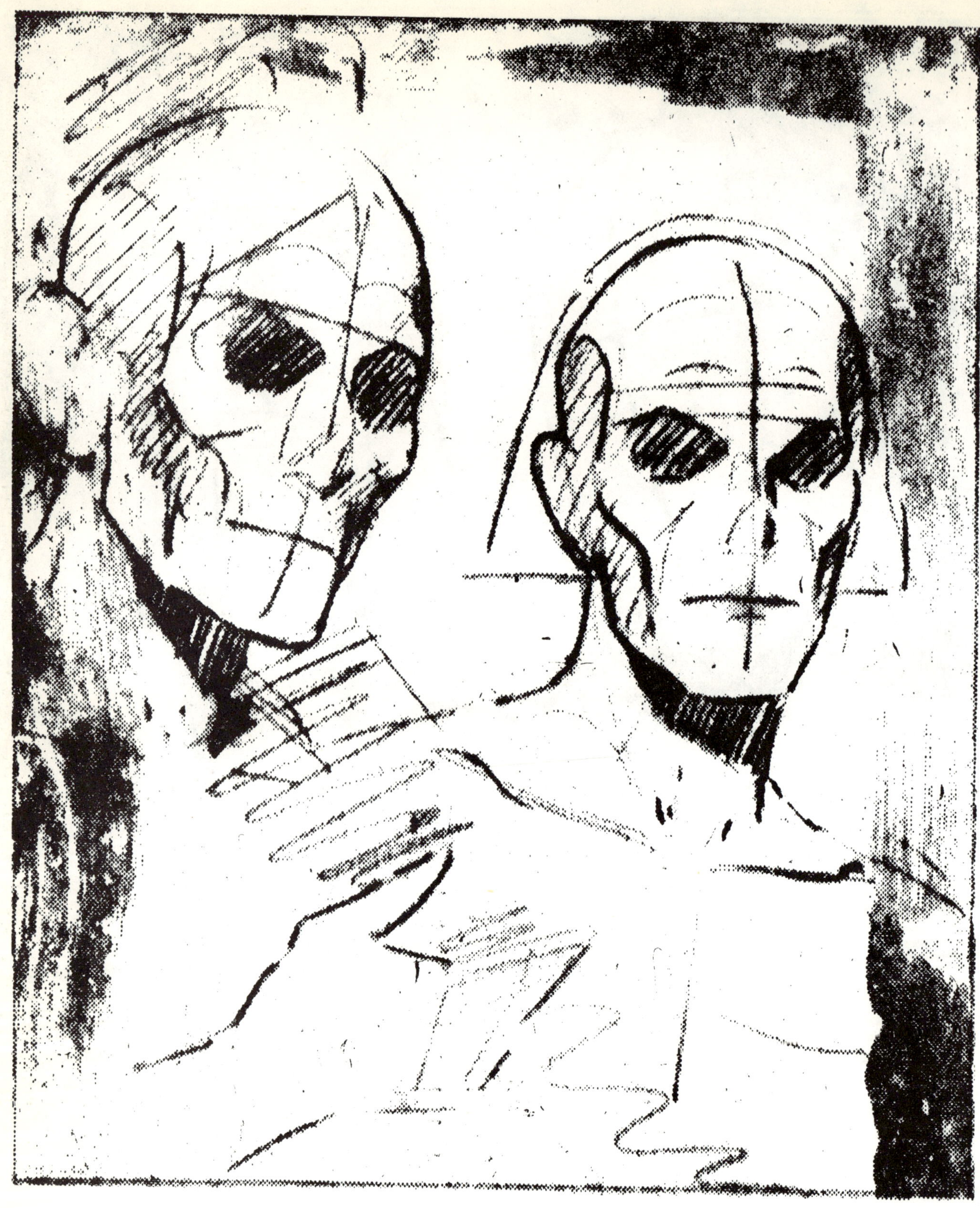

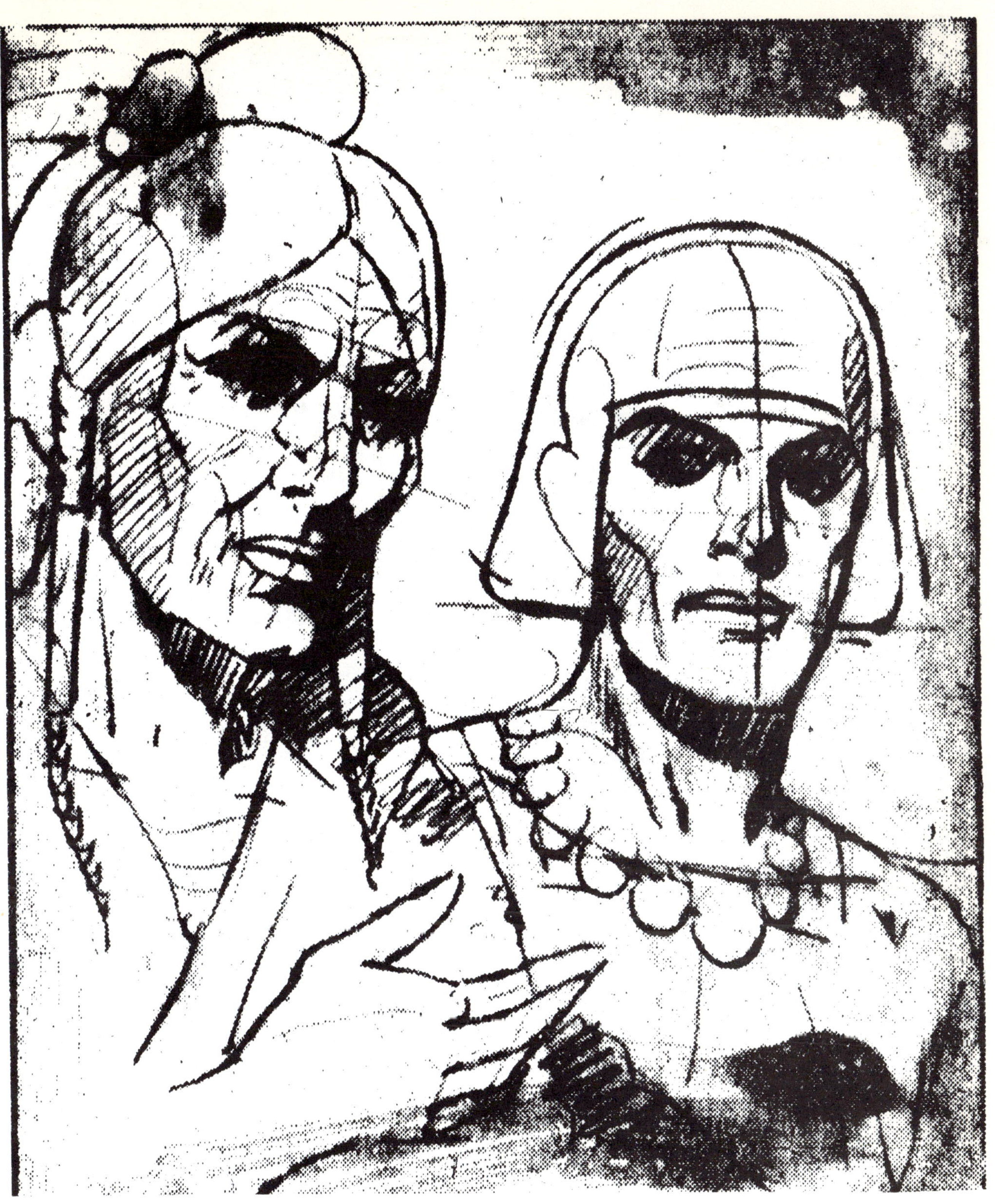

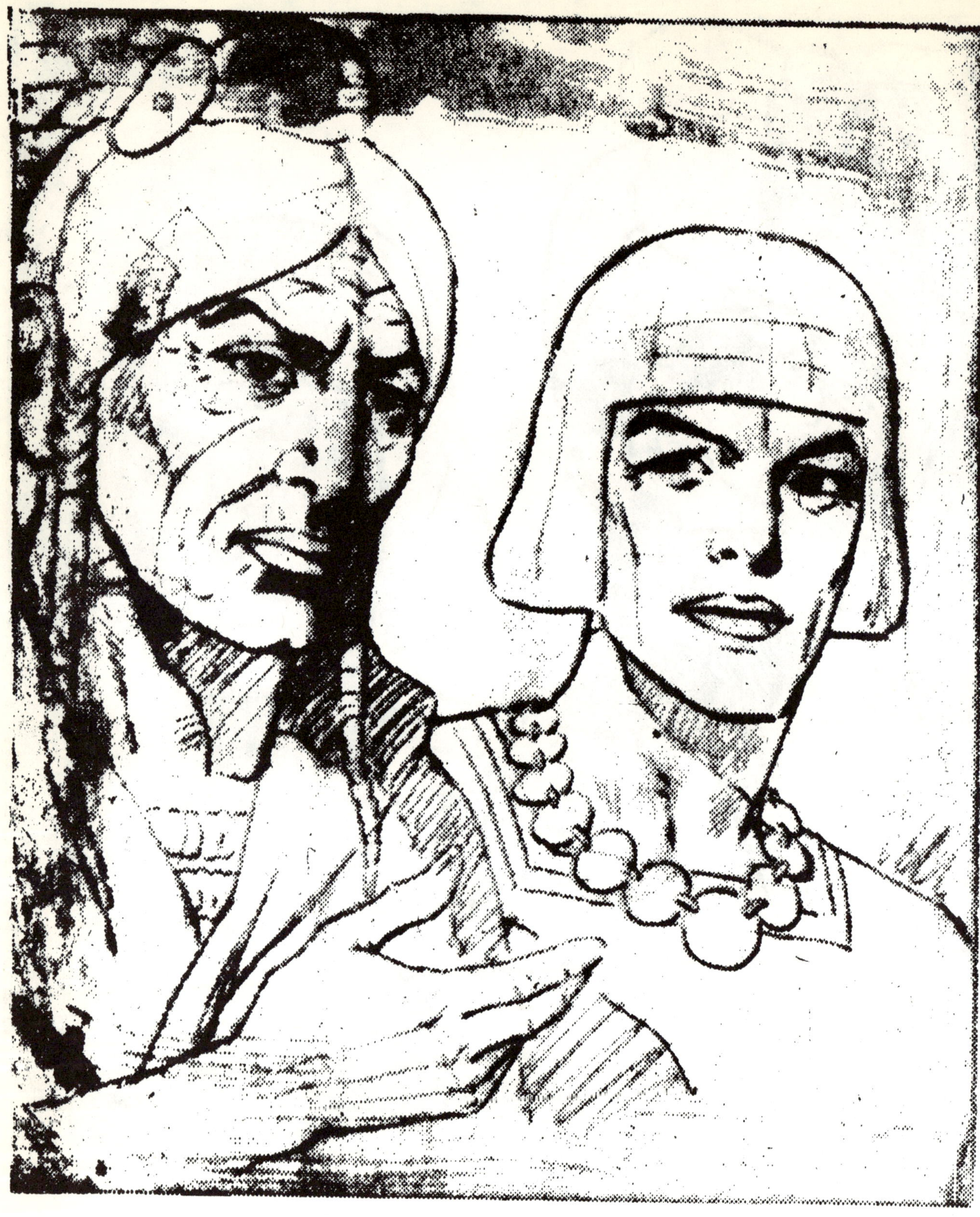

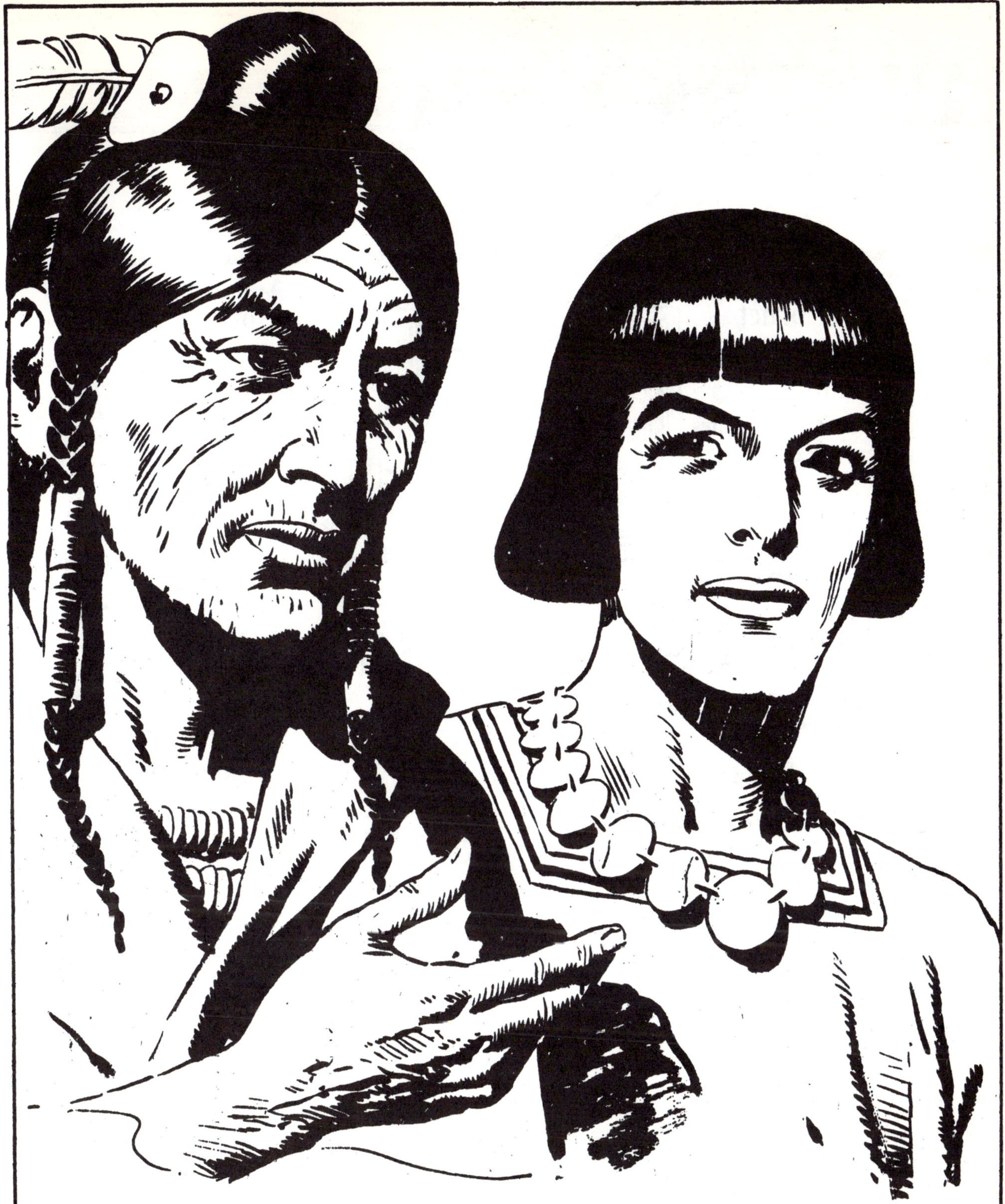

THE CHIEF SHAKES HIS HEAD. *"YOUR JOURNEY DOWN TO THE SEA MIGHT BE PERILOUS, FOR THE TRIBES ACROSS THE GREAT RIVER ARE RESTLESS, OUT OF CONTROL OF THEIR LEADERS."*

SPIES SPIES SPIES SPIE

THE COUCH POTATO BOOK CATALOG 5715 N BALSAM, LAS VEGAS, NV 89130

The Phantom
The Green Hornet
The Shadow
The Batman

Each issue of Serials Adventures Presents offers 100 or more pages of pure nostalgic fun for $16.95

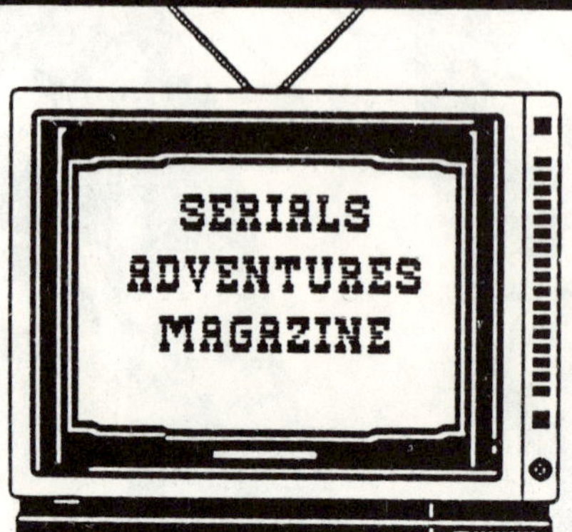

Flash Gordon Part One
Flash Gordon Part Two
Blackhawk

Each issue of Serials Adventures Presents features a chapter by chapter review of a rare serial combined with biographies of the stars and behind-the-scenes information. Plus rare photos. See the videotapes and read the books!

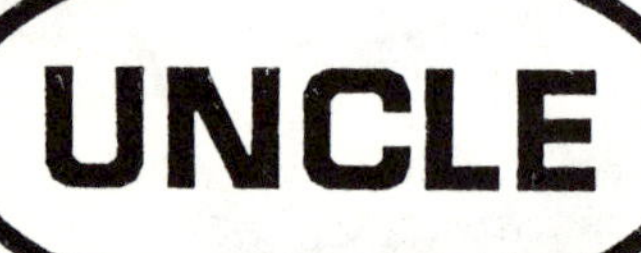

THE U.N.C.L.E. TECHNICAL MANUAL

Every technical device completely detailed and blueprinted, including weapons, communications, weaponry, organization, facitilites... 80 pages, 2 volumes...$9.95 each

PRISONER

NUMBER SIX: THE COMPLEAT PRISONER

The most unique and intelligent television series ever aired! Patrick McGoohan's tour-de-force of spies and mental mazes finally explained episode by episode, including an interview with the McGoohan and the complete layout of the real village!...160 pages...$14.95

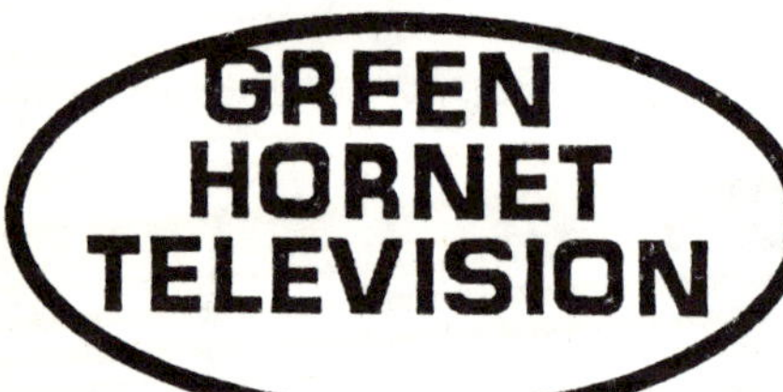

THE GREEN HORNET

Daring action adventure with the Green Hornet and Kato. This show appeared before Bruce Lee had achieved popularity but delivered fun, superheroic action. Episode guide and character profiles combine to tell the whole story...120 pages...$14.95

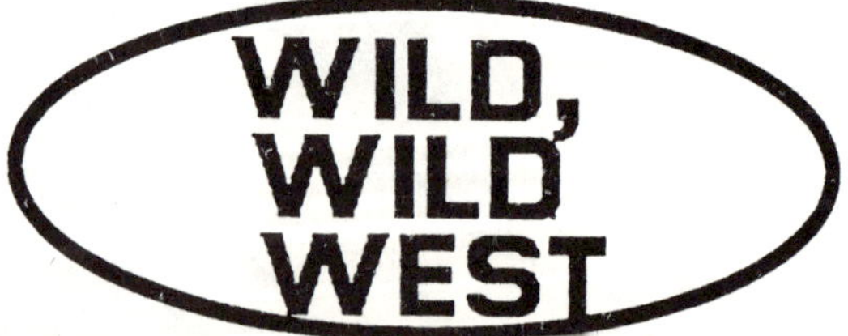

WILD, WILD, WEST

Is it a Western or a Spy show? We couldn't decide so we're listing it twice. Fantastic adventure, convoluted plots, incredible devices...all set in the wild, wild west! Details of fantastic devices, character profiles and an episode-by-episode guide...120 pages...$17.95

THE COUCH POTATO BOOK CATALOG 5715 N BALSAM, LAS VEGAS, NV 89130

SPIES SPIES SPIES SPIE

THE ILLUSTRATED STEPHEN KING
A complee guide to the novels and short stories of Stephen King illustrated by Steve Bissette and others...$12.95

GUNSMOKE YEARS
The definitive book of America's most successful television series. 22 years of episode guide, character profiles, interviews and more...240 pages, $14.95

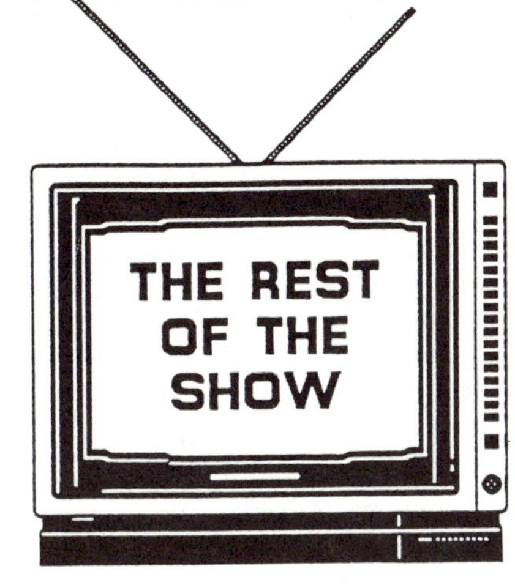

THE KING COMIC HEROES
The complete story of the King Features heroes including Prince Valiant, Flash Gordon, Mandrake, The Phantom, Secret Agent, Rip Kirby, Buz Sawyer, Johnny Hazard and Jungle Jim. These fabulous heroes not only appeared in comic strips and comic books but also in movies and serials, Includes interviews with Hal Foster, Al Williamson and Lee Falk...$14.95

Special discounts are available for library, school, club or other bulk orders. Please inquire.

IF YOUR FAVORITE TELEVISION SERIES ISN'T HERE, LET US KNOW... AND THEN STAY TUNED!

And always remember that if every world leader was a couch potato and watched TV 25 hours a day, 8 days a week, there would be no war...

Boring, but Necessary Ordering Information!

Payment: All orders must be prepaid by check or money order. Do not send cash. All payments must be made in US funds only.

Shipping: We offer several methods of shipment for our product.

Postage is as follows:

For books priced under $10.00— for the first book add $2.50. For each additional book under $10.00 add $1.00. (This is per individual book priced under $10.00, not the order total.)

For books priced over $10.00— for the first book add $3.25. For each additional book over $10.00 add $2.00. (This is per individual book priced over $10.00, not the order total.)

These orders are filled as quickly as possible. Sometimes a book can be delayed if we are temporarily out of stock. You should note on your order whether you prefer us to ship the book as soon as available or send you a merchandise credit good for other TV goodies or send you your money back immediately. Shipments normally take 2 or 3 weeks, but allow up to12 weeks for delivery.

Special UPS 2 Day Blue Label RUSH SERVICE: Special service is available for desperate Couch Potatos. These books are shipped within 24 hours of when we receive your order and should take 2 days to get from us to you.

For the first **RUSH SERVICE** book under $10.00 add $4.00. For each additional 1 book under $10.00 and $1.25. (This is per individual book priced under $10.00, not the order total.)

For the first **RUSH SERVICE** book over $10.00 add $6.00. For each additional book over $10.00 add $3.50 per book. (This is per individual book priced over $10.00, not the order total.)

Canadian and Foreign shipping rates are the same except that Blue Label RUSH SERVICE is not available. All Canadian and Foreign orders are shipped as books or printed matter.

DISCOUNTS! DISCOUNTS! Because your orders are what keep us in business we offer a discount to people that buy a lot of our books as our way of saying thanks. On orders over $25.00 we give a 5% discount. On orders over $50.00 we give a 10% discount. On orders over $100.00 we give a 15% discount. On orders over $150.00 we give a 20% discount. Please list alternates when possible. Please state if you wish a refund or for us to backorder an item if it is not in stock.

100% satisfaction guaranteed. We value your support. You will receive a full refund as long as the copy of the book you are not happy with is received back by us in reasonable condition. No questions asked, except we would like to know how we failed you. Refunds and credits are given as soon as we receive back the item you do not want.

Please have mercy on Phyllis and carefully fill out this form in the neatest way you can. Remember, she has to read a lot of them every day and she wants to get it right and keep you happy! You may use a duplicate of this order blank as long as it is clear. **Please don't forget to include payment! And remember, we *love* repeat friends...**

ORDER FORM

______The Phantom $16.95
______The Green Hornet $16.95
______The Shadow $16.95
______Flash Gordon Part One $16.95______Part Two $16.95
______Blackhawk $16.95
______Batman $16.95
______The UNCLE Technical Manual One $9.95 ______Two $9.95
______The Green Hornet Television Book $14.95
______Number Six The Prisoner Book $14.95
______The Wild Wild West $17.95
______Trek Year One $10.95
______Trek Year Two $12.95
______Trek Year Three $12.95
______The Animated Trek $14.95
______The Movies $12.95
______Next Generation $19.95
______The Lost Years $14.95
______The Trek Encyclopedia $19.95
______Interviews Aboard The Enterprise $18.95
______The Ultimate Trek $75.00
______Trek Handbook $12.95 ____Trek Universe $17.95
______The Crew Book $17.95
______The Making of the Next Generation $14.95
______The Freddy Krueger Story $14.95
______The Aliens Story $14.95
______Robocop $16.95
______Monsterland's Horror in the '80s $17.95
______The Compleat Lost in Space $17.95
______Lost in Space Tribute Book $9.95
______Lost in Space Tech Manual $9.95
______Supermarionation $17.95
______The Unofficial Beauty and the Beast $14.95
______Dark Shadows Tribute Book $14.95
______Dark Shadows Interview Book $18.95
______Doctor Who Baker Years $19.95
______The Doctor Who Encyclopedia:The 4th Doctor $19.95
______Illustrated Stephen King $12.95
______Gunsmoke Years $14.95

NAME:______________________

STREET:____________________

CITY:______________________

STATE:_____________________

ZIP:_______________________

TOTAL:__________ SHIPPING__________

SEND TO: COUCH POTATO,INC.
5715 N BALSAM, LAS VEGAS, NV 89130